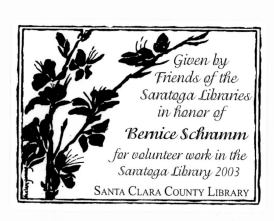

Seattle

and the
Demons of Ambition

Also By Fred Moody

The Visionary Position

I Sing the Body Electronic

Fighting Chance

Seattle

and the
Demons of Ambition

a love story

FRED MOODY

Permission to print the letter on pages 297–298 is kindly granted by the letter writer, James L. Acord.

www.stmartins.com

ISBN 0-312-30421-8

First Edition: September 2003

10 9 8 7 6 5 4 3 2 1

For Anne

Once the people here did find a short cut to riches. From a red-brick hotel down the street, Swiftwater Bill Gates, the Dawson plunger, showered nuggets on the Seattleites who gathered in the streets below.

—MURRAY MORGAN, 1951

Contents

Acknowledgments

There is no end to the number of people who aided me in the production of this book. First and foremost among them is the late Don McLeod, who taught me how to write and live properly in the Pacific Northwest, and whose love, support, and guidance still sustain me, every day.

Heartfelt thanks for their generosity and help are also due Glen and Jean Moehring; my agent, Nat Sobel; my editor, George Witte; Marie Estrada; Brad Wood; Marc Romano; Henry Kaufman; and my neighbor, John Eckert.

Many people stepped forward with timely and invaluable help in researching the city's—and my—past. Chief among these are Kathy Andrisevic, Katherine Long, and Sandy Freeman at the *Seattle Times*; Art Thiel; the Special Collections staff at the University of Washington Libraries; the creators and maintainers of www.historylink.org; and Karen Steichen, Kathryn Robinson, and Frank Abe.

Finally, there are those who provided inspiration, energy, or emotional support in various ways, sometimes inadvertently: Anne, Erin, Caitlin, and Jocelyn Moody; Anh Tran, Bruce Erickson, Sally Hewett, Zelfa Liebchin, Ryan O'Leary, U.S. Coast Guard LTJG Samuel Hudson, Doug Picha, Frank McGee, Anna Margaret McGee, Leah Preble, Jenine "Woodchuck" Adam, Claire Colegrove, Claire Hudson, John Flodin, George and Rosemary DeCuir, Ryan O'Leary, and Jesse and Dave, who were Mac 'n Jacks before Mac 'n Jacks was cool.

Seattle

and the
Demons of Ambition

Apocalypso

Utterly disbelieving, I made my way through exuberant rioting throngs to the corner of Fourth and Union, near the heart of downtown Seattle. When I turned east there, to go up Union, I came face-to-facemask with a wall of policemen in black riot gear, standing behind huge shields and wielding massive batons, guns, and tear-gas launchers. They looked like mannequins in a wall-to-wall Darth Vader display.

In a city where the public face of the police has always been more or less avuncular, this was an amazing shock. Seattle, after all, is the birthplace of the bicycle cop—that singularly benign public servant who tools around the streets in little bicycle shorts, helping the elderly cross streets and occasionally chasing a purse-snatcher down a downtown alley. It took a superhuman leap of imagination to picture the same officers in this futuro-fascist getup.

But as if to hammer home the point that this was real, one of them began broadcasting a loud, barely understandable warning through his bullhorn: "You have two minutes to disperse . . . We will begin firing tear gas in two minutes."

Hard as it was to take him seriously, I thought it best to scurry up the hill—and upwind. Friends had been fired upon with rubber bullets earlier that morning, and I had little reason to believe the police were bluffing now.

In the days leading up to the November 1999 World Trade Organization convention, there had been a great deal of debate about the form and scale of the attendant demonstrations. It is safe to say that no one at City Hall or in the media expected anything like this. My daughter Caitlin's high school AP Government class had been preparing for weeks for the convention and demonstrations as a kind of live-history-as-it-happens class project, and now I was frantically fighting my way through the riots looking for her; she had come downtown to walk in an organized parade. On the ferry over to Seattle that morning, she and her classmates had been happily making signs to carry in the orderly march they thought they'd be attending. Now, for all I knew, she had been arrested, injured, or killed.

Note to her teacher: *"What the hell were you thinking?!"*

Half a block away, I turned and watched the police lob the promised tear-gas canisters into the crowd. The mist scattered and softened the unusually harsh winter light, blurring the shadows around and distinctions between the rioters and the police. Then I watched the horde of demonstrators come running out of the cloud toward me, past me . . . to regroup with the crowd already occupying the next intersection. Watching the cloud drift past downtown's splendid new storefronts (practically everything downtown looked new, part of a spectacular, dot-com-boom-delivered revival), seeing in the mist the ghostly silhouettes of protestors and gas-masked police, I thought I was looking at a weird experimental overlay: a 1960s Detroit riot set against a 1990s Seattle background.

I was watching one of the biggest stories in Seattle history unfold around me, and I couldn't help but note with a certain irony that it was taking place on the day I was walking away from eighteen years in journalism for what I had thought would be a far more exciting life in the New Economy.

It proved impossible to discern any kind of strategic rationale behind the police's actions. Thoroughly outnumbered—there were 50,000 protestors and only 400 Seattle police officers, with police from the suburbs and the King County Sheriff's office being rushed in to help—a group of police would seem to decide arbitrarily to form a line in the middle of the melee, beyond which they would not allow protesters to move. The protesters then would fill the intersection directly in front of the police line and begin performing chants, songs, dances, harangues, and other forms of deafening noise that often took on a cadenced, musical coherence. When bodies and cacophony reached a certain critical mass, the police would issue their warning, fire their tear gas, and watch the demonstrators move out of range and regroup. Then the police would start the whole thing over again, one block away.

What had been envisioned as yet another showcase for Seattle as an emerging world-class city had turned into an epic disaster. The WTO convention was all but shut down, and Seattle was being exposed to the world as an overreaching dunce. From Third Avenue to Eighth Avenue, from Stewart Street to Cherry Street—the central square mile or so of downtown Seattle—Apocalypse rocked. The streets were packed with unkempt hordes, and windows everywhere were shattered. Virtually every intersection was blocked by a throng of protestors, in the center of which sat, in a circle facing outward, people linked together by foam tubing in which they all had inserted their arms, fixing the ends to their shoulders with duct tape. I would walk up to these groups and note with astonishment how impassioned they were, and how young, and how much fun they were having. It was impossible not to remember being their age, dressed as they were, marching in anti–Vietnam War demonstrations, and impossible not to root for them now.

The closer I moved to the Washington State Convention Center, at the upper end of downtown just as it begins turning up into Capitol Hill, the more crowded the streets became. The convention center was the locale for the WTO meetings, and demonstrators were intent on keeping delegates from getting in. (One frustrated delegate pulled a gun, causing the rioters to scatter almost as fast as if the visitor had whipped out a cigarette in a Seattle restaurant.) The streets were littered with overturned Dumpsters, many of which were aflame, and the storefronts—the newest and glitziest in new, glitzy Seattle—had their glass either shattered or boarded up, and were covered with graffiti in either case. The symbol for anarchy—an "A" enclosed in a circle—was painted everywhere. I walked past a looted Starbucks, its windows shattered, the machinery and crockery and display cases on its counters destroyed, and much of the store's merchandise, furniture, and equipment tossed out in the street.

I kept seeing the oddest things in the cloud of chaos. Kids would come running past me with their faces coated in surreal slime—the result of the body's response to tear gas. I saw a helmetless policeman on one corner tenderly washing out the eyes of a protestor while the riots raged around them. He looked like a solicitous dad tending to his fallen son on a crowded playground. I saw Krist Novoselic, the ex-bassist from Nirvana, wading through the melee in gigantic bright yellow boots, aiming his video camera every which way. In the middle of incredible tumult, I saw an orderly line of customers at an outdoor espresso stand. And when I came to the corner of Eighth and Pine, which appeared to be the head-quarters of the protest organizers, I stood in the middle of the intersection, surrounded by chanting, singing, dancing demonstrators, and watched protest leaders employing cell phones to direct troops to the doors of a particular downtown hotel where a delegate was attempting to get out of the building. Minutes later, I watched them joyfully receive the report that the delegate had been forced back inside. "We stopped him!" one leader announced to the crowd. "He couldn't get out!"

Downtown Seattle had spent the 1990s undergoing a depressing renaissance. By 1999, it sported arguably the spiffiest, newest, most fashion-forward and prosperous major urban retail core in the country. National chains moved here in droves, the past few years having seen Barney's New York, FAO Schwarz, Banana Republic, Nike, Sega Gameworks, Planet Hollywood, Restoration Hardware, Tiffany's, and other upscale merchants set up shop, muscling out locally owned businesses. The metastatic transformation of downtown was set in motion by the Seattle Silicon Rush, the technological revolution—spawned by Microsoft—that had suddenly enriched and exposed to the world a city and region that until then had been an economically risible, nearly invisible backwater.

Now, the newness and grand scale of these stores, set against the crowds rampaging happily in the streets, added to the apocalyptic eeriness of the scene: This was not some fading old civilization being trashed by rebellious hordes. Instead, it was a nascent empire, waxing rather than waning, stopped suddenly in mid-wax by a furious resistance it hadn't even known existed.

It is impossible to overstate the obliviousness of Seattle in the days leading up to the WTO riots. The worst that city fathers and journalists alike had expected was a large, parade-like series of protests in the streets outside the WTO meeting halls, with the police having to intervene occasionally to keep demonstrators from spilling out over prearranged boundaries. Most concerned were the downtown merchants, fearful that traffic and crowd problems would keep Christmas shoppers away on the busiest shopping days of the year. Seattle Mayor Paul Schell, long derided by citizens for his self-styled "visionary" aspirations for the city, and for what now looked like a decidedly Panglossian optimism, expected the convention to be virtually trouble-free, declaring in advance, "This event is a momentous, exciting affair for Seattle. It speaks to the growing stature of Seattle's place on the world stage, and it shows impressive confidence in our ability to serve as gracious and competent hosts for international dialogues."

Seattle police, trying to be gracious, had worked out a plan in advance with protest organizers that allowed demonstrators to briefly block intersections, then submit to mass arrests. But the event itself proved not only out of the police's control but also out of the organizers', and now the police, clearly panicked, were resorting to tear gas and rubber bullets. It was the essential paradox of the riots: The police's trust and solicitude had led them inexorably to overreaction and violence.

It later would come out that Seattle had resolutely ignored warnings from elsewhere that the city was getting in over its head. More than a month before the conference, Seattle assistant police chief Ed Joiner—who was tasked with preparing for the onslaught—e-mailed desperately to Mayor Schell, insisting that the city was underprepared. "I hope that someone is considering what Seattle is going to look like—and what kind of economic damage it will suffer—if this event gets out of hand," he wrote.

No one was, save for the unfortunate Joiner. The convention was widely seen as a chance for Seattle to show the world its laid-back, civil way of settling disputes and debating issues. One of the more comic developments, in retrospect, was the event that led to Joiner's alarmed e-mail: The Seattle City Council had been preparing a resolution welcoming the protestors to Seattle and inviting them to camp out in city parks. Warnings from the FBI and police agencies from around the world—even from agencies that had dealt with previous WTO riots—were laughed off by condescending Seattle politicians and boosters, who were as convinced that the rest of the world didn't understand enlightened Seattle as the WTO-weary elsewhere were convinced that Seattle had no idea what was headed its way.

I was just as disdainful of the warnings, but for different reasons. Having grown up in the Northwest since the mid-1950s, I had long since grown weary of Seattle's reflexive tendency toward hopeful hype. Everything anyone ever planned for Seattle was trumpeted in advance as The Thing That Would Put Seattle on the Map at Last. I had seen it happen again and again over the years. There was the 1962 Seattle World's Fair and its "transportation of the future," the Monorail. After 37 years, that little mass-transit prototype had grown all of three blocks longer, to .9 miles, and still ran back and forth between only two stops. In 1969, it was the awarding to Seattle of a Major League Baseball franchise, the Seattle Pilots. One year later, they became the Milwaukee Brewers. Then came the Supersonic Transport that Boeing was going to build in the early 1970s; when it failed to get off the ground, Boeing crashed spectacularly, and Seattle went into one of its worst-ever recessions. In 1976, it was the brand-new Kingdome and its coming new tenants, Major League Baseball's Seattle Mariners and the NFL's Seattle Seahawks; then there was the 1979 NBA championship won by the Seattle SuperSonics, the 1984 and 1989 NCAA Final Four men's basketball tournaments, the 1990 Goodwill Games. . . . The pattern was always the same: Local boosters would proclaim the value of the exposure the Next Big Thing would bring, the Thing would be launched with tremendous fanfare, and few outside the Puget Sound basin would notice. Why, I reasoned, should the WTO be any different?

This shamefaced Northwest tradition of excitedly spawning duds is almost as old as the mid-nineteenth-century establishment of white civilization here. The first full-blown attempt to turn the Northwest into a model civilization for the rest of the world to emulate began in 1885, when messianic settlers from the east established a series of utopian communities in the Puget Sound basin. For some reason, American communitarians and socialists around the country—including Eugene V. Debs and Emma Goldman—decided that Washington would be the ideal state for socialists to "colonize" by setting up utopian communities that would grow both in number and population to the point where socialist representatives would eventually constitute the majority in the state legislature. The strategy held that the state was unpopulated enough, rich enough in natural resources, and had enough cheap land to allow these communities to get a foothold, sustain themselves, and grow rapidly while generating income from timber harvesting, farming, and fishing. Once the state went socialist and showed the rest of the nation how to live the enlightened life, the entire country would follow suit.

These utopias, eight of which rose to prominence from 1885 to 1915, ranged from the purely idealistic to the crackpot mix of idealism and land-rush opportunism. All were launched with tremendous fanfare, attracting hopeful romantics from around the country, and all enjoyed relatively short life spans before devolving into real estate ventures. Among the first to be launched was the Puget Sound Co-operative Colony, founded in 1886 by former acting Seattle City Attorney George Venable Smith and others on the Olympic Peninsula, west of Seattle. "[A]s mankind grows better, juster, kinder and more confiding in each other," the *Daily Call*, a cause-friendly newspaper of the time, had it, "that [communitarian] idea will spread and grow." Smith's idea was that the colony would acquire land, develop and populate it, and that its denizens would work in exchange for free lodging, meals, education, and other goods and services, with the enterprise harvesting and selling natural resources—particularly timber—to support itself. The reality was that "the innate selfishness of the human race" (in the words of an early colony skeptic), combined with the quiet horror of getting through eight months of incessant Northwest winter and spring rain without adequate shelter, had these ventures foundering in obscurity almost from the day they were established. It didn't take long for Debs, et al., to start looking elsewhere for solutions.

Paul Schell had made a long career out of spinning George Smith–like fantasies as a city bureaucrat in the early 1970s, as a failed candidate for mayor in 1977, and as a real estate developer into the 1990s. He had been one of the authors of *Seattle 2000*, a document written in 1973 that spun a vision of Seattle as an emerging center of culture on a more or less European Renaissance model. He had lobbied hard to bring the 1990 Goodwill Games to Seattle on the theory that once the world saw how enlightened Northwesterners fostered diversity and consensus, the Cold War would end and Seattle-style harmony would spread outward, forever transforming the planet. He often spoke of forging a kind of regional nation-state, called Cascadia, extending from Vancouver, British Columbia, to Portland, Oregon, that would be an environmental and cultural utopia—a place to which the rest of the world would look for leadership in cultivating the good, cultured, ethnically diverse, and peaceful life. A self-proclaimed "vision guy," Schell liked nothing better than philosophizing endlessly about "ideas."

So it was a bit of a stunner for the WTO events to unfold on his watch. Schell spent the three-day riot invoking his credentials as a former Vietnam War protestor and expressing his utter bewilderment at being mistaken for a member of the establishment. By nightfall on the first day of the riots he would take a turn for the vengeful, allowing Washington Governor Gary Locke to call in the National Guard, then sealing off the downtown area and turning loose his reinforced police troops. In their menacing Vader getup, marching in a kind of goose-step chorus line down vacant downtown streets, beating in unison their Plexiglass shields with their nightsticks, the constabulary furnished dramatic televised evidence to the world that Seattle was an out-of-control police state.

It was an odd spectacle reminiscent of the two faces of George Venable Smith. As Seattle City Attorney, before heading off to the Olympic Peninsula and his new life as a humankind-loving idealist, Smith had helped plan and lead the Seattle Anti-Chinese Riots in 1886 and had consulted with his fellow civic leaders in nearby Tacoma when that city expelled its Chinese. A few years later, he came back to the Republican Party, resolutely refusing from then on to acknowledge his radical middle years.

Schell's whiplash act was even more reminiscent of Seattle mayor George Cotterill, who in 1913, in the wake of a riot in which various anarchists and Wobblies were attacked and beaten by patriotic mobs after a series of IWW rallies, filled downtown with crowd-controlling police and firemen, and suspended liquor sales, public meetings, and distribution of the *Seattle Times* within the Seattle city limits. Just as Cotterill was moved from his ardent free-speech position in defense of the IWW and various anarchists to more or less shutting down the city, so now Schell was moved from welcoming activists and anarchists to abruptly driving them and everyone else out of downtown and subjecting anyone caught there after curfew to immediate arrest.

You had to wonder: Did hell have no fury like a Seattle politician burned? Was there a truncheoneer lurking beneath the surface of every Northwest utopian?

Standing now in the midst of the violence, I began to see that my skepticism about the pre-WTO hype—a skepticism widespread among Northwest natives—was a brand of cynicism as old as Seattle itself. It was the mirror image of Schell's and the rest of the Seattle establishment's fatuous civic pride. Just as there had always been types, like Smith and Schell, who thought the Northwest could lead the rest of the world into an Age of Enlightenment of one kind or another, so there have always been their opposite numbers here, who insist that obscurity and under-achievement are the enduring values of the Northwest. Both attitudes struck me in mid-riot as different forms of the classic Middle American "it can't happen here" mentality, opposing versions of provincialism—provincial puffery in the establishment's case, provincial self-loathing in mine.

After the riots, when Seattleites started demanding an accounting from their leaders, we were to learn that Seattle "won" the WTO convention because no one else wanted to host it. The World Trade Organization had taken us in like the rubes we were. So eager were we to legitimize ourselves in the eyes of the world that we never bothered to notice what exactly the WTO was, and how reviled it was around the world. Nor did we notice how desperate the WTO was when it started casting about in the mid-1990s for a place to hold its next conclave. It is one of those rare organizations that draws the ire of everybody from every segment of the political spectrum. The right wing sees it as a shadowy, conspiratorial, New World Order–kind of invisible government. The left wing sees it as a means for corporations to circumvent national environmental and labor laws, be accountable to no nation's legal authority, and violate every moral dictum held by virtually every liberal activist organization in the world. The WTO had become the biggest lightning rod in history, attracting legions of protestors that effectively crippled whatever city they invaded, and no city anywhere in the world that was at all in touch with reality wanted to host it.

Enter Seattle—a reality-free environment! "We blew this WTO gig," *Seattle Post-Intelligencer* columnist Art Thiel would write a few days after the riots. "Big time. Because our civic ego ran amok."

For now, though, demonstrators were running amok, with increasing energy and glee as the merry hours passed. By evening, the police—and I—would be getting a close look at the innate mischievousness of the human race, as the rioters grew more and more celebratory. (They also now apparently included my daughter, who, according to a classmate thoughtful enough to call her panicking parents, was dancing ecstatically in the streets at the onset of evening—a charge Caitlin eventually would strenuously deny.) Seattle, famed for civility, was collapsing under the forces of anarchy and adolescence, and it was going to take an unimaginable level of police violence to drive the invaders out. I spent the day walking through the riots, taking everything in, and surrendering to an excited feeling of kinship with the rioters—a feeling that grew more and more puzzling as the day rioted on.

At some point toward evening, I came full circle and found myself back in front of the looted Starbucks, up the street from Nordstrom, down the street from the newest section of downtown—a section now occupied by Niketown, Planet Hollywood, and other outlets of that ilk. I looked down toward Starbucks and Nordstrom, and was struck by something I hadn't noticed before: Mixed in with the celebratory glee on the faces of the rioters was real rage—the kind furious children direct at adults, and righteous students at the establishment. How weird, I thought, to see Seattle, of all places, being the target of anti-establishment rioting!

I realized that, until that moment, in my mind Seattle had always been, if not outright anti-establishment, then certainly aslant of the establishment, determined to live outside the American status-seeking norm. Once a hotbed of IWW-led labor-union activism, in 1919 it became the first city in the U.S. to be shut down completely by a general strike. It was the leading city in the state, toasted in the mid-1930s by the

U.S. Postmaster General as "the soviet of Washington." It had elected, in Schell's predecessor, the nation's first African-American mayor to be voted into office by predominantly white voters. Its county executive was African-American and its state's governor was Chinese-American. It had engendered and nurtured grunge rock, one of the most rebellious, anti-materialistic, and anti-upward-mobility rock movements in history. I was standing within a canister's throw of four Northwest companies—Nordstrom, Nike, Starbucks, and AT&T Wireless—that all had at one time been brash, romantic startups determined to rebel against the status quo in their businesses and deliver something previously forbidden to the beleaguered and deprived citizen-consumer. Now, all four were reviled as oppressors of customers, competitors, employees, former employees, contracted third-world employees, or all of the above. I remembered then too that Microsoft, Amazon.com, and McCaw Cellular (before AT&T bought it and turned it into AT&T Wireless) had once been popular Seattle startups, freedom fighters in the corporate age, wresting power over information and communication from the hands of previously indomitable corporations and putting it in those of ordinary citizens. My city had long been virtually synonymous with rebellion. How could such a place have turned into such a willing symbol of repression?

Watching yet another tear-gas fusillade, I fell to wondering what had happened to Seattle and why no one here seemed to have seen how dramatic the change was, or how much different our self-image was from the image outsiders had of us. How had I not noticed, for example, the stories coming out of other cities insisting that Starbucks was a huge, powerful corporation muscling local coffee outlets out of their own downtowns? How had I not noticed that Microsoft chairman Bill Gates had morphed from the boardroom version of the kids in the streets around me into a latter-day John D. Rockefeller, under antitrust siege from a federal government that enjoyed the support of virtually every computer user in the country? Seattle, long a haven for dropouts and rebels, had turned into a high-tech Rome, begging to be sacked.

I turned a corner and found myself looking at the grotesque, outsized Banana Republic store. Then I remembered with a pang what it had been only a few years before: The Coliseum Theater—the last of the grand old downtown movie theaters—anchoring what was then a quiet, homey section of downtown Seattle. I was a self-employed typesetter then, working out of my home, devoid along with most of the city of any measurable ambition for myself or for Seattle. And I stood here now amid the rioting, while my mind wandered eagerly back to the day in 1981 when I heard a knock at the door that was to change my life forever. I realized now that people all over Seattle were being unwittingly summoned, as I was that day, back to the beginning of the bacchanal.

Knock, Knock

It was a weekday in September 1981, at ten or eleven or so in the morning. I had come up from my basement office after spending a couple of hours working, and was chasing my two-year-old daughter Erin around the house. My workdays, such as they were, consisted largely of relaxation and play, the morning runaround with Erin usually being the only appointment on any given day's schedule.

So when the knock—which sounded unmistakably peremptory and businesslike—suddenly rang out, it brought us both to a dead stop. Erin and I stared at the door, transfixed and puzzled.

My mind, having its own agenda, fell to reflection and reminiscence. I began thinking about how I had left Seattle in disgust after graduating from college in 1973. My institution of higher learning—Fairhaven College in Bellingham, eighty-five miles north of Seattle—had disgorged my soon-to-be-wife, Anne, and me into a job market that had no jobs of any kind for anyone, let alone a youngster with a newly minted English literature degree and a minor in high dudgeon. Seattle had been on the skids since "Century 21"—the 1962 Seattle World's Fair—and its boosters' promise to make our town one of the great cities of the world. Never the liveliest place on earth (not, at any rate, since it shut down its thriving brothel trade in 1911), Seattle felt particularly dead in the wake of the 1969–71 Boeing Bust, a company collapse that saw Boeing gut its work-force, laying off nearly 60,000 of its 101,000 employees. In a company town like Seattle, where it seemed that the vast majority of citizens' lives were plotted along the same curve—they grew up, went to work either for the "Lazy B" or one of its suppliers at a job that left them plenty of time and energy for hiking, boating, and fishing, and stayed on there until it was time to retire with a good pension—that kind of retrenchment is dev-astating, and it felt as if the collapse was all but killing the city. Some 35,000 people in related support industries and services also lost their jobs, and the ripples spread outward until unemployment crept up over 12 percent—more than double the national average. Although they did so in smaller numbers than was the case in other economic collapses in other cities, a noticeable number of Seattleites started doing the unthinkable: piling their mattresses on top of their cars and leaving paradise for less splendid settings, in search of work. My uncle, a Boeing engineer, moved to the southwest Washington hinterlands and bought a motel, where he and my aunt were to live out the rest of their lives cosseting tourists. They were among the more than 10 percent of the city populace that fled dur-ing the Bust years, which hit a nadir of sorts when two local wags bought a billboard and posted the sign, "WILL THE LAST PERSON LEAVING SEATTLE PLEASE TURN OUT THE LIGHTS?"

Even if times had been good, I would have been desperate to leave. I grew up disgusted by and enraged at the complacency and smugness that characterized Seattle throughout the fifties, sixties, and seventies. I spent my college years counting the days until I could graduate and move east—to the land of action, excitement, and ambition. No self-respecting ado-lescent could help but bridle at the maddeningly slow pace of Northwest life and the widely held conviction among our parents' generation that life couldn't possibly get any better than it already was. It was infuriating to live in this best of all possible worlds, where restlessness was frowned upon and ambition was an outright disease. The only cultural values apparent in 1970s Seattle were moderation and politeness. You believed that you could never advance any kind of debate in politics, art, or civi-lization because it was impolite to argue or even raise your voice in pas-sionate enthusiasm for anything.

This oppressive probity seemed particularly ironic in light of what the city had been in its early years. Seattle once was a wide-open, nearly law-less town, inhabited and governed by the irreverent, the rebellious, and the ribald. The teens and twenties here had been dangerously entertaining, with the Skid Road district down by the waterfront a freewheeling realm of burlesque houses, gambling dens, and illicit booze joints. When police chief William Meredith tried to clean up the place in 1901, he was fired, and when in revenge he tried to kill John Considine, the leading brothel/boxhouse owner on Skid Road, he ended up losing his life in a botched shotgun ambush. City government was both in thrall and in the pay of the Skid Roadsters, with my favorite Seattle historical moment being this one, in 1911, as recounted by Murray Morgan in his classic "informal portrait" of Seattle, *Skid Road*:

> The Improvement Company purchased several acres of land in the southern part of town and hired architects to plan a model red-light district. The central feature in the planned community was to be a five-hundred-room brothel, the biggest in the world. When construction was about to begin, the contractors found their work would be simpler if they were to build eighty feet west of the original site. There was one trouble: most of that eighty feet was occupied by a Seattle street, so the city council thoughtfully granted the Hillside Improvement Company a fifteen-year lease on the thoroughfare. A contemporary observer remarked, "American cities have voted away their streets to gas companies, electric-light lines, and street railways, but Seattle is the first one that ever granted a franchise to a public thoroughfare for the erection of a brothel."

Those were the days when Seattle city fathers thought big, by God! Unfortunately for them, their visionary tendencies proved costly: Seattle city government was overturned in the reform-driven 1912 election, and the city was never quite the same again (although Skid Road did keep a bustling alcohol trade alive during Prohibition). There was a brief spasm of grandiosity between 1897 and 1910, when city engineer R. H. Thompson worked his will, building a ship canal and locks between Puget Sound and Lake Union; developing a hydroelectric power system that drew on water from the Cascade Mountains; leveling Denny Hill—one of the four steep hills in central Seattle—and dumping its dirt into the sound, so as to give Seattle more developable land near the waterfront; and shaving off large portions of Beacon Hill, in south Seattle, with which he filled in the tidal flats below.

By the 1960s, though, Seattle had reversed gears, refusing to entertain any illusions about becoming a real metropolis with real metropolitan transit and freeway systems. Voters rejected attempts by civic leaders to build a rapid-transit system and a new freeway (to be named the R.H. Thompson Freeway) to accommodate the massive growth their leaders envisioned. By the 1970s, voter passage of funding for a little pier-mounted waterfront park was about as visionary as things got.

By then, it was inconceivable that anything exciting or outrageous or culturally worthwhile could ever happen here. The Seattle 2000 Commission, a citizens' group led by Paul Schell and other downtown interests, had spent months meeting and working on a symptomatic book entitled *Goals for Seattle*, which was adopted by the mayor and city council and published in 1973. Noting that the Boeing collapse had reduced Seattle's population to levels lower than it had been in 1950, the commission's population group "agreed unanimously that further increase in the population of Seattle (and its surrounding communities) would have a net unfavorable effect on the quality of life of its residents. . . ." The city should therefore find "various ways in which the city could limit or discourage further population growth and achieve an optimum ratio of people to resources—economic, social and aesthetic." Among the program initiatives: "avoidance of pro-natalist bias" ("pro-natalist" defined in a footnote as "birth-promoting") in the city's tax code and social programs, and policies that would help in the effort toward "discouraging immigration."

In other words, Seattle was determined to seal itself off from the rest of the world and keep everything just the way it was. The city wanted to remain a backwater. The only concession to progress the commission seemed ready to make was one that struck me as mildly alarming: "The nation is expected to double its energy demands by the year 2000 and Seattle might be expected to do the same. The additional electricity would probably come from nuclear generating stations, maybe located in Western Washington."

I was graduating from college when *Seattle 2000* came out, and the report convinced me that Seattle would forever be a grim joke. My favorite college professor, Don McLeod, a master of digging up the ridiculous, got the biggest laugh of his career when he unearthed a *Criswell Predicts* promise that Seattle would be the "cultural center of the world" in 2000. To those of us who had grown up here through the 1950s and 1960s, the idea that Seattle would ever have even a measurable culture, let alone an interesting one, was hilarious. Most culture lore involving Seattle tended to cast the city in a ridiculous light. Everyone knew the story of how a furious Sir Thomas Beecham, who conducted the Seattle Symphony from 1941 to 1943, had labeled Seattle on his way out of town an "aesthetic dustbin" inhabited by "illiterate, incompetent, unmusical" critics and audiences. Nothing much had happened since to rebut that assessment. When the "Northwest School" artists Mark Tobey, Morris Graves, Kenneth Callahan, and Guy Anderson first began drawing attention from New York critics and collectors, the *Seattle Times* marked their achievement by inadvertently printing a photo of one of Graves's paintings upside down. The 1962 Seattle World's Fair, mounted as an effort to vault Seattle into the urban big leagues along with New York, Chicago, and San Francisco, instead offered, with breathtaking lack of imagination, a trite vision of twenty-first-century civilization as a Jetsonsesque era of monorails, Bubbleators, and Space Needles. Now, the fair-drawn tourists having come and gone, Seattle was forever stuck with that hackneyed needle as its most visible symbol, the only culturally memorable legacy of the fair being the introduction to the Northwest of Belgian waffles. In 1969, still desperate to be taken for a real city, Seattle boosters brought to town a Major League Baseball expansion franchise, the Seattle Pilots, and put it in a slightly reconfigured minor-league ballpark. After a single season, baseball spirited the Pilots away to Milwaukee, leaving Seattle, in the words of local author Roger Sale, looking like a victim of its own "abject desire . . . to become big league." It was that kind of aspiration, he added, that is "often seen by those in older cities as the needs of rubes."

Sale saw the Seattle of that time as a city that could never have the will or imagination to turn itself into a great metropolis. Something about the collective civic character of the place seemed to stunt its growth. It was as if the natural splendor surrounding Seattle was so spectacular as to be overwhelming: It wasn't that the water and mountains made Northwesterners too complacent to want to build a better city; it was more that the landscape made them despair. How could anything they built ever measure up to the surrounding majesty? Sale would deliver a telling—if tortuously rendered—insight about the city and its spectacular surroundings at the conclusion of his *Seattle: Past to Present*, published in 1976. "I know no one," he would write, "native or newcomer, who has been touched deeply by Seattle who has not felt this sense of life falling short of its possibilities even as there is so much that is to be enjoyed."

When Anne and I decided to head east after graduation, we felt the same way: If we were ever to make something of the possibilities of our lives and our youth, we would have to do it elsewhere. I regarded it as highly symbolic that the most famous Seattleite of the day—D. B. Cooper, the inventor of airplane hijacking, who made history on Thanksgiving 1971—was immortalized for trying to leave town. Sure, the city occasionally attracted the admiring attention of outsiders—as when the Seattle engineering firm Skilling, Helle, Christiansen & Robertson was tabbed to engineer construction of the 110-story World Trade Center towers in New York, and Seattle's Pacific Car & Foundry was among the fabricators picked to supply steel for them. When the towers were finished in 1973, they were in many ways regarded as "Seattle buildings," and locals took considerable pride in the fact that Seattleites had helped build the tallest skyscrapers in the world. But that just seemed proof positive to me that Seattleites were always having to do their best work in other cities because they were never allowed to reach their potential here.

So we took off for the East Coast within days of graduating. After less than a year in New York, we came back to Seattle, married, then turned around again and left for Ann Arbor, Michigan, where we were to live the next six years.

I've spent a good deal of time since trying to understand why we never really took to being away. There is no question that life outside the Northwest's landscape, waterscape, gray skyscape, and year-round wet weather is an acquired taste—particularly if you're transplanted to parts of the country where the weather is prone to violent mood swings. But it also seemed that Seattle started coming out of its chronic lassitude during the latter half of the 1970s. The *Weekly*, an alternative paper modeled on New York's *Village Voice*, was launched in 1976, signaling the presence of a new cultural element in the city. Sales's history was published that year, and he noted that "days of new possibility or reckoning are only now, in the 1970s, approaching for both Portland and Seattle, [and] it is too soon to say what their outcome will be." The University of Washington Huskies upset the University of Michigan Wolverines in the 1978 Rose Bowl—the Huskies' first win there since 1961. The Seattle Sonics won an NBA championship in 1979—the first major pro championship in the city's history. I was beginning to think that I had forsaken my homeland just as it was finally beginning to grow into a reasonable place to live. And when Mt. St. Helens erupted in 1980, I decided that I'd missed out on enough by being gone.

Our longing for the comforts of home was considerably intensified by my job in Ann Arbor. I was working for Ardis Publishers, a publisher of suppressed Russian literature—Russia in the 1970s was still under the totalitarian thumb of the Soviets—and I spent most of my time among eloquent and lugubrious Russian émigrés. Russian history is a nearly endless story of imprisonment, exile, and intense longing for home—the Russians, in fact, have forever made a high art of homesickness. When we finally decided to return to Seattle—a decision I resisted for years because I regarded it as failure—I attributed my sudden intense longing for home to the influence of all those damned Russians.

There was one incident, though, that would return to my mind whenever I thought about those years away from Seattle. Early one winter Sunday morning, I was walking along a nearly deserted street in Albany, New York. My mind was dwelling on the most salient difference between Seattle and other American cities: driving habits. I was remembering how in Seattle you never, under any circumstances, hear a car horn, how weirdly solicitous of pedestrians Seattle drivers are, how slowly they traverse their freeways, and how the Seattle definition of "gridlock" is two drivers at an intersection, each waiting for the other to go through first. The Albany street I was walking along was wide and straight. I saw a car approaching from the distance, drawing nearer. Then I noticed another—parked—car starting up. As the moving car was about to draw even with the parked car, the driver in the parked car—who had turned his head, seen the approaching car, and turned instantly back, suddenly hurrying—floored his accelerator and came squealing out into the street in front of the moving—and now ferociously honking—car. Thirty yards further down the road was a traffic light, however, and it was red; the intruding car had to slam on its brakes, the screech shattering the Sunday-morning silence, in order to stop in time, and the two cars sat there furiously idling as they waited for the light to change. The aggressor had gone to all that panicky trouble to stop thirty yards down the road a single car-length earlier, and from then on that act came to serve in my mind as the perfect symbol for life in the eastern United States.

It didn't take long before I started believing that everywhere I went—to movie-theater lines, classes, meetings, grocery stores—I could hear the roar of that engine and the immediate squeal of those brakes in the background. Everywhere I looked I saw in people there that same intense—and intensely futile—struggle: extravagant effort and emotion thrown into acts of striving for material gain, striving for advantage over others, striving for job advancement, striving for money . . . always this tremendous rage and anxiety for the sake of infinitesimal gain.

On top of that, I became intensely preoccupied with easterners' apparent distaste for one another. It was as if all human contact back there were abrading—not only among people engaged in business or other more or less formal transactions, but among friends and family members as well. One Thanksgiving, while guests in a Staten Island home, Anne and I watched the family's mother and daughter argue constantly and ferociously with the father. At the emotional peak of the holiday, while we were all seated around the Thanksgiving table, we watched the mother and daughter entertain themselves mightily by making little tic-ridden faces at one another. They were imitating Daddy's post-stroke symptoms.

This little vignette served as my other constant symbolic vision of life outside the Northwest. And while the Midwest didn't quite approach that level of misery, it did seem that whenever we ventured outside of Ann Arbor proper we encountered similar disgruntlement and anger—at the weather, at the crowding, at the conditions of the infrastructure, at one another. Six years after leaving Seattle, Anne and I were no more acclimated than we had been at the beginning of our exile, and it was only a matter of time before I would turn thoroughly bilious.

In 1980, we decided to return. We told ourselves that we were coming back for the sake of our daughter Erin, who was born in Ann Arbor and would be eighteen months old when we came back home. We couldn't bear watching her grow up in what seemed to be an emotionally menacing environment. But I also had to admit that I couldn't stand living away from my own kind anymore, and my fear of turning into a rude eastern American, chronically disgruntled and proud of it, had become overwhelming.

It wasn't until we were settled again at home that I began understanding why it was so hard for Seattleites to contend with the world outside the Northwest. I was struck by how the vast majority of people in Seattle had moved from either California or points east. I noticed that when people were introduced, the first question they would ask one another was, "Where are you from?" It was generally accepted that no one had grown up in Seattle, that everyone had moved here within the past few years, and that their move Northwestward had been as much a flight from hell as a flight to paradise. I never met anyone who moved here because he or she found a new job or had been sent here by an employer—always, newcomers had decided to move to Seattle because they wanted a better life, and figured they would eventually find reasonable work. It was clear that even people native to the outside world felt more at home here than there. The two terms you heard over and over again when newcomers rhapsodized about their new Seattle home were "laid-back" and "nice," the clear implication being that, outside the Northwest, people were "aggressive" and "mean."

Again and again I heard transplants describe the same rite of Northwest passage: In talking about how hard it was to make friends when they moved to Seattle, they invariably described an episode in which, after a few awkward months here, they were taken aside by a kindhearted, more Seattle-savvy acquaintance at work or in their neighborhood, and told that they had to "tone it down," "dial back," or "turn down the aggression" in order to survive socially.

Gradually, I began to see how this personal psychological state filtered out to the broader Seattle culture, gaining expression in its media and the public images of its leading personalities. I understood now that either Seattle or I had evolved during my wandering years, for what I had regarded before I moved away as disgusting smugness and complacency now struck me as a kind of agnostic enlightenment. Now I saw Seattle as a city where people chose to cultivate the mind and the soul, disdaining standard American upward mobility and status-seeking for a life in which people were essentially sympathetic with one another rather than competitive, and in which all the city's residents shared the understanding that you measured the worth of people not by what they achieved, owned, wore, or drove but by what they *were*.

There were three leading public presences who defined, with their images and their lives, the essence of Seattle in the 1970s. One was restaurateur Ivar Haglund; one was newspaper columnist Emmett Watson; the last was the Nordstrom family.

Born in 1905, Ivar Haglund grew up on Alki Point, where in 1851 Seattle's first white settlers had established the tiny four-cabin community they called "New York Pretty-Soon" (either Seattle's first act of delusional civic boosterism or its first act of reflexive irony). The most important and compelling of those founders, Doc Maynard, eventually sold his Alki Point land to Ivar Haglund's grandparents. That provenance, and that Scandinavian name, all but predestined Haglund to grow up to be an archetype: The Avuncular Old Salt Who Embodied Seattle. It also happened that Haglund had a gift for eccentricity and a peculiar kind of ambition that assured him a preeminent place in the Seattle firmament. In his youth, he was a folk singer of some regional renown, and was friends with both Woody Guthrie and Pete Seeger. He survived the Great Depression living on modest rents he collected on the various properties he had inherited from his parents. In 1938, against the advice of his friend Mark Tobey, who insisted Haglund was "destined to play the guitar," he opened an aquarium on the Seattle waterfront's Pier 54. He would charge ten cents (five cents for kids) for admission to his sidewalk attraction, sitting outside on a stool, wearing the ship captain's hat that became his trademark, playing his guitar and singing folk songs he'd written about the creatures in his tanks. He described running an aquarium as a simple enterprise: "Just pump the environment out of the harbor, circulate it around the tank and back out. All you have to do is feed the critters." He added Ivar's Fish Bar, a fish-and-chips stand, then grafted onto that enterprise a seafood restaurant named Ivar's Acres of Clams in 1946. He opened two more restaurants—Ivar's Captain's Table and Broadway Ivar's—then a fourth and more fabled: Ivar's Salmon House, on the north end of Lake Union (Haglund had tried without success to get a permit for a floating restaurant). In 1976, now wealthy, he bought the landmark Smith Tower, which had been the tallest building west of the Mississippi when it was built in 1914. Almost immediately, he got into a highly public dispute with the City of Seattle when he violated its historic landmark ordinance by flying a sixteen-foot-long salmon windsock from its pinnacle. The hearing, held before a packed house, was resolved in Haglund's favor.

Haglund had charisma to burn. Rotund, amiable, and silly, he aggressively cultivated the image of a genial fuck-up. He was utterly without pretension. While building his business and holdings into a multimillion-dollar fortune, he gave the impression of someone sailing fecklessly through life in his captain's cap and nautical jacket, strumming his guitar and promoting his business with low-brow publicity stunts. He once dressed a hair seal in a pinafore and pushed it in a stroller to visit a department-store Santa Claus. He staged a "wrestling match" between a worn-out prizefighter named Two Ton Tony and Oscar the Octopus, a popular resident in his aquarium. (It subsequently turned out that "Oscar" was played by a dead stand-in.) When a freight-train tank car spilled thousands of gallons of syrup onto the tracks across the street from Ivar's Acres of Clams, Haglund was photographed sitting blissfully in the middle of the stream on a crate, wearing an enormous bib, ladling the spilled syrup onto a plate of over-sized pancakes. Reporters so loved hanging around him that at one time the *Seattle Times* editors instituted a ban on Ivar stories, only to rescind it shortly thereafter because they didn't like losing readers to the rival *Post-Intelligencer*. Throughout the 1950s, he appeared regularly as First Mate Salty on *Captain Puget*, a popular children's TV show, where he crooned his compositions and accompanied himself on guitar.

His restaurants were decorated in maritime themes with a middle-

American cornball twist. They were packed with nautical stuff—fishnets, lanterns, ship's wheels, oars, barometers, all mounted haphazardly and crowdedly on the walls—and uncompromisingly tacky signs, one of which limited husbands to three or fewer cups of Ivar's "Ever-Rejuvenating Clam Nectar" unless they had a note from their wives. Some of the signs were just plain nutty, as in "Seafood is Brain Food. Be wiser at Ivar's." Others were head-scratchers like "Where Clams and Culture Meet" (a play, with typically dubious wit, on the menu item "cultured clams"). The slogan that became his most famous was "Keep Clam." And when he began underwriting Seattle's Fourth of July fireworks display in Elliott Bay, just offshore from his Acres of Clams, the event inevitably was called "The Fourth of Jul-Ivar."

The oddest thing about Haglund was that he grew more popular and more revered as Seattle outgrew the 1950s and strove toward worldliness. Instead of trying to consign him to oblivion, out of embarrassment and nouveau sophistication, the city embraced him all the more warmly as it "matured." Even Haglund was baffled by Seattleites' love of him—in 1983, when as a joke he ran for Seattle Port Commissioner, he was horrified when the voters elected him by a wide margin even after he tried to withdraw. (He was to die two years later—possibly of shock.)

Seattleites' enduring love for Haglund was largely a function of his unpretentiousness and constant self-deprecation. It also partly stemmed from his intense love of Seattle and its humble roots; partly from the zest with which he played the Dumb Swede, that stock "Ya sure, ya betcha" character in a thousand Seattle jokes; and partly from his appropriation of a song, the "Old Settler's Song," that he turned into an evocation of the Seattle temperament, a homespun delineation of the difference between a Northwesterner and an ordinary, beleaguered, disgruntled, chronically restless American.

The song, which Haglund and Pete Seeger each claimed to have taught the other and which is printed on Ivar's restaurant placemats to this day, is sung by an old prospector who has spent the best years of his life futilely "prospecting and digging for gold." He washes up in the Pacific Northwest, where he gives in to the temperate climate and bountiful tidal flats and realizes the folly of his ways. Why work for food when Northwest Nature gives it to you for free? And why go to the trouble of getting rich, anyway? Now, newly enlightened and laid back, he articulates the abiding happiness that every Northwesterner feels:

And now that I'm used to the climate
I think that if a man ever found
A place to live easy and happy
That Eden is on Puget Sound

No longer the slave of ambition
I laugh at the world and its shams
As I think of my pleasant condition
Surrounded by acres of clams.

That forswearing of ambition, of course, was the defining characteristic of a Seattleite. Haglund's was a tradition that extended back to the beginning of recorded Northwest history. Even the native tribes here had been exceptionally pacific. It was a given that those who moved here now were more than willing to settle for jobs with lower salaries than they could command elsewhere in the country, the loss in income more than offset by the environmental perks that delighted employers called the "Mt. Rainier factor." People were willing to take substantial cuts in pay and career opportunities for the privilege of living "easy and happy" in the shadow of the nation's most spectacular mountain, and surrounded by some of the world's most beautiful waterways and forests. In adopting a more relaxed, pleasurable way of living and working a lot less hard for a lot less money, it seemed that Seattleites were spreading their retirement over their entire adult lives, savoring the joys of idleness during a portion of each working week rather than waiting until retirement to take the time to smell the huckleberries.

That, at any rate, was the plan Anne and I had made. When we moved back to Seattle, I leased a typesetting machine—manufactured by AM Varityper, it was about the size of a large desk—and set up a business in my basement under the name of Melmoth Typesetting. The typesetting process was relatively cumbersome: I would sit at a keyboard and CRT screen and type text that could be stored on a plastic disc and burned through a camera lens and type-font apparatus onto photographic paper stored on a roll inside the machine. Then I would run the paper through developing tanks, paste up the developed copy on boards in the layout a customer wanted, and send it off to a printer. It was easy work, and with two or three relatively large customers, I could undercut more respectable typesetting shops with their higher overhead and make enough money working at home to pay our bills and spend ample time on my quest for easy and happy living.

It was a measure of the attitude toward ambition in Seattle that my approach to business was more or less mainstream—an editor, for example, did not find it all that unusual to have to drive out to a house in a Seattle neighborhood to get typeset copy from some somnolent bearded guy working in his T-shirt and jeans in a cramped basement office. And I was soon to find a ready supply of graphic artists and others more than happy to work part-time for me, for little pay, their material ambitions being more or less in line with mine.

In short, the Seattle economy seemed ideally set up for people with no measurable drive.

There was, however, danger on the horizon, and the writer Emmett Watson, for one, was tirelessly raising the alarm in his *Seattle Post Intelligencer* column. The danger, in Watson's eyes, was that the rest of the nation was fast catching on to Seattle's scam and people were moving here in numbers large enough to destroy our ease and happiness. Due to the strenuous efforts of civic booster groups, property developers, travel agents, and just about any lucky soul who landed in Seattle on a business trip, the word was getting out that Seattle was a place where people had it made in the shade. "Those damned Californians are overrunning us now, and the trend must be stopped," Watson wrote in one typical tirade. The theme in his columns was unvarying: Growth and progress were evil agents out to destroy the Seattle Way of Life, and every newcomer to our shores was another nail in the coffin of the Northwest dream.

Born in Seattle in 1918, Watson attended the University of Washington, where he played baseball, then played briefly for the Seattle Rainiers of the Pacific Coast League before going to work for the *Seattle Star* in 1944. From there, he went to the *Seattle Times*, then to the *Post-Intelligencer*, where he gained fame with his "This Our City" column, a three-dot-item column like Herb Caen's in San Francisco. He made the national stage in 1961 when he broke the story that Ernest Hemingway's death had not been an accident, as claimed by his widow, but a suicide.

Watson was a witty and curmudgeonly writer, particularly when taking on, as he put it, "boosterism of a kind that would shock George F. Babbitt." The 1950s had seen the rise of a booster group called Greater Seattle, run by downtown interests, and in reaction Watson and a group of his drinking buddies almost immediately formed a counter-group called Lesser Seattle. Lesser Seattle was dedicated to spreading the news, largely through Watson's column, that it rained almost constantly in Seattle and that Seattleites were unfriendly, potentially violent people who hated outsiders, committed acts of vampirism on tourists, and made life miserable for new neighbors. "Have a nice day—somewhere else" became the group's mantra, and Watson labeled Lesser Seattle's primary effort the "KBO" (for "Keep the Bastards Out") movement. Part of the KBO agenda was to stop any development or progress that would accommodate a larger population. In 1957, when Seattle was in the midst of a debate over whether to build a second bridge across Lake Washington linking Seattle with its fast-growing suburbs to the east, Watson editorialized in the *Times* that "if there's one thing that splits Seattle wide open with controversy, it's our unholy urge toward progress and more progress." Not only should we not build the second bridge, he went on, "it's absolutely necessary that we start over by dismantling the existing span. . . . Let's purge ourselves of Lake Washington bridges for all time."

At every turn from then on, Watson would leap to the defense of Old Seattle against the pipe dreams of Greater Seattle. (Eventually he would come to refer to that group as "Grosser Seattle.") When downtown money interests forced through construction of a new sports stadium called the Kingdome, and managed finally to snare an NFL franchise for it, Watson suggested the new team be called the Seattle Stoics—a name, he wrote, that "is symbolically pure. Utterly appropriate to the team we will have—and the fans who will support it." Every time a national publication wrote a piece rhapsodizing about Seattle, Watson wrote a rebuttal. In 1977, when the first "most livable city" designation came out for Seattle, Watson reacted with appropriate alarm: "The powerful 'Eastern Establishment' press is in a conspiracy to overcrowd us. The *NY Times* extolled our cultural sophistication, the *Washington Post* raved about us only the other day." Whenever possible, he promoted the idea of spreading bad rather than good news about Seattle, on the theory that it would scare people away from the idea of moving here. "Our suicide rate is one of the highest in the nation," he wrote in 1969. "But we can be No. 1. Subtly, we could lure a better class of suicide here. Let two or three international celebrities knock themselves off in Seattle during a gloomy December and we'd have it made. They couldn't keep us off the front pages. Using our rain properly, we could become a proud, distant, forbidding community. Seattle's explosive growth could be slowed."

Over time, Watson's calls to arms grew more and more impassioned. By the late 1970s, the sense in Seattle that the End Was Nigh was more prevalent than was the sense that the city's greatness lay ahead. "Let us pray that the Mariners go on losing, to avoid national attention; regard every Seahawk fumble as a patriotic sacrifice for our city's oblivion," he wrote in a 1977 column. "Be surly in victory, malevolent in defeat. Snarl at strangers, glower at outsiders, write plaintive, complaining letters to our neighbors abroad. Let us dirty the streets, neglect our parks, magnify our problems. In short, we may have to destroy the city in order to save it."

I loved reading these perorations, even though I regarded the danger as minimal. True, the city did seem inhabited almost entirely by newcomers, but they seemed to grow moss in short order and melt into the scenery. Things went comically wrong whenever the boosters tried improving the city's image. The Mariners in particular had turned into such a hapless operation that whenever their name was in the national news, it inextricably linked Seattle with futility, failure, broken dreams, disappointment, and a whole host of other unsavory and un-American attributes. And the Seahawks, while more entertaining, were owned primarily by the Nordstrom family—certainly the oddest among pro sports franchise owners. Most owners craved the limelight, but the Nordstroms insisted on near-invisibility. They had bought majority interest in the Seahawks as a civic gesture, and wanted none of the attention that came with NFL team ownership. Descended from a young Swedish immigrant who came to Seattle after striking it moderately rich during the Alaska Gold Rush and who opened a downtown shoe store in 1905, they had all gone to work in the family business and by 1980 had parlayed it into a hugely successful retail clothing chain. But the Nordstroms, being classic Seattleites, were almost pathologically shy. They nearly never were quoted in the press, and were photographed even less. They steered clear of the reporters covering the Seahawks, talking with only a select few sportswriters, and always on the strict condition that they not be quoted. They were the only team owners in the NFL not to be named or photographed in their team's media guide. They were like human versions of Mt. Rainier—a spectacular regional asset that remained obscured most of the time.

In a city where even the successful promoters were that shy, it seemed to me that we would always be able to evade legitimately dangerous attention from the outside world. Between the weather outside and the mental makeup within, I reasoned, Seattle would forever be safe from the dangers posed by ambition.

My reverie over, I finally reached out and opened the door in answer to that knock. Standing on my porch was an editor I had typeset for at Butterworth Legal Publishers, which at the time had been pretty much my only customer.

"Hi!" she said. "Remember me?"

I did.

"I'm working right across the lake now, at this new company, called Microsoft? Have you heard of it?"

I hadn't.

The Funeral of Bobo

In early eighties Seattle, status-consciousness was all but forbidden. The closest a Seattleite could come to snobbery was a smug sense that he or she lived in paradise. What I had regarded ten years before as intolerable complacency I now embraced as a virtue: Let the rest of the country consume itself in the quest for status symbols—we Seattleites were living in a place so marvelous that standard American joys (money, lavish wardrobes, new cars, massive homes) weren't worth the effort it took to acquire them. Our down-at-the-heels clothing and down-at-payscale incomes were reverse status symbols, declarations of disdain for consumer comforts that paled in comparison with our God-given creature comforts.

Trying to work as little as possible, I found a ready supply of kindred spirits—overqualified and underambitioned labor—willing to ease my burden. I hired a part-time employee, Rick Herman, who liked to spend his time hiking, boating, and writing, and preferred to work only as many hours as he needed to feed himself, pay a few bills, and keep his recreational machinery operating. "What I do most isn't all that lucrative," he told me in the conversation we had in lieu of a job interview one day. "But it's how I prefer to spend my time. So I don't want to spend too many hours working."

Whenever I had a typeset book to paste up, I would rely on the services of Connie Butler, who had moved to Seattle with her boyfriend Rick Downing some years before. Both were college-educated and literate, and Butler had been a successful artist in Chicago. But the two had come to Seattle more or less to drop out. They bought a little rundown house in Wallingford, a working-class Seattle neighborhood. Downing bought a small commercial gillnetter and fished for salmon a few months each year, doing woodworking and fixing up their house in his off-season, and Butler did design work and paste-up for small magazine publishers and little typesetting shops like mine.

Occasionally, someone from Chicago would track down Butler in her Seattle hiding place and cajole her into accepting a commission to do a painting. One day, over her protests, Downing took me back to the little room that served as Butler's studio and showed me what she was working on. It was breathtaking—a softly hued, highly realistic, and romantic picture of a young woman in a rowboat, looking at once dreamily and somberly off to one side of a languid river overhung with lush trees. It spoke simultaneously of life's almost infinite possibilities and the odd comfort we can take in disappointment—a pretty nifty trick.

Stunned, I started praising it extravagantly, asking Butler why she didn't devote any promotional energy to her art, and why she spent any time at all doing the kind of work she was doing for me instead of painting and drawing masterpieces for the world. But she seemed both burdened and embarrassed by my enthusiasm, and I never brought up the subject again.

Like me, Butler worked out of her home and took in as little paying work as possible. Whenever I brought work over to her, she and Downing and I would spend hours sitting around talking about books—Butler and Downing were avid readers—and sharing Seattle Mariners baseball stories, the M's being arguably the most hapless team in the majors, if not in major-league history, and knowledgeable Seattle fans being both hard to find and gifted with a perverse ingenuity about the game. To be a Mariners fan was not only to have a taste for macabre humor; it was to be more a connoisseur of losing than of baseball itself.

Seattle in those days seemed to me almost entirely populated by people like Herman, Butler, and Downing: intelligent, talented, perceptive, literate, and far too wise to give in to the temptations of acquisitiveness and ambition. We were dropouts, and relatively righteous about it: I always felt that what we defined as "workaholic" the rest of the country defined as "normal,""acceptable," "admirable," or "American."

Those anomalous Seattleites interested in upward mobility and upscale appearance, however, had only to make a short drive across Lake Washington on Watson's reviled Highway 520 floating bridge to find the standard American middle-class determination to look like you were living large. Here were the bigger homes set farther back from the street behind bigger hedges and bigger lawns of the sort you associated with California. Here were the cul de sacs—exotic little circular dead ends of a kind found nowhere in Seattle proper. On the east side of the lake, everyone seemed to be striving to do materially better. The suburbs there had actually grown in population during the Boeing Bust, and by the 1980s they had emerged in the Seattle mind as tacky, menacing proof that "Californication," as Seattleites started calling the population growth and cultural changes they were beginning to see everywhere in their beloved city, was as real as Emmett Watson had so long insisted it was.

Small wonder, then, that I had never heard of Microsoft—it was located on the side of the lake I resolutely ignored. All I knew about the company was what the inquiring editor had told me: that it wrote software for personal computers—new machines that I had heard a little bit about, since they were just starting to make national news. Curious, I drove over a few days after her visit and made my way to the address she had given me.

The company was housed in a long, brown four-story building that stretched out behind an old Burgermaster drive-in. The building was typically nondescript—a bland concrete-and-glass suburban office structure of the sort you could see all along the highway on the east side of the lake. I made my way past the Burgermaster, pulled into the parking lot—it was less than half full—and walked through the double glass doors at the entrance.

The lobby was dark, crowded, chaotic, and as remarkable as the outside was unremarkable. Electronic equipment was piled everywhere, both in and out of boxes. There was no receptionist and no security—I could easily have walked out with all the computers I wanted. Kids looking like the "Frodo lives" freaks I remembered from college were running in all directions. Eventually, I found some signs with numbers and arrows on them and made my way down the appropriate hall to my editor's office.

The hallways were long, running interminably between rows of individual offices. There wasn't a cubicle or shared office in sight, Microsoft deeming it important to give every employee a private office, however small. My editor's was one in a row of editorial offices at the far end of one hallway, where *Star Wars*, *Star Trek*, and medieval-themed office décor gave way to posters of authors, folk singers, and floral arrangements—the stuff I remembered from girls' dorm rooms in college. All the editors down here were women, their little cluster of offices an oasis of femininity in a vast desert of male nerdulinity.

Microsoft at the time had not yet entered the word-processor and other application-software businesses that eventually would vault personal computers into the mainstream. It was focused on an operating system, MS-DOS, and personal-computer-language software programs (Pascal, COBOL, FORTRAN, BASIC) that were sold, as were personal computers at the time, mostly to hobbyists or curiosity-seekers with a lot of money.

These editors were working on booklets for programming minicomputers, as people were calling personal computers then, with languages like COBOL and BASIC. Computer programmers, it turned out, were helpless when it came to the English language, and Microsoft had hired a large number of English majors to keep these booklets coming out as fast as their software programs did. People who bought personal computers would also get a package of five-inch-square, soft plastic discs, like the ones I used in my typesetting machine, and a binder full of these little manuals; you would use one disc to boot up the machine and load its operating system, then eject it and replace it with the disc containing whatever program you wanted to use.

I couldn't believe there was any company anywhere that was hiring so many English majors. And when the English major who had called me out to Microsoft sat me down and explained what she wanted me to do, I couldn't begin to believe how much she was willing to pay me.

Like all phototypesetters at the time, I charged a set amount for typesetting and pasting up each page, my per-page fee averaging $5—a dollar or more below the average among my competitors. The price covered the cost to me of typing and formatting my customer's copy, running out proof sheets, photocopying them, bringing the copies to my customer for proofreading, and paying Butler for paste-up. After getting back the proofread copies, I would type up the corrections and changes, then cut out incorrect words or lines with a razor blade, stripping in the corrected copy. I charged 75 cents per correction for errors my customer made, and charged nothing to correct my own.

People at Microsoft didn't want to be bothered with that much accounting. They simply wanted me to run out an entire new page whenever anything—even if only a single punctuation mark—had to be corrected, and they wanted to pay my full per-page rate every time I had to rerun a page.

In other words, the place was a money machine. A single fifty-page manual, which might take two weeks from beginning to end of the project and would require only a small portion of each day in the bargain, could bring in a couple thousand dollars—more than I sometimes made in a month of full-time work for other clients. And these editors always paid immediately, never bothering to give one of my invoices more than a cursory glance.

This was a working arrangement, I decided, that I could happily indulge in for the rest of my life.

How can I explain how strange it was to have something like Microsoft suddenly land in Seattle? Nothing about the place was normal: A typical Seattleite got by on very little money and had all the time in the world to accomplish whatever it was he or she wanted to do. But the people in this place were the opposite: They had all the money in the world, and were desperately short of time. They worked around the clock—before long, I found myself making deliveries as early as six in the morning and as late as ten at night—and never under any circumstances showed any concern of any kind over money. It was as if they were looking for ways to get rid of it—in the hopes, maybe, that it would buy them more time.

The other odd thing about Microsoft was the incongruous connection between its appearance and its drive. The people wandering frantically around Microsoft's hallways looked just like normal (if nerdish) Seattleites. They were dressed in jeans, sweatshirts, T-shirts, flannel, boots, sneakers, wore their hair unkempt, and were often sloppily bearded. They sported, in other words, your basic laid-back Seattle look. Yet they crackled with purposefulness, ambition, and fervor. They looked and acted like people who knew they were on to something unimaginably big, and they had the passion of True Believers. They always needed everything immediately, and were convinced that they were doing work that would change the world—an attitude that by definition was hilarious in a Seattleite.

I found out during one of my visits that the company was run by a twenty-six-year-old named Bill Gates—who, I was told again and again, was both a genius and a wacko. He had been raised in Seattle, gone to Harvard, dropped out after one year, and moved to Albuquerque, New Mexico, where he founded what then was called the Micro-Soft Corporation. After two years there, he came back home—he had done his forty days in the desert and had had enough.

It was clear that Microsoft was headed for success-territory the likes of which had never been seen in Seattle. The excitement there was infectious and exhilarating—this amazing little emotional and financial boom exploding on the quiet eastern shore of Lake Washington. I kept waiting to feel in my heart the thrill I could see everywhere around me whenever I went out there. But, instead, the more of it I took in, the more I found myself recoiling from it.

At first, I thought it was simply that I couldn't imagine spending as much time away from home as these people had to spend. By now, we had two daughters, and being at home during the day, working mostly when the girls were asleep, left me exposed almost constantly to irresistible charm. Erin ran around the house all day either narrating her life in the third person ("'Hi Dad!' said Erin. Then she ran quickly into the kitchen . . .") or explaining the world around her, as in: "This is the permanental fur cat; its fur is permanental soft. As it grows, its fur will usually grow soft. These are the ears. As the cat grows, it will usually get dots on its ears. This is 'iminie,' from playing roughly with other cats. And its tail is the usual soft, slim, round part of the body." Meanwhile, her little sister Caitlin toddled around calling me "Little Shat" and taking me by the hand whenever I came upstairs from the basement, leading me to a couch, sitting me down, and correcting me as if I were a wayward child ("Now, Little Shat . . . you know that was a *very* bad thing to do"). The opportunity to give that up for the company of hyperactive computer geeks and endless work on algorithm-bedecked paragraphs about BASIC and COBOL was horrifying.

Yet it was hard not to see that my customers at Microsoft were destined for wealth and success beyond the reach and imagination of your basic English major, and I felt sorely tempted again and again to apply for work there. I could see that it would be the end of the financial struggles that dogged my half-hearted business venture. Microsoft editorial jobs consisted mostly of checking grammar and punctuation in extremely straightforward prose—not a daunting task, except for the risk of death by boredom—and the payoff was potentially immense. I was always trying to talk myself into being interested, asking myself why I had such an adverse reaction to the idea of working there, gradually coming to suspect that my fear of the place stemmed from more than just wanting to spend time with my family. (The thematically useless idea that Microsoft had no interest in hiring me has never occurred to me.)

Erin had a way of timing her pronouncements to coincide in eerie ways with my preoccupations. I was sitting around the house one day, inwardly moaning about having to go out to Microsoft and all it represented, when she popped in, stood staring intently at me, and intoned:

"Erin looked concernedly at her daddy. 'You must go into the Dark Phoebus,' she said."

I was pondering my ambivalence with particular frenzy one day when I came walking out of the Microsoft building and fell prey to one of those timely memories that always occur to people who inhabit memoirs. I found myself recalling Doc Maynard, the hesitantly legendary settler here who gave Seattle both its name and its collective consciousness.

In 1850, unhappily married and mired in debt, Dr. David Maynard set off for California and its fabled gold rush. His wife Lydia and their two children stayed behind. On the way west, he fell in with a family headed for Puget Sound. The group was decimated by a cholera epidemic, and Maynard fell in love with one of the survivors—Catherine Broshears, who was widowed by the epidemic—and followed her to her brother's home on south Puget Sound. The brother ran Maynard off when he learned he was married, and Maynard eventually made his way down to California. A friend there told him the real money to be made was back up in the Pacific Northwest, where a man could get rich cutting down trees and shipping the lumber to San Francisco, which was undergoing a massive construction boom. After returning to the Northwest, Maynard settled in Olympia—near the Broshears' settlement—and promptly went broke trying to run a store. His habit of extending unlimited credit and selling goods at cost made him too popular with customers and too unpopular with competitors, one of whom finally persuaded him that he would do better up at New York-Alki.

The short story about Maynard from then on is that he laid claim to 640 acres of land that eventually would be worth $100 million, and frittered away all of it, dying more or less in poverty. The long story—told with mythic power and poignancy by Murray Morgan in *Skid Road*—was that Maynard was an epic dreamer undone by visionary tendencies, insufficient greed, ambition for everyone but himself, and drink. On the one hand, Maynard had great instincts: He changed the name New York-Alki to Seattle, rather than Duwamps, as the territorial legislature tried to do, because Seattle would sound more alluring to potential commercial developers; he gave some of his best waterfront land away to newcomer Henry Yesler so that Yesler could build the region's first steam-powered lumber mill there—a move, Maynard knew, that would vault Seattle ahead of the other settlements of equal size along Puget Sound in the race to become the region's leading city. He sold land and a fully equipped building for $10.00 to an itinerant blacksmith so that Seattle would have a resident one. He was the first settler to establish commercial ties with San

Francisco and its money. Maynard dreamed big dreams for Seattle, and lived to see them more than realized largely because of the moves he made in the settlement's early years.

But Maynard also found it impossible to keep for himself any of the wealth he brought to Seattle. In 1855, the Washington Territory started forcing Salish natives onto reservations. Maynard—who had been the first settler there to employ natives, who had learned their language and counted many natives among his good friends—stocked Chief Sealth (after whom Maynard would eventually name Seattle) and the other natives being sent to a reservation across the sound with enough supplies from his store to get them through their first winter away from their homes. When he sought reimbursement from the territorial government, he was rebuffed. He also was stigmatized as an "Indian lover" in the wake of that incident and ostracized by the rest of the city. Alienated, he traded away his Seattle land for a slightly larger and considerably less valuable parcel on Alki Point—site of the original New York-Alki settlement, now across the Duwamish River from Seattle proper—where he and his now-wife Catherine tried to make a go of farming. That venture failed largely because Maynard was an unenthusiastic farmer who gave away to less fortunate people most of what he managed to harvest. Finally, his house burned down and he and Catherine moved back to Seattle and opened a hospital. That enterprise went under in short order, even though Maynard's reputation was restored among Seattleites, because he hated billing his patients.

Eventually, Maynard ended up afoul of the courts when his first wife, Lydia, came west to lay claim to half his land. Maynard had finagled a divorce out of the territorial legislature even though, as one of the dissenting legislators objected, his wife didn't know she was being divorced. The dispute over his land dragged on for years, until finally the courts decreed that neither of Maynard's wives was entitled to any of his land, since the first had never lived on it and the second hadn't been married to him when he took a married man's claim to 640 acres. Therefore, the state decreed, he had to give half his original claim back to the government. Since by then all Maynard had left were a few parcels scattered around Seattle, the rest having been given or traded disadvantageously away, he found himself destitute. When he finally died in 1873, Maynard was as broke as his city was prosperous. He was revered by his contemporaries as much for his misfortune as for his generosity, and all of Seattle turned out for his funeral.

The most fitting memorial to Maynard—a puzzling tribute left by an anonymous worshipper not on Maynard's tombstone but on his wife Catherine's—reads, ambiguously and hilariously, "She did what she could."

Seattle was only 130 years old on the day I was standing outside Microsoft remembering Doc Maynard. The shadows of the other original settlers—Lee Terry, C. D. Boren, his sister Laura Boren, Arthur Denny—loomed everywhere in Seattle, in the form of downtown-Seattle street names, district names, and prominent families. But Maynard, whose only visible legacy was a six-block-long South Seattle street and a single Pioneer Square building, loomed immensely larger in the Seattle imagination. He was the only one among Seattle's founders who remained a genuinely compelling figure—a man who, in Morgan's words, "tried to get rich and instead brought wealth to others," who "was Seattle's first booster, the man who was sure greatness could come," but who "dreamed the right dreams too soon." For a long time, Seattle was divided economically and socially by Yesler Avenue, the street down which Henry Yesler skidded logs to his waterfront mill. North of Yesler was respectable downtown Seattle, all gleaming office buildings and upscale retail outlets; south of Yesler was a disreputable district of squat, decrepit brick buildings known as Skid Road, the "place of dead dreams," as Morgan called it. Until a concerted renewal project began in the early 1980s, much of the area was a slum. The district had been called by many names over the years (the Lava Bed, the Tenderloin, the Great Restricted District), but when it was first named, it was named Maynardtown.

There was something admirable not only in Maynard's generosity and the breadth of his vision but also—more so, in fact—in his haplessness, which as time went on came to seem a profound discomfort with success and wealth. Maynard died a material loser and a spiritual winner. The charm that endured about him, the element in his legend that invariably brought a fond smile to your lips when he came to mind, was the involuntary nature not only of his losing but also of his winning. Something in his soul kept him from realizing the dreams of wealth and success that he harbored for himself and for his settlement. At every step of the way, some act of his (most often, as was the case in his dealings with the unfortunate Salish natives, an act of generosity) undid him and left him materially worse off than he was before. He was at the pinnacle of his fortune the moment he first registered claim to his land—the same moment, of course, when his coevals were at the nadir of theirs. They parlayed their land into vast personal fortunes; he parlayed his into a great city—and a dubious legend.

Whatever Maynard's dreams for himself and his legacy, he lives on in Seattle as a classic divided soul: a man who always managed to work at cross-purposes with himself, consistently undoing his own designs in one way or another. He was Seattle's first underachiever. And I found myself wondering, standing there that day in the Microsoft parking lot, if Lesser Seattleites—the only true Seattleites—were not still somehow so in thrall to Maynard that we reflexively turned away from chances at wealth or success. In the words of another of my old college professors, a Yale expatriate named Rand Jack, we were "a city of underachievers." Was our collective lack of ambition a psychological trait inherited from Maynard? More to the point—was mine? Had Maynard so formed his city's soul that Seattleites forever afterward would yearn more for disrepute than fame and fortune?

It was undoubtedly the Maynard in me that led me to join and lend my typesetting services to a group called Invisible Seattle, which had been formed in 1979 by Philip Wohlsetter and James Winchell, the latter a friend of mine from college. Through most of the 1980s, Invisible Seattle published and performed pieces combating the takeover of Visible Seattle by developers, gentrifiers, and other promoters of pretension. The group published a newspaper, *The Zeitgeist*, issued proclamations, renamed Seattle landmarks, and put Seattle political and cultural figures on mock trial. Invisible Seattle rechristened the Monorail the "Disorient Express"; set up a network of personal computers at Seattle's annual Bumbershoot arts festival so that anyone could sit down and write, the collective work eventually compiled, edited, and published as a massive collaborative novel entitled *Invisible Seattle*; and popped up everywhere in the city, performing various disruptions of one kind or another.

Much of Invisible Seattle's effort was directed toward honoring the memory of the most important celebrity and symbolic presence in Seattle history: Bobo the Gorilla, who held sway over the regional imagination from his arrival here in 1951 until well beyond his untimely death in 1968. Bobo had been captured in Africa when only two weeks old—he was the youngest gorilla ever to have been captured alive—when his father was killed and his mother captured by William "Gorilla Bill" Said, a self-styled adventurer who made his living selling gorillas to zoos. Said sold Bobo to Raymond and Jean Lowman, a couple living in Anacortes, Washington, some sixty miles north of Seattle. The Lowmans tried raising Bobo as if he were a human child. They dressed him in slacks, shirts, and cardigan sweaters, and he lived with them in their home until his habit of breaking everything he touched (his favorite activity was throwing) led them to build him a house of his own, adjacent to theirs. The Lowmans and Bobo were a considerable tourist attraction; it was not uncommon for the family to look up from Sunday dinner to see out-of-towners clustered at their window, snapping pictures.

Bobo soon grew to unmanageable proportions, though, and the Lowmans sold him to Seattle's Woodland Park Zoo in 1953. There, he proved to be a showstopper—so much so that the zoo was able to mount a prodigious fund-raising campaign centered on Bobo's charisma, raising enough money to build a new house for its primates.

Bobo, wrote "Citizen of Invisible Seattle" David Humphries in the *Weekly* early in 1981, was Seattle's "unrivaled star celebrity in residence. . . . Surrounded by an indefinable aura of joy, he was loved by all who knew him. . . . Bobo was the biggest attraction the Woodland Park Zoo ever had. But he was much more than that. He was a community asset, a hero to children, a mascot. His widely publicized zoo antics so delighted Seattleites that a citywide cult of Bobo imitators developed. . . . Before the Space Needle went up or the Pike Place Market was redeveloped, before the Sonics or the Seahawks, Bobo *was* Seattle, and Seattle was infected with a mad passion, Bobomania."

People traveled from all over the Northwest to see Bobo, and he outperformed even Ivar Haglund in Seattle newspapers and on television. *Seattle Times* reporter Tom Robbins, in a typical 1962 accolade, wrote that Bobo put to shame human Seattle's promotional efforts. "It has taken millions of dollars and seven years of hard work to fill the World's Fair grounds with visitors," Robbins wrote. "There is a big fellow in North Seattle who, with no help and no money, could empty those grounds in less than 10 minutes. . . . It is understandable that a chap that can bend iron bars and stretch truck tires as if they were rubber bands might be unimpressed by the accomplishments of puny humans. While we race like schizophrenic squirrels in a revolving cage filled with status symbols, time clocks, tax forms, and parking meters, he relaxes in uncluttered, air-conditioned comfort and reigns in quiet majesty as king of Woodland Park Zoo. His name is Bobo."

Humphries came closer than anyone to elucidating Bobo's mysterious charm. "Maybe it was Bobo's Pepsodent playboy smile," he wrote, "or it could have been his eyes; most male gorillas have a mean, malevolent look in their yellowish, bloodshot eyes, but Bobo's were Marie Osmond white. Whatever the reason, most everyone agreed: Bobo was a looker."

His looks, unfortunately, were something of a false advertisement. In 1956, the zoo imported a female companion, named Fifi, in the hopes that

Bobo would produce more marquee idols that would further burnish the zoo's image and heighten its popularity and fund-raising capacity. But Bobo refused to have anything to do with Fifi, who would grace his cage and futilely pursue him to the day he died. Bobo spurned Fifi's often frantic sexual advances by throwing her off, screaming, threatening her, and sometimes beating her up.

The entire city followed the doings of Bobo and Fifi as if they were the last surviving members of the Royal Family. Seattle newspapers and television stations chronicled every twist and turn in the sexual saga. Interpretations abounded. Everyone had a theory about Bobo's obstinate celibacy—the prevailing belief being that Fifi lacked looks, grace, and charm—and a veritable cottage industry of pop primate psychology took root in 1960s Seattle. Bobo's zookeepers tried various stratagems in their increasingly imaginative attempts to stimulate the big lug's libido: They placed infant gorillas outside his cage at one point, in the hopes that Bobo would feel sexually inspired by paternal stirrings, and they rigged up a television monitor in his cage, through which they broadcast romantic scenes from classic movies. But Bobo remained unmoved, and died heirless.

An autopsy lent something of a tragic twist to what had become an increasingly comic story: It turned out that Bobo had an extra female chromosome, caused by a little-known condition called Klinefelter's Syndrome.

Upon his death, Bobo was given to the University of Washington's Museum of History and Industry, which stuffed him and put him on display. He stands there still. "Alive or dead, Bobo is still a terrific drawing card," noted the *Seattle Times*. Visitors flocked to the museum, which had hitherto been a little-visited, arcane institution, to pay homage. "Some Bellevue teenagers," the *Times* reported shortly after his posthumous debut, "burst into tears upon seeing Bobo."

Humphries and Invisible Seattle, in honoring Bobo, understood that they were paying homage to a beloved Seattle that was vanishing against its will. In posing the question why a city bent on sophistication would be so in thrall to something so lowbrow, Humphries observed, "But that's what makes Bobo interesting: he was a reflection of ourselves, of the city in which he lived. In the 1950s and 1960s, Seattle was filled with families with children, and the kids had this big, childlike, show-off gorilla to look up to. With the declining birth rate, we have no need for such heroes now. We've gotten more worldly and grown-up. But in Bobo's heyday he was a lot like Seattle: friendly, growing, unsophisticated, a little clumsy, good-hearted, and gladly willing to entertain visiting relatives."

When not mourning Seattle's past through Bobo worship, Invisible Seattle was looking to the city's future with some trepidation. Across the nation, rock music was moving from disco to mindless, formulaic pop that eventually would take the form of inartistic exuberant male big-hair extravaganzas. The country as a whole was moving—largely through the spread of television—to a uniform popular culture that was rapidly eroding the nation's separate and distinct regional cultural traditions. Seattle, in spite of its boosters' desire to meld with the American mainstream, had a thriving rock-and-roll countertrending underground in the early 1980s, and I often joined Invisible Seattleites in forays to the Rainbow Tavern, in the University District, where we took in the act of the best of these groups, Red Dress.

Fronted by a skinny, bald Roosevelt High School graduate named Gary Minkler, Red Dress sported a loud, aggressive, thundering, intricate, and angry sound that merged punk and sixties rock in a musical melee that had its audiences screaming, leaping, and bouncing off walls and one another in a frenzy. The Red Dress themes, both sonic and lyric, tended toward darkness, futility, and cheerful fear of the future. One song, entitled "Bob Was a Robot," was a wailing number sung by a boy to his girlfriend, who has left him for a robot; another, "Teenage Pterodactyls," grafted adolescent angst to dinosaur myth; and a third, "I'm Not an Astronaut, I'm a Nut," screamed out a Seattlesque take on the American lust/hatred for celebrities:

> *I'm gonna blow a hole*
> *In a famous face . . .*

Invisible Seattle's greatest triumph was the highly publicized mock trial of Tom Robbins, who came to fame in the early 1980s with two novels, *Another Roadside Attraction* and *Even Cowgirls Get the Blues*. Robbins had been a colorful newspaper writer and art critic for the *Seattle Times*, and had been largely responsible for bringing alive the Seattle visual-arts scene of the 1970s through his reviews. He left journalism in the late 1970s after, as he put it, "calling in well" one morning, and began publishing fiction. With the success of his novels, he discovered that he had an overpowering taste for celebrity. By 1984, he seemed to be everywhere, zestfully posing for photographs and spouting such self-consciously cute aphorisms as "It's never too late to have a happy childhood." Since he had become the headline-hungry antithesis of a Seattleite, a Bobo without portfolio, and since his books were distasteful enough to become best-sellers, an outraged Invisible Seattle prosecuted him and put him on trial. After months of pretrial publicity in the local press, to which Robbins reacted with increasing bewilderment, Invisible Seattle staged its trial at Seattle Center, before a packed house and a rigged jury. Winchell was judge, Wohlstetter prosecutor, the jury a gospel choir, and a parade of witnesses was played by various members of Seattle's underground arts world. Robbins wisely declined to attend; Invisible Seattle summarily found him guilty of being "completely visible."

By 1983, Melmoth had two customers: Microsoft and Butterworth Legal Publishers, the latter publisher primarily of a book-thick periodical enti-tled *Land Use Board of Appeals Reports*, LUBA being an Oregon govern-ment agency. Between the two, Melmoth was bringing in nearly $100,000 per year. I was able to get a bank loan for a new $30,000 state-of-the-art typesetting machine, complete with a modem, and thus could receive files electronically from capable customers rather than having to retype their manuscripts.

Microsoft began showing that year what a force it and its industry promised to be, predicting it would post an impressive $70 million in software sales in the coming year and announcing that it was about to take what the *Weekly* saw as a colossal gamble, moving into the "application software" market against such solidly entrenched competitors as Visicorp, Micropro, and Digital Research. With its operating system, MS-DOS, installed in "40 percent of all microcomputers sold," the company wanted to expand the reach of its operating-system sales and strengthen its posi-tion against more established software companies. To do that, Microsoft would have to hire and train legions of sales representatives (in 1983, the company had only twenty-seven) and learn how to sell directly to cus-tomers—"called, at Microsoft, 'end users,'" wrote *Weekly* reporter Joey Pious. MS-DOS had been sold almost exclusively to microcomputer manufacturers, who installed the operating system on computers before shipping them to retailers, and Microsoft lacked experience in the retail market.

Gates was defiantly optimistic. "A revolution is taking place in the world of computers today," he told Pious, "and software is where the innovation is coming from. No longer do we need to go out and build better, more powerful hardware to achieve productivity improvements. We simply develop a new software package, and people can put it to use immediately on their existing machines. The revolution is here—and it is soft."

Pious was skeptical. "The competition is here, too," he wrote, "and it is hard."

Aside from their English-major ghettoes, Microsoft and Butterworth had nothing in common. Butterworth, in fact, was as moribund as Microsoft was thriving. Two years in the typesetting business had taught me to recognize the signs of incipient business failure—I once had delivered a typeset book about NASA's cover-up of the civilization the Apollo astronauts had found on the dark side of the moon to a publisher whose door was padlocked and festooned with notes from outraged creditors—and I could see Butterworth's demise coming. This was distressing not only because the company was subsidizing half of my sloth, but because a good number of fellow faint-hearted, underachieving English majors worked there.

Chief among these was Jan Allister, a newcomer to Seattle from Chico, California. Allister had been a divorced mother, named Jan Willis, of three, and teaching at California's Chico State College when she remarried. Soon after, she moved to Seattle with her new husband, Mark Allister, who came to the University of Washington to work toward his Ph.D. in creative writing. Jan was working at Butterworth to help put him through school.

Whenever I came out to Butterworth, Allister and I would start talking about writing and books like two language-lorn English-speakers who suddenly encountered one another in a remote foreign country. And somewhere along the line of exchanging book recommendations and life stories, I told her about my years at Ardis, in Ann Arbor, and she passed that story on to one of her co-workers, Ann Senechal.

Senechal was a newcomer to Seattle who had taken a temporary job at Butterworth while she was waiting for her new job as managing editor of the *Weekly* to begin. I spent a lot of time at Butterworth explaining the salient points of Seattle culture to her—particularly the rich, astonishing, and Seattle-appropriate record of futility being compiled by the Seattle Mariners—and she always listened with intense interest. But nothing I told her interested her nearly as much as something Allister told her about me: that I had known the poet Joseph Brodsky when I lived in Ann Arbor.

I was in the Butterworth offices one afternoon when Senechal came up to me and asked, disbelievingly, if what she had heard was true—"that you know Joseph Brodsky?" I was acutely embarrassed by the question because it made me feel as if I had been boasting, intent on making myself seem more interesting than I really was—no self-disrespecting Seattleite, after all, would ever stoop to name-dropping.

Nevertheless, I *had* let that slip to Allister, and now I admitted to Senechal that the improbable claim was true.

It turned out that Senechal was asking not out of curiosity but because Brodsky was coming to the University of Washington for a reading, and the *Weekly* wanted someone to cover the event. "Is that something you could do?" she asked.

I couldn't tell whether she was asking if I'd be willing or if I had the writing ability. In any event, I immediately said yes.

In due course, Brodsky came to Seattle, read to a packed house at the University of Washington's Kane Hall, and spent a day walking around Seattle with me and talking. At one point we wandered into Ye Olde Curiosity Shoppe, a cluttered waterfront emporium packed with classically tacky souvenirs and famed for its signature attraction—a mummified corpse with a bullet hole in its chest. Brodsky was enthralled. He bought two little boxes made from seashells for himself and a coonskin hat for Erin.

For all the time we had spent together in Ann Arbor, I had never asked to hear the story of Brodsky's expulsion from Russia. He always seemed to hate playing the romantic figure of the Russian Exile, which was something of a stock character in seventies and eighties America, and he preferred suffering his homesickness in silence. But now he seemed in the mood to reminisce, and he told the whole sordid story, his voice lapsing into stunned gloom only once, when he was recalling how the secret police were insisting that he fill out a form consenting to be exiled. "How shall I describe myself here?" Brodsky had asked, pointing to a blank line on the document. "Just sign, 'Joseph the Jew,'" his interrogator answered.

Like every Russian I knew, Brodsky had taken to the U.S. with enthusiasm for everything but the location. He had happily become a citizen and settled into the life of an increasingly prominent Russian-American poet. He was studying English frenziedly and beginning to write poetry in English as well as Russian. He loved being free of government scrutiny and able to vote in elections that mattered. He was passionately conservative, as were virtually all exiled Russians I knew—I remember him saying, when Jimmy Carter defeated Gerald Ford in 1976, that he'd "have to find a new country to live in"—and he still was saddled with an amazing, made-in-Russia addiction to cigarettes. His Edgewater Hotel room was filled with bottles of heart medication—he had had two bypass operations by then—and packs of cigarettes.

He also had not shaken his conviction, universally and passionately held among Russians, that ethnic divisions were Everything. We walked over a good deal of downtown Seattle and the Seattle waterfront that day, with Brodsky expostulating constantly about Seattle's charms. "It is so beautiful here, Fred! So peaceful! I might move here, actually . . . it's a perfect place. And you know what I like best about it, Fred? It's that there are no swarthy people here!"

I was less dismayed by the sentiment itself—I had long since grown used to hearing such pronouncements from even the most enlightened Russians, including Russian Jews—than I was by what it indicated to me about Seattle. My years east had been eye-opening in good part because racial and ethnic divisions were so open and so deep back there. In Albany and Ann Arbor in the 1970s, I routinely heard whites and blacks alike refer to blacks as "colored," and I had developed the widely held self-image among Seattleites of our city as an exceptionally enlightened, bias-free utopia. But Brodsky, however inadvertently, was gracelessly pointing out that Seattle was less enlightened than overwhelmingly white, Seattle tolerance being more a function of uniformity than diversity. It's easy to tolerate people, after all, that you never have anything to do with. Could it be that Seattleites were no less racist than the rest of the world, the only thing setting us apart being the lack of opportunity to express racist sentiment?

With its population 83 percent Caucasian, Seattle was the second-whitest in the nation among large cities, trailing Indianapolis by less than 1 percent. I wondered if we weren't too inclined to take credit for things beyond our control when it came to our pretensions to tolerance. In matters of race, we were tolerating the absent. It was a little like our self-satisfaction over how nice everyone in Seattle was—how hard is it to be nice when you live in such a stress-free city, free even from immoderate weather? Brodsky made our self-satisfaction feel unwarranted, and I was reminded in that connection of yet another line from Murray Morgan: " 'To hear you people talk,' an easterner told a Seattle friend, 'you'd think you *built* Mt. Rainier.' "

It turned out that the *Weekly* liked my Brodsky piece enough to ask what else I wanted to write about, and within a matter of months I was freelancing regularly there, supplementing my typesetting-business income and setting off on a steep learning curve about Seattle and its possibilities.

The ascendance of the *Weekly* can be seen now as a sign that Seattle was on the threshold of massive change—moving from a big provincial town to something like a major American city. Even in 1976, when the *Weekly* was founded, it wasn't clear that Seattle was ready for a publication offering an alternative to the complacent coverage sold by the city's dailies—nor that there was enough cultural life in Seattle to sustain a culture-centric weekly. But by 1983, when I began working half-time for the *Weekly*, it was the city's leading cultural voice, and the paper's offices were filled with the kind of high energy that ascendant organizations always have. We were on a roll at the *Weekly* and we knew it—and we sensed that Seattle was, too.

The more time I spent at Microsoft, meanwhile, the clearer it was to me that the company was going to be a solid success. Every time I went out there the place was packed with more people. Microsoft kept offering me more and more work from more and more editors and hiring people at an ever-more-blistering pace. My friend Jan Allister was growing increasingly miserable at Butterworth, so I told her about Microsoft and introduced her to the head of its editorial department. The woman hired Allister almost immediately after giving her an editing test. I might not have had the stomach to work at such an emerging colossus myself, but at least now I was assured of getting all the typesetting work I needed.

This was vitally important. Writing was proving to be immensely pleasurable, and my wife, with career ambitions no greater than mine and with an even greater desire to stay at home playing with our daughters, began doing adoption counseling part-time, generating the same puny income I was earning with my writing. So it was typesetting that was paying our bills. And as long as I could keep cash-spewing Microsoft as a customer, I could avoid the distasteful ritual of getting into my business costume—an old, ill-fitting jacket-and-slacks outfit I had bought years ago for some adult social occasion—working myself into an optimistic lather, and making sales calls on potential customers. Nothing was more depressing. I had only had to try that a few times, and every depressing attempt left me feeling like Willy Loman without the charm.

Taking Stock

David Brewster in Seattle was like the Warner Brothers' Tasmanian Devil in a narcolepsy ward. He was short and frantically energetic, with the Tasmanian Devil's oversized round head and twisted mouth, and he spun ideas and words out of his head at almost supersonic speeds. He was consumed with positively Criswellian ambition for Seattle, determined to help make it a Great Cultured City on the order of Paris or Rome. And everywhere he turned, he butted heads with an establishment and population that really didn't want to make that much of an effort to change their sleepy little hometown into another East Coast–style city full of smog, smartasses, smarminess, and self-importance.

Although Brewster was one of a kind—particularly when it came to intellectual energy and the determination to see his ideas through to the end—he also was a Seattle type: the overeducated newcomer from the east, lured to the frontier by its rough-hewn charms but determined nonetheless to bring it the civilized values he fled—particularly when it came to restaurants and the arts. Roger Sale and Paul Schell were others of that ilk—eastern transplants in love with Seattle on the one hand, dismayed by its complacent disdain for progress and learning on the other. They had come west not so much to flee unpleasantness as to enlighten natives kept by an excess of pleasantness from reaching their intellectual and cultural potential. These carpetbaggers, with their infuriating habit of constantly telling Seattle it had a lot of growing up to do before it could be taken seriously as a city, and their even more infuriating habit of mentioning the college they'd attended whenever they were introduced to someone, were very much fixtures in 1980s Seattle, and objects of disdain.

Brewster was different. Although Yale-educated, he never included "Yale" in his personal introduction. He lacked pretension—particularly when it came to his wardrobe, which featured horn-rimmed, greasy glasses, rumpled clothing, and a haircut that looked like a practical joke. He insisted that people call him "Dave" rather than "Mr. Brewster." He was legitimately brilliant rather than the kind of earnest, over-read, and underimaginative alum East Coast schools kept sending Seattle's way. He was unstoppable in his ambition, and his enthusiasms were infectious even to Seattle natives.

Most would-be sophisticators of Seattle eventually lapsed into resigned grumbling intended more to showcase their own alienated cultural enlightenment than to effect any real change in the city. But Brewster was the kind of dreamer who couldn't rest until his dreams had taken a turn for the tangible. And he loved his adopted city too much to let it remain benighted. So with his 1976 launch of the *Weekly*, he helped set in motion a Seattle cultural shift on a par with the one set off in 1926 by the election of reformer Bertha K. Landes, the mayor who killed off Seattle's brothel industry for the last time.

After graduating from Yale, Brewster had wanted to move to San Francisco, but settled on Seattle because the University of Washington was the school closest to San Francisco to offer him a job. He arrived at the UW in 1968 to teach English and finish his dissertation, but soon soured on his academic ambitions and dropped out. After a stint at the *Seattle Times* as a copy editor, he moved to *Seattle* magazine, a glossy monthly published by Stimson Bullitt (a Seattle institution, the Bullitt family owned Seattle's KING Broadcasting and ran various foundations and arts enterprises), until the magazine foundered on Brewster's habit of running stories and setting an editorial tone that his advertisers abhorred. They eventually killed the magazine by boycotting it.

In 1971, Brewster left for KING-TV, and his fellow *Seattle* writer and friend Gordon Bowker left to start a gourmet coffee company called Starbucks. After a brief stint at KING as an assignment editor, Brewster went to work for *Argus*, a downtown Seattle publication, as a writer and managing editor. He left there in 1974 and published a Seattle restaurant guide, *A Gourmet's Notebook*, that elicited bemused howls from Seattleites.

The notion that their city harbored either notable restaurants or diners who could tell struck everyone but Brewster as hilarious.

When he got around to founding the *Weekly* in 1976, it looked as if Brewster had figured out how to make publishing work as a business proposition. Publishing newsprint rather than a glossy magazine cut production costs; cultivating legions of small and large advertisers rather than a few major ones kept his revenue streams diverse enough to prevent any one of them from drying up and killing off his business. And the editorial mix he developed—serious, opinionated, and thorough political, arts, and issues reporting mingled on his pages with the salacious, advertiser-friendly, and frivolous, with opinionated events listings and immensely entertaining personal ads thrown in as well—brought in a broad (and advertiser-beloved) mix of baby-boom readers from all over the city. By 1982, when I wrote my first piece for the *Weekly*, Brewster was one of the biggest stories in town.

Modeled editorially on New York's *Village Voice*, alternative newsweeklies had sprung up all over the country in the late 1970s. Drawing their income from commercial advertisers and personals, they featured subjective reporting and aggressively stylish writing, with a focus on arts, entertainment, and cuisine, that offered relief from the bland, objective fare served up by daily papers. Brewster, characteristically, had higher-than-national-average aspirations for his paper. His was the only weekly in the country, other than the *Village Voice*, that was not given away free to readers. While most weeklies paid substantially less than living wages, constantly turning over their staffs so as to keep low-cost young writers on the payroll, Brewster wanted to pay his writers enough to keep them at the *Weekly* for their entire careers. He was intent on developing a core group of writers so skilled that readers would pick up his papers because the writing—no matter on what subject—was so striking. And he wanted his paper to be taken as seriously as the mainstream media when it came to covering Seattle arts and politics. (For that matter, he wanted Seattleites to start taking arts and politics seriously—a tall order, given the city's history.)

I met Brewster after having published three or four freelance columns, all assigned by Ann Senechal. I had heard quite a bit about him by then—he was notorious as a City Hall gadfly and a goad to the downtown establishment, and his pretensions to grandeur for both the *Weekly* and Seattle were well known and widely viewed as delusional. He wanted to talk with me about becoming a quarter-time staff writer, and I came down to the *Weekly* offices one afternoon to meet with him. He ushered me into a glass-walled-and-ceilinged room, evocative of a tent, that had been artily retrofitted into an old Seattle building's spacious office. He sat down across a conference table from me and began talking . . . and talking . . . and talking. He talked about Seattle. He talked about journalism as practiced by the two Seattle daily papers. He talked about the Vision (always pronounced by Brewster with a capital V) of alternative journalism. He talked about the *Village Voice*, the *Atlantic Monthly*, *The New Yorker* and *The New Republic*, making it clear that he wanted his *Weekly* to be of that quality—an attitude that came across as completely insane in the Seattle of 1982. He talked about Seattle historical figures, politicians, business leaders, fads, trends, churches, bars, sports teams, schools, and neighborhoods. He talked about the *Weekly*'s mission to shake things up in Seattle, make people think about and challenge and question the status quo. He talked about Seattle's potential for greatness and his refusal to countenance the city's traditional complacency. Then he asked me only three questions:

"Did you study journalism in college?"

"No."

"Good! Where did you go to college?"

"At Fairhaven, in Bellingham."

His jaw dropped. "You mean . . . you went to college *out here? Really?*"

It was always that way with newcomers: The California immigrants couldn't believe Seattle natives could ever be hip, and the East Coast immigrants could never believe we were educable.

But Brewster was ranting again. I sat there agape, taking it all in. One minute I would feel like his therapist, charged with letting him vent until he had exhausted his manic state. The next I would feel like his patient, sent to him to be shock-treated out of my depressive state. At some point near the end of our session, I began to understand that the latter view was closer to accurate—but that it was all of Seattle who was his patient.

By the time Brewster was finished with me, I was so uncharacteristically energized that I agreed to the salary and work regimen he suggested without even hearing what exactly it was. Then I set off to wake up the city! Shake people up! Make things happen!

Brewster was the strangest mixture of imagination and cliché that I've ever met. He managed to keep his writers intellectually engaged with their work while also getting them to create copy commercial and schlocky enough to sell to the masses. There were days with him when I felt like I was working for a publisher who was half Bertrand Russell, half P. T. Barnum.

One of my first *Weekly* cover assignments was a classic case in point. A little less than a year after our first conversation, Brewster invited me to a meeting of his editorial staff and asked me to unearth a Hmong refugee family to feature. The early 1980s saw a heavy influx to Seattle of Hmong from Laos and Vietnam, driven out of their homeland in the wake of the American war effort there and their unfortunate allegiance to our side. Refugee families were growing increasingly visible—particularly in Seattle's crafts markets, where Hmong women sold gorgeous, oddly moving, mysteriously symbolic embroidery on jackets, blankets, quilts, and little cloths. They were part of an increasingly visible Asian influx that was lending Seattle tremendous color, light, energy, culture, and great food. "Go out there and find them," Brewster said excitedly. "Tell us how they live, where they came from, how they got here, how they're assimilating. I want to know about the uncle who's working at the gas station, the kid who's finding his way in high school, the grandparents who can't learn English. . . ." On and on he went, sketching out a struggling immigrant story packed with every cliché save for the passage through Ellis Island.

But I also felt this strange kind of infectious energy filling me as he was talking, and I left the meeting more excited than cynical. Part of it was that he didn't give me a deadline, telling me simply to take as long as I needed to write a satisfying story. He also didn't set any word or space limits; he apparently believed enough in me to send me out with virtually no instruction, secure in his faith that I would deliver something good.

Most of my excitement, though, stemmed from the odd spell he cast on me, and it was to remain true for the next fifteen years that whenever he talked to me long enough, he put me into a manic trance.

I started making calls and was led in short order to Dorothy Kelly, a Seattle woman who did volunteer work with refugee families. She led me in turn to the Lees, a large extended family living in homes in Seattle and out in Carnation, a rural town twenty miles east that was just outside the Seattle suburban growth envelope. Kelly arranged for me to meet with Yeng Lee and his family in their tiny Seattle apartment. Lee and I talked while his wife sat silently next to him and his daughters Michelle and Gloria (they were given American names because they had been born in Seattle) watched *Spiderman* on their little television.

A week or so later, after Lee secured permission from his uncle, Tuxao Chasengnou, for me to meet with him and his family in Carnation, I drove out there with the *Weekly* photographer—a newly out-of-college kid named Pete Kuhns. We made our way through California-esque suburbs to the swampy cow pastures, remnants of forests, farmland, feed lots, and collapsing barns and sheds that butted up against the eastern edge of our civilization. Finally we got to a little tract-house development on the edge of Carnation that looked like it had been built in the early 1960s, in anticipation of a suburbanization that never quite materialized. Now the homes were lapsing into decrepitude, their roofs mossy and their siding grimy and flaking.

We knocked on the door of the Chasengnou family home, explained in extremely slow English who we were, and were ushered inside. The house was dark, the only light coming from an occasional candle and a television set in the living room. The fireplace was set up for cooking, with a homemade contraption over the fire for suspending pots, and the family appeared to have finished dinner a few minutes before our arrival. There were three generations living in the house and nearly all the inhabitants were clustered in front of the TV set, which was broadcasting the Academy Awards. I asked Chasengnou why they didn't have any lights on and why they didn't use the stove in the kitchen. He commenced a long, halting speech about the silliness of electricity, this invisible force that came mysteriously into your house, and ended with a rhetorical question: "Why depend for everything on one single thing like that?"

From my conversations with the Lees, the Chasengnous, Kelly, UW professor Marshall Hurlich, and various other local Hmong and experts on Hmong culture, I pieced together a story of horrifying psychological and cultural dislocation. The Hmong had been nomadic farmers for centuries, without a written language until 1976, their religion being a form of animism in which virtually every object and body part is inhabited by a soul or ancestor spirit, and virtually every question can be answered, obstacle overcome, problem solved, or decision made by prayer or sacrifice to one of these spirits. They had been forced into the Vietnam War by Americans intent on shutting down the Viet Cong's and North Vietnamese Army's supply lines from Laos, and when the Americans fled in 1975, the Hmong were forced to choose between flight to Thailand or gradual extermination at the hands of the vengeful Vietnamese and Laotian governments. The Thai government was willing to let them stay in refugee camps only long enough for them to arrange transfer to the United States. By 1984, more than half the 350,000 Laotian Hmong were gone, with the world's largest Hmong exile community, numbering 24,000, being Seattle's.

Once they left their land, the Hmong were cast psychologically adrift. Their ancestor spirits could not make the journey with them. Now, Chasengnou explained to me, there were no spirits to provide guidance to him and his family, and when he died, his children—being raised in America and cut off from Hmong tradition—would not know how to guide his spirit to heaven. Added Yeng Lee's father, "Now you feel like you can't control what happens to you anymore. You never know what the next day will be like, or if you will die tomorrow."

Lee, Chasengnou, and Kelly, in telling me the details of the thirty-four-member extended family's gradual move to Seattle, enumerated endless episodes of depression, trauma, and confusion. Lee's wife, Yee Lee, had come down with a mysterious stomach pain that doctors ultimately attributed to depression—a problem so widespread among the Hmong that it engendered a medical specialty in Seattle studying and treating "somatization," the manifestation of unrecognized and untreated depression in the form of such physical symptoms as stomach pain and, in some particularly dramatic cases, psychosomatic blindness. The Lees' only son died in infancy early in their exile—an event they attributed to an angry ancestor-spirit—and Yee was to suffer six miscarriages before giving birth to another son, the quest for a male child throwing the family's animist faith into disarray. They had consulted a Hmong shaman in Portland at one point, and now, Lee said, "Maybe I believe it helped and maybe I don't." The UW's Hurlich added, "The Hmong lapse into a kind of fatalism here, and adopt a mechanistic view of the world. It's no longer clear that they can do anything to influence the world."

A few days later, I was sitting in the Lees' living room when Yeng Lee told me about a letter his sister, living in Portland, had sent him when he was still in the Thai refugee camp. "She explained that there is a satellite that can see everything that we do. It can take your picture. If you drive far out into the woods, out where there are no people for miles around, and you cut down a tree, even though there's no one who can see you, they'll still know you cut the tree; and when you get home, the police will be waiting for you with pictures of you cutting the tree. Is it true?"

"No," I answered.

A few days after that, while talking with some other members of the family with the television on in the background, I realized that—aside from the time I'd seen the family watching the Academy Awards—superhero shows had been on every time I'd been in a Hmong home, and the reading matter I'd seen most often in these homes had been superhero comics. One eighth grader, Ker Lee, told me that his favorite movies were *Super-*

man II, *Superman III*, and *Return of the Jedi*, and that his favorite reading was *Spiderman* comics. And it all seemed to make perfect sense: Here was a people whose lives, more or less unchanged over centuries, had been destroyed overnight by invaders with—from the Hmong point of view—superhuman powers. Given what had happened to them, they probably regarded the superhero genre as nonfiction.

I was mulling all this over when Ker Lee came up to me and said, "Yeng says you don't believe in the satellite." I confirmed that I didn't, surprised that this had been a topic of family discussion. "Do you really not believe in it?" he asked. "Why?" There was an edge of anger in his voice.

The Hmong are generally slight, short people, and I am relatively tall. I towered like a giant over the people in these families. And now, standing in the midst of them, with everyone staring intently at me while I looked down at this satellite-worshipping boy, I realized that it was impossible for the two of us to understand one another. We were on opposite sides of an ontological barrier.

I was seized then with a tremendous vertiginous sensation, followed by something I can only call a conversion experience—this weird and wonderful moment when an overpowering notion hits you with the force of revelation. You can never tell whether these things come from the heart or the head—when they hit you, they feel God-delivered—but they are shocking and deeply pleasurable. You feel blessed—like you've suddenly been given a look beneath the skin of the universe.

I had been reading Mircea Eliade's *The Myth of the Eternal Return*—a book explaining the difference between primitive and modern cultures—and realized now that the Hmong had suffered a far more devastating loss than I ever imagined. Eliade notes that "primitive" people—as he calls pre-moderns—lived in a world where time is circular; where every gesture, every action, every thought is part of an orderly ritual, a repetition of something archetypal, in perfect harmony with an infinitely harmonious universe. Life there endlessly circles around, repeating itself, from birth through death and back to birth; and every object is inhabited by a god. The Hmong's had been a world of ceaseless comfort, where suffering and setbacks were part of a system that sustained the soul, and where death eternally gave counsel and sustenance to life. The modern world, by contrast, is a march through linear time to an undeserved, undesired death, after which there is nothing. The modern inhabits a world devoid of gods and meaning, hostile to the heart, and one that forces you constantly to ask the question "Why?" without ever allowing you to expect an answer. The primitive enacts with his or her life an endlessly repeated ritual, endlessly meaningful; the modern is born without reason, lives a linear life of meaningless consumption, grows old, and dies disappointed.

For much of the world, this transition from the primitive to the chronically disgruntled had taken twenty-six centuries or so; for the Hmong, it had taken days. They had been thrown thousands of years into the future and now were stranded here, bewildered, bereft of their gods, and in trying to make sense of it all were resorting to cargo-cultish forms of worship. The material changes and physical dislocation in their lives, terrible as they were, were nothing compared with the ontological dislocation.

Wracked, ecstatic, horrified for my hosts, I stared at their loss in all its glory and felt at once mournful, envious, guilty, and nostalgic. I also felt ashamed, said my good-byes as fast as I could, and fled.

I'm still dissecting the experience. But in the days immediately afterward, my guilt gave way to a deep desire to repeat it. That was as close to religious ecstasy as I'd ever come. "If this is what journalism with David Brewster can give you," I thought, "sign me up!"

The contrast between life in Microsoft's building and life in its Seattle-area surroundings seemed to grow more jarring every time I drove over there. I would sit around at home in the morning, doing what work insisted on being done, working on *Weekly* articles, sitting through Little Shat sessions with Caitlin, then eventually would make my way out of my quiet little neighborhood, across placid Lake Washington with its pleasure boats, wind down behind the Burgermaster, and come driving into a parking lot full of telephone-company vans, cars, and people scurrying anxiously in and out of the building. The halls inside Microsoft were always packed with people either hurriedly moving from one office to another or hurriedly whacking one another over the head with foam-rubber swords. It was a place where even tension-relief was done in haste, there never being time to do anything carefully or at leisure.

The editors I served in 1983 and 1984 were turning inexorably from arty English majors into anxiety-ridden middle managers. Their speech grew more and more clipped, their panic over the tiniest details on my typeset pages more and more pronounced. I found myself (happily and lucratively) driving back and forth over the lake for the sake of running out an entire page over again because an editor wanted a section heading moved one-quarter of an inch lower, or because she wanted to change a single word or alter slightly the order of words in a sentence. Week by week, the editors grew more tense and less given to conversation, and the deadlines grew shorter.

The one exception was Jan Allister, who took in the atmosphere and tension around her with a combination of detached amusement and out-right distaste. She had grown up in rural central California, and still culti-vated a distinctly down-home manner. She played folk guitar, baked her own bread, canned her own vegetables and fruit, spoke with a faint twang, and liked to listen to "Prairie Home Companion" on Saturdays because Lake Wobegon was "just like Chico." The technology fixation at Microsoft was more baffling than exciting to her, and she found it hard to feel inspired by the vision, so aggressively fostered at Microsoft, of a future with "a computer on every desktop, running Microsoft software."

I used to greatly enjoy lingering in Allister's office, partly to hear her Microsoft stories and partly to watch the parade of tense co-workers coming through. After less than a year there she was designated a "Senior Editor"—Microsoft was hiring at such a furious pace that seniority lead-ing to promotion was measured in hours rather than years—and she was responsible for a number of the company's important publications. She worked on FORTRAN and COBOL manuals, the first *Flight Simulator* manual, and Microsoft's early C programming manuals. She survived the experience by ignoring the content of these publications, concentrating on language, grammar, and punctuation, and telling herself constantly that she was suffering for the sake of a greater good: the support of her family and her husband's education.

There was, however, no getting around the worthlessness of the work—it was hardly as if she were advancing the state of Literature—and the strangeness of the place. Allister and her fellow editors, being in their thirties, were ten to fifteen years older than the programmers, who either were newly out of college, still in college, or just out of high school. The programmers tended to be as adrift outside the world of algorithms as the editors were in it. I was sitting in Allister's office one day when a nineteen-year-old kid in a fringed leather jacket and thick glasses came in and asked if she'd go out with him that weekend and watch his band play. He thought she'd enjoy sitting adoringly and girlishly at the foot of the stage, talking with him between sets. "Good God," she said, "I'm old enough to be your mother!" The kid looked at her in confusion, trying to figure out whether she was telling him the truth or inventing an excuse not to date him.

There was a great deal of such cluelessness about women in those days at Microsoft. But to Allister, the clueless programmers, being exotic, were more interesting than offensive. Less charming were the supervisors and marketing people who were constantly importuning her for copy. Everything to these people was a crisis, every request an emergency. You would have thought the fate of the company—and, for that matter, the world—depended on whatever document they wanted at the moment. Allister and her cohorts—who were older, wiser, and (being English majors) considerably more cynical than the company marketers about their employer, took more and more refuge in satire, the best example being a faux memo Allister wrote one day. "Ask them for a deadline," the memo read, "and it's always the same: ASAP. When do they need copy? ASAP. What is the date by when they need the material? ASAP. You work through the weekend to get a copy on their desk by Monday morning, the day they said they HAD TO HAVE IT AT ALL COSTS, then when you bring it as promised they are out for the day. The only date or measure of time they seem to know is ASAP—which is what you will be if you bother getting it done on time."

Time and again during Allister's tenure there, I would feel these spasms of temptation to apply for work at Microsoft. The money was astoundingly good, the other editors smart and companionable, the atmosphere charged and exciting, and there was more and more evidence every day that the company was going places. In 1983, I had bought my first personal computer—a used first-generation IBM, with the word-processing program Spellbinder, and it had already changed my writing life. It was clear that the machines were going to grow more powerful and less expensive, the way calculators had, and that the day was coming when everyone would have one. It was clear, too, that Microsoft was going to supply the operating system for most of them. People were starting to talk about the possibility that Microsoft would be issuing stock one day, and that in advance of that time employees would be allowed to buy shares for a price that would be far lower than the eventual price to the public. So it might be possible in two or three years to make a fair amount of money over and above your salary by staying there.

But I saw Allister working ever-longer hours at work that was ever-less intellectually satisfying, and I saw her co-workers getting increasingly stressed and taking on more of the automaton-like mannerisms of the programmers. And it seemed to me that many of the editors were giving in to the temptation of ambition: ambition for impressive job titles; ambition for money and financial security; ambition for Microsoft. Something about it all seemed creepy, almost, as if the good and pure parts of their souls—preoccupied with spiritual and intellectual pleasures—were being subsumed by ego, greed, and slavishness. Their work was becoming the most important thing in their lives—unthinkable in a Seattleite.

Whenever I was in the Microsoft building, I felt as if I could hear Seattle whispering urgently to me: "Come back . . . come back." My return trips across the lake would be like escapes to paradise, where an afternoon spent playing tennis, wandering in a park, walking along a shoreline somewhere, playing with the wife and kids, or just sitting around idly, doing nothing worthwhile, was far more sensible and sane than frantically advancing my career prospects in an upwardly mobile corporation. Seattle kept tugging me back to sanity whenever I was tempted to cast my lot with the juggernaut across the lake. I began seeing the choice in terms of Seattle's founders: Did I want to be remembered, as Doc Maynard was, by a spouse's tombstone resonating ambiguously, tantalizingly, with "She did what she could"? Or did I want to be remembered as the unimaginative builder of a vulgar, overstated mansion like the ones built on Capitol Hill by early Seattle settlers with their we-were-here-first money?

As if the choice weren't clear enough, I came driving home from Microsoft late one night, in deep darkness, and pulled up to the curb in front of my house. Our front door had a glass pane that extended its full length, and I watched as my youngest daughter, Caitlin, two years old, parted the curtain over the glass and stood there, a tiny wistful girl bathed in intense warm household light, trying to see out into the darkness where she had heard her father's car drive up. She was wearing bright-red Oshkosh B'Gosh overalls and had her little hands pressed up against the glass. Groping in dreamy confusion, unable to see beyond the pane, she looked like she was trying vainly to see the reason why I preferred the cold comfort of work to the productivity-free idylls of home and family.

I had no doubts that Microsoft was going to succeed spectacularly. Allister came to our house one day, tormented over the question of what to do if Microsoft wanted her to pay cash for her stock options. She was barely managing to keep her family afloat with her salary, and the idea of setting a portion of it aside to buy stock in a company that might never get around to issuing it publicly was daunting. I felt this rush of excitement when she was detailing the problem—an English major on the verge of incredible riches! "God, Jan," I said, "even if you have to borrow from your parents or friends or a bank or anybody, you should do whatever it takes to get together the money to buy it. It's going to be worth a ton."

As long as Rick Hermann was happy desultorily setting type in my basement, it was easy for me to subsidize my ego-gratification with Melmoth income while I spent increasing portions of my days and nights covering sports, social issues, art, culture, lifestyle, and Seattle readers' favorite subject: themselves. Brewster and I settled into an odd and exciting synergy. He was like the human embodiment of the ambition gland I was missing. No matter what idea he came up with, all he had to do was talk about it with me for a few minutes to get me infected with his contagious excitement. Time after time, I would walk out of his office convinced that he was boring, crazy, east-coastern, trite . . . and my heart would be pounding with joy and exuberance. And, time after time, I would stumble blindly through the initial phone calls and research on one of his notions, having no idea where I was headed, then turn a corner one day and find myself standing in the midst of a mother lode of great-story material.

The Brewster-assigned story that was to absorb a good part of my imagination for the next six years began with the 1983 pro football season—the first under new Seattle Seahawks head coach Chuck Knox, with whom the entire city had fallen wholeheartedly in love the moment he was hired. "If ever a man had a town pulling for him," *Sports Illustrated* had written when Knox's hiring was announced shortly after the end of the 1982 season, "it's Knox."

That a coach of his stature would come to Seattle spoke volumes about both the city's delusional self-image and the coming of age of its football franchise. The more I pondered Knox's presence here, the more I began to understand that NFL teams take on the identities of their respective cities, and that the reportage of a given team's games and fate in the local press constitutes a civic myth—a city's description to itself of its soul, its struggles, its values, its aspirations. (Football, for some reason, is more this way than baseball, basketball, or hockey.) The Pittsburgh Steelers are always a blue-collar team, famed for fundamentals, defense, and hard work; the Los Angeles Rams were flashy, glamorous, building their image around the theatrical long pass and big play; the Oakland Raiders, hailing from the home of the Hell's Angels, are always outlaws . . . and the Seattle Seahawks are thoroughly out of their league when competing against teams from older, more established, often larger, and always more storied cities.

From the early 1960s until the announcement in 1973 that Seattle would be awarded an NFL expansion franchise in 1976, city boosters had been insisting with increasing volume that Seattle could never be a legitimate American city without a pro football team. But at the same time, despite having plenty of families and businesses wealthy enough to buy and run a franchise, Seattle lacked any with both sufficient money and sufficient ego. The city suffered from a high-roller shortage, a lack of interest in ostentation. There also was a good deal of resistance among the general population to the idea that Seattle should try to join something as highfalutin as the NFL. The struggle to be awarded a franchise was as much an internecine struggle as it was a struggle of Seattle against the NFL establishment. Twice in the 1960s, Seattleites had voted down proposals for stadium bond issues. Only when King County floated a domed-stadium bond issue in 1968, with the idea that it would house both pro baseball's Seattle Pilots and a future pro football team, did voters finally buy into the notion of lending tax dollars to the quest for pro sports. And that display of civic pride ended with the Pilots moving to Milwaukee before the new stadium was finished.

In 1971, a group of six Seattle businessmen formed Seattle Professional Football, a group seeking an NFL expansion team. That group struggled to win NFL acceptance until, finally, the Nordstrom family, largely as a civic gesture, agreed to pony up a little more than $8 million to buy 51 percent of the team. But the Nordstroms, with a Seattle-traditional distaste for attention and glory, agreed to invest only if someone else among the owners would actually run the franchise and be ownership's representative to the NFL and the public. The group settled on property developer Herman Sarkowsky, who was also part of the NBA's Portland Trailblazers ownership group. Although owning only 10 percent of the Seattle franchise, Sarkowsky would be its "owner" in the eyes of the NFL.

Once Seattle had its franchise, it set off on a decidedly unconventional development track. Not content with building slowly, as per NFL custom, the Seahawks set out to win as much as possible as soon as possible, and enjoyed unprecedented success on the field. In 1977, Seattle became the first NFL expansion franchise in history to win five games in its second season. In 1978, the Seahawks went 9–7, becoming the first expansion franchise ever, in any sport, to have a winning record in its third season. They went 9–7 again in 1979, winning eight of their last eleven games and beating the Oakland Raiders, 29–24, in the season finale—partly by means of two fake field goals.

The trick plays were typical of the Seattle Seahawks of the era, and the franchise was virtually defined by them. It was as if Seattle redeemed itself for giving in to pretension by refusing to take its newly attained status seriously. The Seahawk attack was built around the gimmick and the improvised pass. In a league known for uniform, often drearily predictable play, the Seahawks were an exception. Seattle became synonymous with weird, wide-open, anything-goes, decidedly irreverent football, employing quick kicks, fake time-outs, tackle-eligible passes, onside kicks in the middle of games, fake punts and field goals, passes to placekickers and from placekickers to quarterbacks, and a roster of other bizarre plays that made them the darling of Howard Cosell's *Monday Night Football*. Coaches and general managers throughout the league railed against Seattle's disrespect for the NFL, but television commentators loved it.

In short order, though, the Seahawks began atoning for their sins against tradition. Since player-draft order and difficulty of schedule are the two means by which the NFL weakens winning teams and strengthens losing ones, thereby enforcing league-wide parity, the Seahawks' two 9–7 seasons dropped them lower in the draft and earned them gradually tougher season schedules. By their fifth year, they were still a talent-weak expansion team, but were drafting and playing from the position of an established, talent-rich team. They were further weakened by improved preparation on the part of their opponents. After falling to 4–12 in 1980, the Seahawks returned to action in 1981 and heard, for the first time in team history, rumblings of discontent from the public. They were playing like the Harlem Globetrotters but compiling a record like the Washington Generals'. Head coach Jack Patera's image as a mild-mannered man of few words, with a mile-wide zany streak, changed to that of a temperamental, eccentric, tyrannical drill sergeant whose coaching methods were hopelessly behind the times. The Seahawks went 6–10 that year, the low point of the season being a 32–31 loss to the Raiders in which Oakland scored 29 straight points and Seattle had a 59-yard trick pass ruled illegal. On that play—sheer artistic genius—the Seahawks had lined up in punt formation with only ten players on the field, then sent a receiver on a pass route from out of the group of players standing on the sidelines. The resulting touchdown was disallowed, and the play came to symbolize everything that was wrong with the Patera-coached Seahawks.

The franchise—and, by extension, the Nordstroms—began paying dearly for having given Seattle a taste of national celebrity. Disgruntled fans started mutilating and returning their Nordstrom credit cards, and the Nordstroms, panicking, responded by trying to sell their half of the team to their fellow owners. When the dust settled, the Nordstroms agreed to remain team owners, but only if they could take over operation of the franchise. The only thing they lacked as much as they lacked lust for celebrity was a sense of humor, and now they were determined to run their football franchise the old-fashioned way: soberly, seriously, and successfully.

The 1982 season was marred by a labor dispute that resulted in the Nordstroms' firing of head coach Patera and team general manager John Thompson, both of whom, in taking rabidly anti-union stances, turned what few fans they had left against them. Mike McCormack, a former player who was soon to be named to the NFL's Hall of Fame, took over, and he immediately courted and signed Knox. Suddenly the disrespectful Seahawks were headed by football people with respectable NFL pedigrees.

The Nordstroms had gone after Knox because he had a well-earned reputation for turning around failing franchises. In both Los Angeles and Buffalo, he had transformed perennial losers into contenders. But that was not what made him seem so well suited to Seattle. If Knox, as *Sports Illustrated* wrote, seemed a perfect match for our city, it was more because of the way futility and failure had come to define his career. Four times Knox had taken teams to the league conference championship game—the last playoff game before the Super Bowl—and four times he had lost, three of the losses turning on inexplicably bad twists of fate. In the most infamous of those games, his Los Angeles Rams had a first down on the Minnesota Vikings' six-inch line, then were penalized five yards before they could snap the ball. Failing to advance from there, they settled for a field goal and lost by four points. The next season, after coming within inches of scoring a touchdown on third down, Knox called for the Rams again to kick a field goal—which the Vikings blocked and returned for a touchdown.

It seemed that Knox, like Roger Sale's Seattle, led a life that persisted in "falling short of its possibilities." He was the NFL's version of Doc Maynard. Years later, in his autobiography, Knox would write, "I'm not a superstar. I'm not a hero. I don't glitter. I survive." Seattle, he felt, was tailor-made for him. "I had heard about Seattle's rain, its gray, its dreariness. I had read about it being so far from the rest of civilization that back in the 1800s businessmen on the East Coast would ship women out there by boat so the lumberjacks would have someone to talk to. . . . [Knox, like the NFL, had a tendency to sanitize history.] This was a program that in the previous three years had gone 14–27. In the seven years of the franchise there had been only two winning seasons, and no playoff appearances. The way things were run, it seemed they hated the idea of succeeding. Most certainly, my kind of team."

To the feelings of kinship he inspired in Seattle fans, Knox added tremendous hope for the future. His first act as head coach was unimaginably bold to a Seattleite: He traded away years of first-round draft picks to move up in the 1983 draft so he could get Penn State star running back Curt Warner. The drafting of Warner—the Seahawks' first superstar—galvanized the city and had everyone in it counting the minutes all spring and summer long until the season-opening kickoff. When it came at last, against the Kansas City Chiefs, Seattle received it, then took the ball on its first play from scrimmage and handed it to Warner, who burst through the line of scrimmage and ran sixty yards—at which point, still untouched by a defender, he fumbled. The Chuck Knox era in Seattle was officially under way.

From Out of the Shadows

The 1980s saw Seattle seem to wake from a long slumber, look at itself in the mirror, turn away in disgust, and resolve to clean up and lose some weight. The city went on a self-improvement binge driven more by vanity than desire for better civic health. While Seattle fell prey to occasional irresolution and argument over whether it really was all that necessary to do *that* much cleaning up, it was clearly determined to make itself more attractive. Slob appeal was giving way to snob appeal.

The city was in the middle of another boom, this one a function of Microsoft's growing economic impact and the dollar's weakness against foreign currencies—particularly the yen. Washington had always been a big exporter to Asia—of agricultural products, fish, airplanes, other state-produced goods, and now software—and the dollar's decline, while not particularly good news for most of the country, was great news for Washington. Moreover, Seattle's was the closest American port to Asia—a day's sailing closer than Los Angeles's—and goods flowing between Asia and elsewhere in the U.S. came through Seattle in ever-larger volumes. By 1980, Boeing employment had inched back up to 75,000; 1982 saw airport traffic up 10 percent, with the city bringing in $900 million in tourist dollars; and in 1983, the Port of Seattle handled 800,000 shipping containers, 13 percent more than the previous year. The ripple effects of all this were noticeable: Downtown saw construction of fifteen million new square feet of office space between the 1971 Boeing crash and 1985, and experts expected to see that much new space built again between 1985 and 2000. In 1984, the seventy-six-story Columbia Tower was completed—twenty-six stories taller than the next-highest Seattle building, the Seafirst Bank tower, it was a grotesquely spectacular structure that could be seen from points on the far side of Lake Washington. Office towers ranging from twenty-seven to forty-two stories tall were sprouting up all over town. The *Seattle Times* counted nine new skyscrapers under construction, along with plans for a new state convention center, a $100 million renovation of historic Pioneer Square, plans for a new Seattle Art Museum . . . all of it adding up to one million new square feet of office space created downtown in that year alone.

As late as 1980, the Seattle skyline had been that of a midsize western city—a commercial cluster set low against the horizon, unremarkable from a distance—with only two exceptions: the Space Needle, north of downtown, and the Seafirst building, which stood out so dramatically from the rest of downtown that it was dubbed "the box the Space Needle came in."

No more. Now, a forest of phalluses was springing up—and people all over the city were excitedly giving in to the sense that Seattle was becoming a legitimate Great American City.

Even so, not everyone was happy about the boom, and it seemed as if Seattle might be resolved to fight off the self-improvement binge of its indefatigable boosters. In 1983, the city wrote a new downtown plan—described in a *Weekly* editorial as a product of "the usual Seattle process of seeking consensus through exhaustion"—that divided downtown into three zones: a retail core, an office core between the retail zone and Pioneer Square, and a mixed residential and retail zone north of the retail core. Faced with the opportunity to make over a faded downtown with gleaming new skyscrapers, the Seattle City Council passed an ordinance confining them to the office core, and limiting the height of new buildings to 240 feet in the retail core and 400 feet in north downtown. The moves seemed a clear victory for Lesser Seattle tradition, a declaration that the city would not give in completely to the quest for money and status. "For every Columbia Tower that goes up," Emmett Watson would write a few years later, "there is a price to be paid on the street." A good number of his fellow citizens were determined to pay as little of that price as possible.

Yet it was hard not to feel that the forces of glamour and civic ambition were running amok. At the end of 1983, *People* magazine delivered a tremendous blow to Seattle's self-image when it designated Bill Gates as one of the "25 most intriguing people" of the year. Suddenly, the arcane personal-computer industry was vaulted into the mainstream, and a local boy who had seemed a classic Seattleite—withdrawn, socially inept, resolutely disinterested in drawing attention to himself—was rubbing elbows in a celebrity magazine with Vanessa Williams, Jennifer Beals, Richard Chamberlain, and Mr. T. Never before had a Seattleite deigned to be celebrated in that manner, and Gates in particular seemed the antithesis of a spotlight-seeker. It couldn't have been any more shocking if *People* had tabbed Ivar Haglund.

The designation was odd enough to arouse the intense interest of the *Seattle Times*, which launched a full-scale investigation into what it called Gates's "allure"—part of which, the *Times* reported, "stems from the fact that Microsoft specializes in software, now the hot moneymaking end of the computer industry. The company's programming discs enable machines manufactured by such giants as Apple to perform a much wider variety of functions."

The other force behind the emergence of Gates's elusive allure turned out to be more . . . *strategic*. Microsoft, it developed, had spent $300,000 in 1983 getting the word about Gates out to the mainstream media. The company had hired an energetic and highly skilled public-relations expert, Pam Edstrom of Waggener-Edstrom Public Relations in Portland, to craft Gates's image. She began spreading stories about the eccentric boy genius to publications, like *People* and *Fortune*, outside the small computer-industry niche. As rendered by Edstrom, the stories were irresistible: Gates the congressional intern who hoarded McGovern/Eagleton presidential campaign buttons, then sold them at an immense profit when Thomas Eagleton was dropped from the 1972 ticket because he had concealed his past electroshock treatment for depression; Gates the Lakeside High School student who volunteered to write a class-assignment software program that eventually made him the sole male student in an English class; Gates's highly successful company, Traf-o-Data, which he and schoolmate Paul Allen founded while still in high school . . . and on and on and on. Edstrom was bent on turning a classic Seattle eccentric, accomplished but uninterested in fame, into an aggressively colorful character, a larger-than-life American celebrity.

I watched all this with equal parts confusion and shock. Many of the stories, rapidly growing into legend, were highly exaggerated at best. It was disillusioning to see an otherwise admirable local figure suddenly reveling in meretricious celebrity. Gates himself seemed uneasy, distinctly out of his element—as if the publicity-craving were being forced on him by corporate strategists. When asked by the *Times* how he felt about his anointing by *People*, he answered, "I was happy that the article talked about what the company was doing instead of just talking about me." Celebrity, in other words, was something to be endured for the sake of advancing Microsoft's prospects.

The Gates transformation, alarming as it was, signaled only a small part of the transformation coming Seattle's way. I got my first real sense of the scale of that change in the spring of 1984, when Brewster assigned me to write a story on the controversy surrounding the future of Lake Union—a small, 1-by-1.5-mile water-jewel set on the northwest end of downtown, almost exactly in the center of the city map. Connected by man-made canals with Lake Washington to the east and Puget Sound to the west, Lake Union had been almost exclusively industrial for most of the century. Its north shore was dominated by the ruins of a huge gasworks, and the lake had been ringed with a motley assortment of maintenance and repair yards, houseboat moorings, and boat-construction and sales operations until well into the 1970s, when rising land prices and an increasing civic concern with the future of the lake began driving the industrial tenants out. The 1970s also saw the eviction of the lake's low-rent houseboat dwellers and their replacement by high-income tenants who could afford to live on the water now that it had turned into some of the city's priciest real estate. Pre-boom tenants had lived on humble boats along the lines of the *African Queen*; the new Lake Union tenant and his or her upscale digs would eventually be captured accurately in the 1993 hit movie *Sleepless in Seattle*, in which Tom Hanks plays a typically upscale man living in a typically splendid Lake Union houseboat.

I took a walk around the lake in the summer of 1984, cataloguing its sights, sounds, and struggles. Walking west from Ivar's Salmon House, I stopped first at a wreckage-strewn, vacant, and inadequately fenced lot in which I could see a tattered, tilted sign: MARINE SERVICE UNLIMITED. The remnants of the building there were decorated with two graffitoed words: BOOM and LUST. From there, I could take in virtually everything on the shore all around the lake. To my left, along the east shore, were ship-repair yards and some yacht and houseboat moorages; opposite me, on the downtown end, sat two enormous rusting ships, a U.S. Navy pier, a park, and the Center for Wooden Boats—a haven for nostalgic boatbuilders and recreational sailors to work at their craft or rent rowboats by the hour. Along the west shore sat a mix of office buildings, boat-sales outlets, new restaurants, a seaplane-charter service, more houseboat moorages, and various other marine-related businesses, growing more heavy-industrial the further north they were along the shore. Interspersed among all these enterprises were a good number of vacant lots filled with wreckage, garbage, rusted cyclone fencing, and other evidence of defeat, neglect, and public-policy paralysis.

The overall impression was one of hopelessness—not the hopelessness of frustrated ambition, but the hopelessness of frustrated stasis. Rather than being directed at the new chic restaurants and yacht moorages flanked by customer-offputting trash, my sympathies went out to the sites trashed by the forces behind the yacht-and-restaurant invasion. Nothing else in Seattle showed so graphically how intent the city was on gentrification, and how much it was losing in the process. The fact that gentrification was not yet fully under way around the lake signaled only that many in city government understood any change there to be change for the worst. Yet their political weapons ultimately would prove powerless in the face of the economic forces behind the invasion. Regulations intended to preserve the lake as a "working lake," as its protectors called it, had served to postpone the inevitable but not to forestall it, for no amount of regulation could reverse the effects of skyrocketing land prices. "Development restrictions," one frustrated commercial realtor righteously explained to me, "limit use of the north end of the lake to marinas, marine retail, and hardware, that sort of thing. But the property is too expensive to sustain that kind of business, so the land sits there undeveloped. I'd like to see all that be high-rises—it's idiotic not to pursue highest and best use of that land. But I don't see anything happening out there for a long time, because nobody ever listens to anybody."

Ultimately, though, new development there seemed predestined. The "anachronisms," as another commercial realtor derisively termed the industrial traces still left on the lake, were doomed. Already, on Lake Union's south end, industry was giving way to grossly glitzy restaurant/retail complexes with piers attached for the mooring of yachts. Within a few years, the boatyards would be gone, replaced by various chain restaurants, including a Burger King, a T.G.I. Friday's, a Benjamin's, a Cucina! Cucina!, and a Hooter's, the last three comprising a singles-scene critical mass impressive enough for the *Weekly* to label it Seattle's "herpes triangle." The H.C. Henry Pier, I was told, had just evicted five boat-repair businesses to make room for a California restaurant chain. Walking around that end of the lake, wallowing self-indulgently in mourning for the working-class refugees-in-the-making, I felt forced to acknowledge the undeniable reality that I bore a significant share of responsibility for their demise. I was working for a paper that marketed itself to the patrons of the trendy restaurants and singles bars coming the lake's way; the advertisers and readers paying my salary were the same people driving out the people I purported to love.

I was in mid-self-abnegation when I encountered a crusty, disgruntled man named Dave Updike, who operated a tugboat and diesel-repair yard there (it was his operation that harbored the two rusting ships symbolizing the lake's current "blight"). Updike was being evicted to make room for a California developer intending to build a restaurant called the Rusty Pelican (a name that said it all about the lake's coming gentriblight) on his domain. Updike had not deigned to return my repeated phone calls—they were, after all, from the publication most aggressively promoting The Enemy—and I approached him with some trepidation. "Yeah, I got your messages," he said curtly, then stood there looking past me. I asked whether he wanted to stay put. "They asked me if I was interested in staying," he answered. "And I was—but not at the price they were asking." What did he think about the lake's future? "They want to put a *restaurant* in here," he said, as if it were the most sacrilegious act imaginable. Then he turned and walked away.

Standing there, watching Updike dolefully withdraw, I couldn't help but see myself through his eyes—as an agent of the force behind the lake's and the city's coming demise. The image that came to mind echoed in advance something the British expatriate writer Jonathan Raban would write of his first visit to Seattle a few years later: "All the most important buildings faced west, over the Sound, and Seattle was designed to be seen from the front. You were meant to arrive by ship, from Yokohama or Shanghai, and be overwhelmed by the financial muscle, the class (with a short *a*), the world-traveled air of this Manhattan of the Far West. If you had the bad taste to look at Seattle from the back, all you'd see would be plain brick cladding and a zig-zag tangle of fire escapes."

That backside, I realized now, was the Seattle I loved—the unpretentious part of the city that wrapped itself in flannel against the cold blandishments of ambition and tried to make as little an impression and as little material progress as possible. That determinedly lesser Seattle, understanding that the key to the city's soulful glory lay in keeping secret the marvel of living here, disdained the splashy show the rest of the city was always trying to put on for the sake of tourist and trade dollars. Glamour and attention and gentrification meant that the paradise we had stumbled into here would be destroyed by overpopulation, and the displaced denizens of the wrecked property around the lake were having none of that. Those first new restaurants and yacht moorages that had made inroads among the lakeshore's detritus reminded me of the milfoil and English ivy and blackberry brambles that were rampaging through the Northwest's ecosystems, displacing and destroying native species.

It wasn't just Lake Union, either, that was declining into magnificence. As Raban would note five years later, "Until very recently, it seemed, Seattle had gotten along well enough with its turn-of-the-century Italian Renaissance architecture; but now the terra-cotta city was beginning to look dingy and stunted beside the sixty- and seventy-story towers that were sprouting over its head" in the booming office-tower zone south of retail downtown.

The one indisputable boon delivered by the decline and displacement of Seattle industry was the space it made available to artists. Like alder sprouting up in the remains of a ravaged forest, studios were everywhere around Lake Union in the 1980s, and flourished most happily in the Fremont District, at the lake's northwest corner. I was particularly taken with the burgeoning glass art movement, which spent the 1980s wangling its way from Seattle onto the world stage. Two prominent Seattle galleries—Foster/White and Traver-Sutton—were known primarily for the glass artists they represented; artists came from around the world to learn how to work with glass at Seattle's Pratt Fine Arts Institute and the Pilchuck School, forty-five minutes north of the city; and I spent a good part of 1986 wandering from studio to studio around Lake Union.

My exploration began with an assignment from the *Seattle Times* Sunday magazine, *Pacific*, which contracted with me to write a story on some of the leaders in Seattle glass art. The first name on my editor's mind was Dale Chihuly, who was beginning to make a reputation for himself all over the country, having been the first local glass artist with enough commercial clout to be represented by a New York gallery. By 1985, Chihuly, a Tacoma native who co-founded Pilchuck and had been working in glass since 1967, was selling assemblages of colorful "seaforms"—pieces that looked simultaneously shell-like and like "undersea flowers," in the artist's words—for upward of $20,000 each, a twentyfold increase from what he was getting ten years before.

Chihuly proved as fascinating for his public image and promotional skill as for his art. He had singlehandedly crafted Seattle glass into a Scene and launched the careers of innumerable protégés. Most of the glass artists in Seattle credited him with having created the climate making it possible for them to support themselves with their art. In their next breath, though, they tended to complain that he was suspiciously skilled at self-promotion. There was something disquieting about Chihuly's promotional skill—as if the energy he devoted to selling his art was unseemly not only in an artist, but in a Seattleite.

Indeed, you couldn't help but notice the Barnum in Chihuly before you could get around to appreciating his art—which was, it should be noted, breathtaking. When I called him the first time (and, for that matter, *every* time thereafter), I would get his answering machine. I would only get as far as "from the *Seattle Times*" in the message I was leaving when I would hear him suddenly pick up the phone and greet me happily. When I told him during our first phone conversation that I was researching a story on Seattle glass artists, he asked for my mailing address. The next day, Federal Express showed up with a large package of magazine articles about Chihuly and the Seattle glass scene.

Everything around him seemed staged. It was as if I were following a performance artist. Chihuly glass-blowing sessions were a tremendous production, staged in picturesque studios with furnaces and stereo systems blasting at full volume while crews of photogenic men and women worked frantically and sweatily at cranking out massive Chihuly seaforms. Chihuly himself never blew glass anymore, or even did any of the shaping work with the paddles and other hand tools glass artists used. He had lost the use of one eye—and, with it, his depth perception—in a motorcycle accident, and now acted as head of an atelier, directing the work of production teams in a manner he liked to compare with that of the European masters. A Rabelaisian figure with wild, extravagant, thick, and curly hair, a black eyepatch, stereotypically disheveled and paint-spattered clothing, and an almost constant crooked smile, Chihuly would wander among the ear-splitting noise and hard-working crews in his studio, shouting out occasional instructions, leaning in to watch a piece being shaped in the final tense moments as it cooled into rigidity, and always being in exactly the right spot, and in exactly the right light, when the *Times* photographer was snapping an action shot.

He was enormously exuberant, theatrical, entertaining, and charismatic. Throwing his arms wide as if to embrace the entire artistic world, he would declaim on the magic of glass, with its ability to "eat light," take in and diffuse color, soften and bend into extravagant, impossible shapes, and soothe the soul with a magical luminance. At the same time, he had no interest in the critic's perspective; the closest he would ever come to critical appraisal of his chosen art form was to say, "Glass just seems to make people feel good." And when I asked him whether glass-blowing was an art or a craft, he thundered, "Who the hell cares?"

The man was good copy.

Virtually every other glass artist I met was Chihuly's temperamental opposite. Those not on one of his production teams generally worked alone in small, decrepit studios with a single furnace and barely enough room for the tools and pieces arranged haphazardly on the floor and shelves around them. Sonja Blomdahl, the most interesting of the artists I met, worked in virtual seclusion in a narrow cinderblock shed at the south end of Lake Union, producing subtle glory in the form of soft, bright, large bowls decorated with bands of color. She labored before her furnace quietly and ritualistically, as if she had been standing there for centuries, patiently working these elemental materials—fire and molten glass—performing the same motions over and over again, a figure from Eliade's pre-modern paradise, both enacting and crafting gleaming symbols of the primitive's eternal return.

When I met her, Blomdahl had been making bowls for five years. "I'd always liked bowl shapes," she told me, "so I just started making them, and I enjoyed trying to make them as round and as perfect as I could." Applying two bands of what she called "plain colors," separated by a narrow band of clear glass, she had developed the bowls to the point where they had an unearthly, luminescent quality that made them seem to give off rather than reflect light. There was a profound mystical force in the play of color and light in her bowls and spheres—they always looked to me as if Blomdahl had managed to encase a colorful, shifting cloud in a diamond.

Even Blomdahl couldn't quite figure out what made her keep working at these bowl shapes. She appeared somewhat confused by her own monomania. "I just seem to feel like making these *bowls* every day," she said. "Bowls. They're like mandalas. They're very healing and circular, they show in some way how I like things in my life coming back around in the same circle. Although . . . I don't really know where they come from, only that they come from somewhere in the soul, and that the circles have been going on for centuries."

There was a great deal of enthusiasm in the outside world for her bowls. Blomdahl was fast becoming one of Seattle's best-known artists, and was baffled about her growing reputation. Particularly baffling was the obsessive adulation directed her way by fitness guru Richard Simmons, then at the height of his celebrity. Simmons—who was celebrated more for his lunatic behavior than his ingenuity at exercise—would rave, giddily and loudly, about Blomdahl's bowls to everyone who came near him. He had once jumped out of a car in the middle of Seattle traffic as it passed by a gallery with some Blomdahl bowls in the window; running inside, he immediately bought all the pieces on display.

In what struck me as a classic Seattle attitude toward publicity, Blomdahl shrank away from the self-promotional opportunity Simmons presented her, turning down offers to meet him and turning away writers and photographers seeking her out because they had learned of her through him. When I asked her about him, she just shook her head and said softly, "I don't know what to think about that guy."

What most moved me about Blomdahl was her resolute disinterest in anything other than the forces inside her, driving her art. I was convinced that she would have gone on making whatever she felt like making forever, even if she never sold a single piece. I had visions of gallery owners coming into her studio and gathering up her output without her once even turning away from her work to look at them.

I was struck, too, by one set of pieces lined up on several shelves in a corner of her studio. There were more than a dozen of these things, all of them virtually identical: clear glass penises attached to and draped limply over bright red hearts, as if the hearts were the rest of the male genitalia. On my first visit to Blomdahl's studio, I was accompanied by Betty Udesen, a *Times* photographer. When she saw the "genitals," she burst out laughing. "I'm getting over a relationship," Blomdahl told her, and I stepped back into a far corner of the studio while they exchanged rueful, commiserative smiles. *Men.* The pieces were at once grotesque, gorgeous, witty, disturbing, ingenious, and unlikely ever to bring Blomdahl a dime in income.

Up in the Fremont District, Dick Weiss was absorbed, like Blomdahl, in doing art for art's sake without giving much thought to its commercial potential. Weiss worked in flat glass, making spectacularly colored and patterned panels, windows, glass doors, and murals. He worked in a daylight basement studio in his house, quietly piecing together dazzling arrangements that were being installed all over the region: in residences, University of Washington buildings, a convalescent center south of Seattle, high schools, the Seattle-Tacoma International Airport. He underwrote his passion with carpentry. With his face set in a permanent crooked grin, Weiss loved to talk at high speed with visitors about his work. "Generally I get an idea in my head," he said one day, "and that's all I do for ten years or so. I've got a simple mind!" Like Blomdahl, he was absorbed in circular shapes, his pieces being made up almost exclusively of "rondelles"—spiral patterns arranged in eccentrically shaped leaded panes—and he worked at these patterns day after day, year after year, sometimes because someone had commissioned a work from him, often because that was what he felt like doing that day.

He was a close friend of Chihuly's, whose high rate of production and love of publicity Weiss found hugely entertaining. Like a lot of glass artists in those days, Weiss felt considerable affection and admiration for Chihuly, and was grateful for the attention he had drawn to the region and its artists. But at the same time, he felt that Chihuly's business acumen diminished the inherent worth of his art. "Oh, Dale, Dale . . . ," he would say, shaking his head and smiling as if at an engaging, chronically mischievous child whenever he and his friends talked about Chihuly's publicity hunger. Weiss scrounged for a lot of his glass in the scrap heaps of other artists, and had a room packed with discarded fragments. One day, he gave me one he'd gotten from Chihuly's studio. It was a flat piece from a seaform sculpture that had broken—a common occurrence—and Weiss thought it a particularly humorous and telling artifact because Chihuly had been practicing his signature on it. It was covered with samples of his autograph.

It seemed that whenever I would lapse too far into the self-satisfied sense that life in Seattle was as good as it could get and was unlikely ever to get any worse—my Lake Union experience notwithstanding, I found myself constantly giving in to the temptation to believe that everything would manage to work out for the best, that Seattle would forever be the best of all possible cities—some non-local would show up to slap me in the face. Often, it was Brewster, either by virtue of a story assignment or one of his incessant speeches about Seattle's shortcomings. His loathing of the city's lack of ambition grew stronger year by year; what I saw as virtue, he saw as provincial vice. In a 1984 interview with the *Seattle Times*, he vented his civic spleen the way he did almost every day in the *Weekly* offices. In his view, Seattle was a willfully underachieving city, "a collection of villages, nine Midwestern towns that happen to call themselves Seattle. . . . All things indicate that this still is a city that does not want to have a civic consciousness. . . . There are several profound questions this town has to face. One is whether it's a global, international big city on the world stage, or whether it's still a collection of small towns whose backwardness is its attraction."

Other outsiders saw in Seattle less a potential center of enlightenment than a place of benightedness. *Life* magazine writer Cheryl McCall, a friend of Connie Butler and Rick Downing from their pre-Seattle days, came to the city and moved in with them for a few months, first to write a *Life* story, then to film a documentary on the legions of homeless kids who hung around the Pike Place Public Market. A warren of tiny stores, restaurants, and stalls for farmers and craftspeople connected by a labyrinthine series of staircases and hallways, the Market was built in 1907 at the northwest corner of downtown. It is Seattle's most treasured landmark; one of its best-known tourist stops, it has been rescued repeatedly from attempts to raze and redevelop it and was immortalized in a series of Mark Tobey paintings and drawings done throughout the 1940s and 1950s.

Working with photographer Mary Ellen Mark, McCall documented the heartbreaking lives these kids led—lives rife with drug and alcohol abuse, prostitution, desperation, disease, severe injury, imprisonment, and, often, early death. Rick Herman and I spent hundreds of hours transcribing McCall's tapes on my typesetting machine—the only affordable electronic word processor McCall could find in Seattle.

Their film, *Streetwise*, proved to be a masterpiece of juxtaposition, elements of childhood sharing scene after scene with elements of sordid involuntary adulthood. In one typical scene, a little baby-faced, hard-eyed fourteen-year-old girl named Tiny is wearing a child's sweater, decorated with bunnies, while she details her night life as a prostitute. "Old fucks," she says, are preferable, because they are not as "rough" as "young fucks." You hear her excitedly telling a friend, new to the street scene, how much money a "veterinarian whore" can make. You hear the street musician Baby Gramps, a Market inhabitant, singing a raspy "Teddy Bears' Picnic" as you watch a Cadillac pause outside the Market to let a kid negotiate, then get in. During one of Tiny's attempts at living again with her mother, you hear her say wistfully, on New Year's Eve, "Another year's gone by fast, huh, Mom?"

"Yeah," her mother answers. "Don't bug me—I'm drinkin'."

Streetwise was a sensation. Country music singer Willie Nelson, who helped finance it, flew up to Seattle for the premiere, and it garnered press attention and accolades from all over the country. Seattle was considerably less enchanted. The *Seattle Post-Intelligencer* accused McCall and Mark of manipulating the children in the documentary, staging scenes, exaggerating the problems of Seattle's homeless kids, and in general giving the nation a falsely dark view of life in the city's latter-day Skid Road. McCall saw the criticism as a "get off my turf" reaction against an out-of-town reporter scooping the local press. But I saw it as a classic Seattle denial-reaction, a refusal to let go of a self-image as a nice city full of nice places and nice people. The idea that pedophiles roamed freely downtown, openly picking up hapless kids, and that those kids were declining and dying in the shadow of Seattle's most benevolent landmark in full view of Greater and Lesser Seattleites alike, was impossible to accept.

Seeing the Light

The latter half of the 1980s loom in my memory now as a mass exodus of the wonderful. Jonathan Raban would leave in 1989: His paean to the city notwithstanding, he apparently felt that Seattle's charms didn't make up for its cultural deficiencies. In 1985, Rick Herman and his girlfriend Leigh Willis left Seattle for Bellingham, eighty-five miles north, where they would settle down comfortably, have a son, and raise him in the kind of laid-back circumstances that were fast fading away in Seattle. My *Weekly* editor, Ann Senechal, was preparing to move back east that same year, telling me that Seattle felt like an "outpost," that she had never expected it to be so "small and confining," and that she kept "running into walls here." Her leavetaking would set Brewster to editorializing mournfully that Seattle was suffering a brain and ambition drain. A good friend of my wife's—Marian Docter, a lifelong Seattleite—moved to Alaska because, she said, "All the men in Seattle are wimps." They lacked even sexual ambition. Jan Allister, having been given 1,600 shares of Microsoft stock before the company's 1986 IPO, would resign shortly after the company went public at $21 per share (the stock would close its first day of trading at $27.75, and Microsoft's first stock split would come the next year), turn management of the stock over to her husband, tell him never to tell her how much it was worth, and move with him to the Minnesota backwoods, where they both would take teaching positions at

St. Olaf's College. She had fled the frantic pace and prosperity of California for the remote Pacific Northwest, only to have them follow her here; she wouldn't be taking any chances this time.

The year after Allister fled, Microsoft became the world's biggest microcomputer software company, with revenues of $345.9 million, and it occurred to me that Allister had made a classic Seattle move: walking out on her employer when it became uncomfortably celebrated and successful, as if the company's glory and her attendant affluence tainted her. As the wealth—and the legend—of Gates and Microsoft grew through the eighties, as Microsoft employees grew increasingly, cultishly, devoted to their leader, and as talk spread through the halls at Microsoft that Gates harbored ambitions of growing it into a "billion-dollar company," Allister grew more and more restive, and less and less happy with a work regimen as pointless as it was exhausting. She derived no joy from work whose only reward was monetary. The more successful Microsoft grew, the less she could define her reason for being there. "Why should I keep working like this," she asked me one day, "just so Bill Gates can make another million?"

Even to me, from my safe remove, there was something exhausting and demoralizing about Microsoft's drive. No matter how hard and how well people worked there, no matter how much they accomplished, it was never enough. The company was an incessantly hungry beast. You never saw anything in the way of celebration when a milestone was reached; all anyone ever talked about was the exhaustive list of mistakes they'd made in the course of successfully completing a project, how they could have done better, and how much better they would do next time around. Energetic new faces kept pouring into Microsoft, bringing the kind of excitement and energy that kept company old-timers—people who had been there all of two or three years—anxious and on edge. The editors I worked with seemed to have to pick up and move to a new office every six months or so, and now most of the company was moving out of its building as Microsoft expanded into a large complex of buildings on the other side of the highway. There was never any downtime there, any time for people to put their work on cruise control and concentrate on the rest of their lives, and it didn't look as if Microsoft employees would be relaxing anytime soon.

By 1985, I was juggling assignments from three different Microsoft editors, and depending more and more on the company's money to underwrite a lifestyle that combined low-level literary ambitions with high-level household ambitions. A typical workday consisted of playing with my daughters, checking on my employees' progress (with Herman gone, I now employed two high-school kids and an ambitionless Invisible Seattleite), writing, and going to a Mariners game in the evening on the pretext of covering my sports beat for the *Weekly*. The most demanding part of my regimen was the occasional drive across the lake to collect money from Microsoft.

I made my way over there on one particularly splendid summer day to deliver copy to an editor whose name I no longer remember. I do remember vividly, though, her inviting me to sit down, then telling me gently that Microsoft would no longer be sending out its copy to be typeset. "The people here have set up a system," she said, "that allows us to send what we write directly to computers that can turn it into typeset copy."

Suddenly I was sitting through one of those bottom-dropping-out-of-your-life moments that immediately devolve into despair. It was as if Mt. Rainier, forever advertised as dormant, had suddenly erupted, wiping out all of downtown Seattle. I couldn't imagine life without this little sinecure. It had been an amazing haven from ambition, mobility, effort, and adulthood, leaving me free to play Little Shat whenever I wanted. And it not only had spared me work in general—it also allowed me to avoid making sales calls, the most humiliating and demoralizing activity I could imagine. Now, trying to picture myself as a shabby salesman of an obsolete typesetting service shuffling the Seattle streets trolling desperately for new customers, I could already hear myself lapsing into madness, asking Anne, "Whatever happened to that diamond watch fob?"

I stared at the editor as impassively as I could. I made some bleating noises about how a computer could never replace the kind of service and scrupulous devotion I provided, and about the silly arrogance of these "computer people" who thought their machines could be made to do absolutely everything—"They're going to see," I said, "that it isn't as easy as it looks"—but my heart wasn't in it. The fact is, it *was* as easy as it looked. While it was true that I couldn't imagine a computer ever being able to set type properly on its own, I also knew in my head of heads that my little niche was doomed.

I had a vision of progress then as an accelerating steamroller bearing down on me, with Gates at the helm. Just as electronic typesetting machines like mine had put a generation of linotype operators out of work, so was the personal computer now putting electronic typesetters like me out of work. If only we'd had as long a run as the linotypers had!

Terribly moved by own plight, I could see that there was no end to

Gates's ambition—he wouldn't stop until everyone on earth, save for him, was replaced by software. Then I asked myself the question thousands of stunned competitors would ask themselves in the years to come: How could someone like Gates ever have come out of *Seattle*?

I heard a few days later about another software advance more threatening to Melmoth than even Microsoft's decision. It had to do with Ann Senechal, who was moving back to Seattle less than a year after she'd left. She had settled in Boston, only to find that people there were mean, competitive, and unimaginative. It was the typical escape-from-Seattle experience. Even though she had grown up back east, now she found it practically unlivable. Her days were filled with memories of "the beauty of Seattle and the pleasantness of its people." In a doleful phone call with one of her Seattle friends, she was told about a new company—Aldus— that was working on software for something called "desktop publishing," and was hiring writers and editors. Senechal said it sounded interesting, and Aldus's founder, Paul Brainerd, who was traveling to Boston on business, called on her a few days later.

Brainerd was recruiting people from the publishing industry to evangelize for his company, which was writing software for the Macintosh that would allow people to design and set type for their own publications. Apple was desperate for the software because, while the Macintosh was an ingenious machine with an ingenious interface, it also was relatively useless, since there was very little software written for it. Brainerd was convinced that his product would revolutionize publishing and render the Melmoths of the world obsolete. People would be able to set type at home, getting the same quality from a cheap personal computer that I needed a $30,000 machine to deliver.

A few weeks after that conversation, Senechal was back in Seattle, the sixty-ninth employee at Aldus, laughingly explaining how she hadn't understood anything Brainerd was talking about when he was recruiting her over dinner in Boston. "He kept talking about 'software' and 'stock options,'" she said, "and I didn't even know what those words meant. Finally I just asked him, 'Will you pay for my move back?' And when he said yes, I decided to take the job. I couldn't wait to get back here."

With offices in Pioneer Square and a staff convinced that it was changing the world, Aldus was the best workplace Senechal had ever seen. She noticed, though, that working there had an odd effect on her social life. "When I was *Weekly* managing editor, I'd tell people at parties and stuff where I worked and they'd be fascinated," she said. "Now, someone comes up to me at a party and asks what I do, and I say, 'I work for the

Aldus Corporation,' and they just walk away. And if you try telling someone you make 'software,' they give you this blank look. People have no idea what it is."

The Microsoft and Aldus news, along with this mass exodus of people all around me, set off alarms in my mind. Seattle was being killed off. Microsoft and Aldus were wreaking unimaginable progress, and people were fleeing the city in advance of the resulting carnage without even knowing exactly what it was they were fleeing. Allister and Herman were fleeing advancing prosperity, Senechal and Docter had fled ineradicable complacency—with Senechal returning largely because she'd found a niche of restlessness here—and Raban, I guessed, thought we were irredeemably rustic. Add it all up and it looked as if Seattle were turning into the *worst* of all possible cities: a Paradise Lost inhabited by the intolerably smug.

Raban made an interesting observation on his way out of town. "Booms in Seattle," he wrote in *Hunting Mister Heartbreak*, "had always been triggered from a spot a long way off. It was not so much a place where things happened in themselves as a place that was intimately touched by distant, often very distant, events." As a result, Seattle had always reaped tremendous benefits from booms while paying few of the associated social costs. "Up in Nome," Raban wrote of the Alaska Gold Rush, "men were going crazy, gunning each other to death in bars, jumping claims and hitting the bottle; down in Seattle, the hoteliers, store owners, meat packers and shipping agents went about the quiet business of making money out of the madmen."

It was true. Doc Maynard had set up shop in Seattle to supply timber to booming San Francisco during the California Gold Rush. Seattle had been the money-siphoning gateway and supplier to booming Alaska during that territory's gold rush. World War I, fought in Europe, brought a ship-building boom to the Seattle dockyards. (The ensuing bust did result in the entire city's being shut down by the only general strike in the nation's history, but the strike broke up after a few days without much in the way of incident, Seattle getting back to the business of politely rebuilding its economy, and the leading radical behind the strike, Anna Louise Strong, fleeing town in frustration, eventually making her way to Moscow, Peking, and glory.) And World War II, fought in Europe and Asia, brought a plane-building boom to Boeing (and a property-confiscation boom to the erstwhile friends, neighbors, and landlords of interned Japanese Americans).

Booms here—and busts as well—were more beneficent than they were in other places. The social costs, in the form of the boom's losers, were small enough to be pushed easily out of sight, into Seattle's margins—Skid Road/Maynardtown, the city's small racial-minority enclaves, the shadows of the Pike Place Market—where those of us who didn't want to see them didn't have to. Could this be what set Seattle apart, gave it the magic that held everyone in thrall? Did our sense of ease come from being able to hide our unease? It did seem tied in Raban's mind with what he saw as Seattle's most salient characteristic: "The whole temper of the city was mild. . . . There wasn't a horn to be heard and everyone made room on the road for everybody else. Even on empty streets, pedestrians waited in polite knots for the sign to flash WALK before they crossed."

Still, whenever I attributed Seattle happiness to anything man-made, along would come an outsider to remind me that I was taking my natural surroundings and their power over the soul for granted. This time, it was Brewster, directing me to research and write a *Weekly* cover story on the quality of natural light in Seattle.

As with so many Brewster assignments, this one left me amazed at his infinite capacity for surprise and delight. After living in the Northwest for nearly twenty years, he was still stunned by thoroughly ordinary-to-a-native elements of Seattle's everyday environment—so much so that he actually thought the persistent dimness outside, as much a feature of Seattle life as rain, merited a 5,000-word story.

Brewster's incapacity for jadedness struck me as an entertainingly crippling condition. He resembled the lytico-bodig patient Oliver Sacks would write about years later in *The Island of the Colorblind*, whose memory could never retain anything. "Come again soon," the man said to Sacks at the end of the doctor's visit. "I won't remember you, so I'll have the pleasure of meeting you all over again." There were days when you half expected Brewster to run outside when it started raining, amazed that water in Seattle just came falling right out of the sky! Real water! Just like the stuff in the lakes!

Instead of the embarrassment I expected, though, the story turned out to deliver yet another awakening. Brewster brought up the subject in November, of all times, when Seattle suffers through sixteen hours of darkness a day—hardly, I thought, a propitious time to study sunlight. But when I went outside after our meeting—it was just after noon—I found myself looking around with newly acquired naif's eyes. I was struck by how soft, directionless, lush, luxurious, and romantic the light in the air looked. The buildings around me—terra-cotta, brick—positively glowed, their colors dissolving like colored mist into the air around them.

Now I could see that light in Seattle is amorphous—not so much beamed from a single source as aglow all around. It looks like sourceless light—apparent everywhere, coming from nowhere. It so softens shadows that there is virtually no contrast between light and shade, leaving Northwesterners to move through a dreamily dim, carefully ill-defined world of rounded edges and comfortable contours. Standing on the corner, looking at the soft neon beer signs in the Virginia Inn's window across the street, I could see how our light, being gentle, looks so kindly on flaws and brings the ordinary lavishly alive.

It became impossible not to notice this magical cast of light everywhere I went. I was particularly charmed by the effect I could see on grass and moss—this eerie, unearthly luminescence, this great glow quietly emanating up from the ground, standing out both vividly and subtly from the surrounding gray. It was far more alluring and far less painful to the eye than the sunswept Mexico and California beaches I remembered from visits long ago, with their vicious blinding whites and knife-edge shadows.

Eventually I would talk with a photographer, Bob Peterson, who explained that the glow in the grass was a function of natural "backlighting," brought on by the way the light is diffracted by airborne moisture and made to bounce every which way. Every blade of grass, he said, every strand of moss, was backlit. Photographers, he added, pay thousands of dollars for lighting equipment that delivers effects the Northwest delivers for free. "It's why they shoot so many car commercials here," he said. "It's also why the Northwest has the most beautiful rhododendrons and women's cheeks in the world."

Peterson turned out to be only one among a tremendous number of people in Seattle who were professionally enchanted by the light. I set off on a series of interviews with painters, art critics, photographers, cinematographers, architects, meteorologists, and psychologists whose voices comprised a serial chorus of ecstatic praise.

Even the science and statistics behind the light's magic sounded oddly poetical. Meteorologists at the Seattle office of the National Oceanic and Atmospheric Administration went on and on about how the weakness of Seattle daylight is owing both to cloud cover and latitude. Our sunniest month—July—averages just ten clear days. Over the course of a year, the Northwest averages only fifty-five days without cloud cover. From October through March, it is almost constantly cloudy, there being only seventeen clear days during those six months, twenty-seven days that are classified as partly cloudy, and 137 completely cloudy. December has only two clear days, and March only three.

But even on cloudless days the light here is diffused, explained the National Weather Service's Bruce Renneke, "because of the latitude factor." Between that and the winter tilt of the earth, the sun—which looks on a winter day like it is skulking around the southern horizon, hoping no one will notice it—is made to cast its light down on Seattle at an extreme angle, through a consequently thickened atmospheric filter. Light passing through all those little droplets in the air, Renneke went on, is turned "isotropic"—scattered, traveling in all directions at once. Not only does it grow weaker, but it also casts and reflects horizontally, washing out deep shadows and spreading a wondrously diffuse, subtle, gray-green glow through the air.

All these factors, along with the light-sponging dark-green landscape, conspire to create a highly romantic psychological atmosphere. The effect has people who work with light rhapsodizing about it. I talked with an architect, Mick Davidson, who said that "in other parts of the country, light is pretty much cut-and-dried. Here, it's almost an enigma."

Eventually, I came across a series of paintings entitled "Oyster Light," by Gertrude Pacific. Done in 1976 and 1977, the series, she said, "depicts the color of the light in Seattle, especially at that hour just before sunset. It's that time when there's some kind of wonderful inversion of light. It's as if everything's suddenly lit in a different way. The sun goes down behind the Olympics, but we still have a lot of light—as if the sunlight is directed upward. It's pearlescent—the sky reminds me of the inside of an oyster shell." The light led Pacific to convey in these paintings a certain understated romanticism and mystery that hints—like the light itself in the real world—at ineffable, elusive cosmic portent. "It is a light of expectancy," she said. "You're kind of unsure about what's going to happen. It is also a light of possibility, of the recognition of Nature, of enlightenment."

Something in the light led her to surrealism. All the paintings are evocatively lit portraits of wild animals in urban settings. A bear sits atop Freeway Park, a park built on an overpass over Interstate 5 in the middle of downtown; a snow owl is perched on a downtown parking meter, the street utterly deserted; an eagle stands on a lightpole; a doe, standing on a downtown rooftop, looks up, surprised, at the viewer of the painting.

There is an inversion in the paintings corresponding to the inversion Pacific sees in the light. The animals, inhabiting the natural light, make the place—Seattle, downtown, civilization, human progress, ambition—look, as it should, out of place.

The Seattle light exercise left me brooding about the complex conspiracy of accidents that makes Seattle exceptional. I realized that it is not so much the spectacular accidents like Mt. Rainier that keep you here as it is the near-infinite number of unspectacular ones, setting the sunlight slanting at such an extreme angle through so much airborne water, turning the sun's fire so soft and sweet that you are constantly lulled by it. That diffuse light turns Seattle into a place with no hard edges. Even concrete looks beguiling. With the light-mist soaked into your soul, you can't get worked up about anything, good or bad. Anger seems pointless, exuberance unnatural, outsized ambition not only unnatural but disturbing. How could anyone want to roil the placid waters suspended in the air here, risk tearing apart the cloud-filter that softens everything from sunlight to devastating news?

Nothing in Seattle looked the same to me after working on that story. The splendor of the light, the magic cast I could see everywhere now, seemed to make the artificial, inimical, ambition-borne features of the city—from skyscrapers to scowls—stand out in bold relief, as if clumsily lit by an amateur. Everything good here had been born here, engendered before the arrival of the white settlers, lolling in the downy light like a fat puppy; everything bad here was manufactured and relatively modern— defacements growing more ostentatious and looking more intrusive and out of place by the day.

Not everyone, I had to admit, was susceptible to the light. Everywhere I looked, I saw signs of human culture making deleterious inroads against retreating natural and psychological splendor, then invoking that same splendor as symbolic proof that Seattleites themselves were somehow different from the American norm. It was the same exercise that had the white settlers here killing off natives, then naming cities and parks after them. We are so much in tune with our natural surroundings, the self-imaging argument went, that we are milder, gentler, and wiser than people from elsewhere, and thus are given more to consensus and compassion than self-interest and confrontation.

Seattle in the 1980s, to cite the most egregious example of its false-hearted self-image, loved citing to outsiders the fact that it had been the only city of its size to integrate its schools voluntarily, rather than doing so in response to a court order. Voluntary integration in 1978 was part of the Seattle myth that people recited to themselves as evidence of the wonderfulness of the city and its inhabitants. The myth fogged over our memories of the antibusing demonstrators of the early 1970s, the seven years of prior court battles, and the resignations of three school superintendents over busing controversies. Worse, it almost completely obliterated the voices of panicked and grieving African-American parents. Now, fifteen years after busing began, when I went into Seattle's black neighborhoods and schools to research for the *Weekly* the question of why African-Americans were doing so poorly in the school system—busing had triggered not a rise in grades and test scores among African-American students, as promised, but instead a sharp decline—I was met with a chorus of lamentation. "Busing is destroying our community," parents would say over and over again. "Give us back our children!" While white Seattle was simultaneously congratulating itself on voluntary integration and moving to suburban or private schools to avoid it, black Seattle was putting its kids on buses in the early-morning darkness and watching them be carried off to distant, inaccessible corners of the city because it had no other options.

The city abounded with black heroes and heroines fighting desperately for their children. Most prominent among them was Pat Wright, whose Total Experience Gospel Choir, made up almost entirely of African-American kids, raised money with its riveting performances to fund black students' college educations. Wright made membership in the choir conditional on good academic progress in elementary and high school. Total Experience was the most celebrated African-American performing group among white audiences in Seattle, and served as evidence to Seattle whites that their city was exceptionally tolerant. Wright, though, took a dim view of Seattle's racial attitudes. Having moved here from Carthage, Texas, in 1964, she found the change in racial climate startling. "Racism here is actually worse than it is in the South—even in Texas," she told me. "Because here, you can't tell how someone feels. There, it's out in the open—you know the guy across the street hates you because he *tells* you he does. Here, you don't know until it's too late." What whites took for Seattle niceness, blacks regarded as deviousness. "I'd rather have people just tell me up front how they feel about me," Wright said, "instead of hiding their feelings and doing things to me behind my back."

The quiet horror of Seattle's self-deception was brought home to me by a telling statistic reported in the *Weekly*: The population of children in Seattle had declined by one-third from 1970 to 1985, with 30,000 of the vanished believed to be kids who had moved away. Children were literally fleeing the city. I was out walking early one morning when I chanced upon a glimpse into the life of the kids left behind. Walking by Bryant Elementary School, a crumbling brick building in my neighborhood, I noticed that the school grounds served as a latrine for the neighborhood's dogs. I remembered seeing people—all of them white—walking their dogs there in the evenings. Now, on a Monday morning, the parking strip beside the school was covered so thoroughly with offal that you could scarcely find a patch of clean grass as big as a human foot. I saw a full school bus pull up, and its passengers—all of them black—begin to disembark. It was a glorious morning, the air glistening softly—that magic mist-scrimmed backlight on everything, from every angle—and the kids came skipping off the bus onto a slick sea that had them immediately slipping, sliding, and grimacing in dismay, then disgust.

There, in a single chaotic image, did I see Seattle's anti-natalist—and, by default at least, racist—policies in full flower.

At the time, I was working on a classic *Weekly* story, one of those opportunities we were constantly offering people to read about themselves. This one, about the emotional state of single professional people, explored in excruciating, narcissistic detail the angst brought on our target audience, thirtysomething Seattleites, by their growing financial prosperity and personal freedom. Restless, for the most part unhappy, either unable or unwilling to remain in relationships, they sought solace in entertainment, consumption, fleeting sexual liaisons, and self-examination— that last endeavor generally conducted out loud, ad nauseam.

The interview that stood out most in my mind was with a thirty-year-old woman who was manager of Microsoft's editorial department. I met her for lunch at a restaurant near Microsoft and sat through the meal feeling my astonishment and depression deepen word by word as she talked at a furious pace about her friends, lovers, new condominium, faint hopes, and profound disappointments. "I'm not going to sell my condominium and move to another part of the country with someone who's getting another job," she said. "I mean, that's going to take a lot of commitment." She looked at the satisfactions derived from her work as far more profound than anything she could ever get out of a relationship. "I've always been very much involved in sort of career-interest stuff instead of any kind of monogamous, settling-down stuff. And now I don't think I'm less happy because I'm single. I've really done well with the things I've done. I feel successful in my career—I think I've reached a lot of really major goals and the things I've had to prove to myself."

Then, in the middle of telling me how happy and fulfilled she felt, she began to cry, and kept on crying and talking for several minutes while I sat across from her feeling responsible. Sit in a restaurant long enough with a woman in tears and the withering looks directed at you from all over the room start making you feel like a cad.

I endured interview after interview like that, with people intent on living childless lives devoted to career and material acquisition. They viewed potential lovers as something between objects to consume and business partners, and their relationships were invariably short-lived. Eventually, I talked with a despairing matchmaker who said, "I'm constantly stunned at how people can be so adept in their careers and emotionally be so much like children."

The Microsoft manager's condominium was near Connie Butler's house—in a fabled Seattle neighborhood where old frame homes like Butler's were grudgingly giving way to condominium complexes—and the more she talked (and the more I talked with people who talked like her), the more I saw Seattle giving way to people like her: young, childless, with a lot of money and an apparent determination to spend it all on themselves. It made me see the city forty years hence as a place populated by a million or so defeated and childless elders, rocking in state-of-the-art easy chairs and staring relentlessly at their navels, anxiously looking for flaws.

Clearly, the numbers and influence of these people—the *Weekly*'s target audience—were growing rapidly all over the city. *Weekly* readers were overrunning Seattle, as was evidenced by a 1986 *Seattle Times* story noting that Brewster's publishing company had grown into a $3 million operation.

The self was big business in Seattle. From then on, my *Weekly* writing assignments would either be about the individually prosperous or the collectively poor. If I wasn't writing about yuppie angst, I was writing about the woebegone Mariners—who struggled far more mightily against King County for a better Kingdome lease than they ever did against opponents on the ballfield—or the crumbling, overcrowded, demoralized Seattle schools. I was working on a story about an innovative Seattle school principal one day when I encountered a group of educators from Vancouver, British Columbia, touring her school. One of the visitors took me aside in a classroom and pointed up at a typically decaying section of wall, where water stains and cracks in the plaster were as visible as they were in abandoned downtown buildings. "Is this . . . *normal* for schools here?" she asked, disbelieving. I told her it was. "It's so strange," she said. "You have all this money here . . . we don't have nearly as much, but we would never allow our schools to get like this—it would just be *unthinkable*."

This had become a steadily more personal issue for Anne and me, since our oldest daughter Erin was about to enter first grade. We kept hearing alarming stories: about a man walking down the street in a nearby Seattle neighborhood who had seen a little girl playing in her front yard

and abruptly stabbed her to death (because, he later told police, she had
blond hair) or about the shooting of a child outside T. T. Minor Elementary School—the school to which the Seattle School District intended to
bus little Erin in a few months.

Seattle, clearly, was intent on expelling us. My business was dying, our
friends were leaving, and the city wanted nothing to do with our children.
The better the city's material prospects, the worse its psychological
prospects. I sat up late one night and regarded the history of Seattle as a
history of diminishment, boom by boom. I remembered reading about
the native tribes and their habit of fleeing into the woods and hiding
whenever invading Kwakiutl tribes from the north came down looking to
do battle, and I remembered, too, how the tribes finally were forcibly put
on a boat by white settlers and sent out into the sound, to Bainbridge
Island and the Kitsap Peninsula beyond. Now I saw their expulsion as
equal parts exile and deliverance. They were our first Lesser Seattleites.
Fully aware that a material boom would bring a spiritual bust to their
homeland, they served by their very existence to mock the pretensions of
newcomers intent on bringing civilization and wealth to the Northwest's
paradise.

Now, in 1985, in a move that in retrospect seems to have been
dreamed up and executed virtually overnight, Anne and I packed up our
kids and belongings and followed the exiles over to Bainbridge Island,
thirty-five minutes away by ferry. We bought the first house we found
there: Near the end of a winding, dead-end road, it sat up against a tangled woods and looked across the road at a tiny rotting house mounted on
cinderblocks, overgrown with blackberries, and surrounded by a yard full
of rusting cars and boats. Gentrification and sophistication seemed forever escapable here. We didn't know what was going to happen next in
Seattle, but whatever it was, we thought it best to watch from out here,
out of harm's way. Here, we thought, we could safely ride out the storm
we could feel bearing down on our city.

The Children's Crusade

We had no sooner moved our kids out of the city than Seattle mayor Charles Royer, in league with a citizens' group, declared Seattle a "KidsPlace" and announced his intention to make the city more child-friendly. KidsPlace signs sprouted up all over downtown as the city tried to reverse a dire trend that not only had seen the population of children in Seattle decline by one-third but also had seen twenty-two schools close, Seattle's average household size shrink to the smallest of any American city's, infant-mortality rates begin creeping upward in 1980 after a decade of decline, and child-abuse rates skyrocket. In 1985, the year we moved, the Seattle city attorney's office handled a record 5,600 child-abuse cases—an amount city official Joanne Tulonen characterized as "the tip of the iceberg."

The KidsPlace campaign smacked of desperation and denial, lending all the more credence to our notion that the city had become resolutely antinatalist. Downtown was a construction zone, with new buildings shooting up on virtually every block, a grandiose bus-tunnel system being built underground, Pioneer Square being renovated, and the Square's thriving crack and prostitution trade being forced up into Belltown, right outside the *Weekly*'s door. There was something incongruous about the sight of a KidsPlace sign on a pole in front of a parking lot, flanked by construction sites, where drug deals were being consummated all day long. KidsPlace looked like a city where kids had to run a gauntlet whenever they ventured outdoors. I would walk from the *Weekly* for ten minutes south to the ferry dock, through noise, chaos, rampant ambition, and various other forms of desperation, board the boat, ride over to the island, and enter an entirely different world—one that corresponded almost exactly to the Northwest of my childhood.

Our street was a little haven from ambition. Virtually everyone else in the neighborhood had figured out a way to avoid having a normal job. One couple owned a little glass-art shop in Pioneer Square; the man living in the rotting house across from us worked occasionally in the Bremerton shipyards; the man living in the woods behind us didn't appear to work at all; another neighbor was a seasonal fisherman and part-time carpenter; another owned the Streamliner Diner, a little eatery in the island's tiny town of Winslow; another was a self-employed attorney whose favorite topic of conversation at neighborhood parties was how he was "working too hard." We couldn't have picked a more compatible place, inhabited by more like-minded people, to ride out the restlessness-and-greed boom overtaking Seattle in the late eighties.

Raban would note in *Hunting Mister Heartbreak* that Seattle was a profoundly Asia-looking city. Just as New York and the rest of the eastern seaboard—and, for that matter, most of the country—looked Europeward, so did Seattle look Asiaward. He was to see Asian influences throughout the city and would make a number of friends in the Seattle area's Korean diaspora, which numbered some 40,000. Bainbridge, I noticed, had even more of an "Asian" tradition: Many of the island's most prominent families were Japanese-American, several of the streets had Japanese names, and the cultural and social center of the island—the Town and Country supermarket—was owned by a Japanese-American family. Issei and Nisei Japanese were such an integral part of the island that when the U.S. Government ordered residents and citizens of Japanese ancestry into concentration camps during World War II, the island's newspaper, the *Bainbridge Review*, was the only paper in the country to editorialize against the internment. Filipino farming families—another strong ethnic community on Bainbridge Island—maintained and protected many of the exiled Japanese family properties during the war. Tradition on Bainbridge among Caucasian, Filipino, and Japanese-American alike held that Japanese-Americans returning from internment fared better on the island than anywhere else on the West Coast, including Seattle. While many families elsewhere opted not to return to their prewar homes, and others came back to find their property stolen, destroyed, or defaced, those returning to Bainbridge returned largely to welcoming arms.

It didn't occur to me that not only Bainbridge but also Seattle stood out from the rest of the West Coast when it came to Asian attitudes until I met the Chinese-American writer Shawn Wong in the course of writing about him for *Pacific* magazine. Wong, who had grown up and gone to college in California, came to Seattle in 1977 after marrying a Seattle woman. The percentage of Asian-Americans in Seattle was growing fast—from 2.3 percent in 1950 to 7.5 percent in 1980, nearly 10 percent by 1987, and 13 percent by 2000, by which time Asians would be Seattle's largest minority group—and Wong was stunned to find Asian faces everywhere in the mainstream. "I noticed it right away when I got up here," he told me in 1986. "There's really more of a sense here of presenting the true picture of the community in the news or whatever. People in Seattle, I noticed, knew the names of Asian-American artists, like George Tsutakawa, and knew that they weren't from Japan. You didn't have to fight that stereotype of being *foreign* here. There were Asian-Americans on TV and in the news that weren't just pretty faces. There were Asian-American reporters at the newspaper. There were articles about Asian-American writers. It was shocking! In San Francisco, they really try to project an image of Chinatown that's more popular than true—that it's this exotic, foreign place."

Among the more abiding Seattle-Asia connections was one begun by Oregonian Harry Holt in the wake of the Korean War—the adoption of Korean orphans by Northwest families. Through Anne's work, we had met countless families with adopted Korean children, and eventually we decided to adopt as well. Korean adoption at the time was incredibly easy— some 400 Asian babies per year, most of them from Korea, were coming to Washington State—and it took only a year or so and about $4,000 to complete an adoption. We sailed through the preliminary application process, then had to put everything on hold until we could come up with the final payment of $3,173. This was a daunting task, given my suddenly uncertain income and the fact that our only asset of any size was an utterly useless typesetting machine, and it threatened to derail our adoption entirely.

Months passed. Korean babies—any one of whom, given better cash flow, could have been ours—kept pouring into Seattle. But then one day someone unexpectedly emerged to buy my typesetting machine.

The purchaser was a Japanese-American kid who worked for the machine's manufacturer, AM Varityper. We met in a Seattle bar to complete the transaction. He knew as well as I did that the machine had no future and that it certainly wasn't worth the $4,000 I was asking. Yet for some reason he was more than happy—eager, almost—to write me a check. When his check cleared, we paid the agency and concentrated on waiting anxiously for our long-awaited new baby to arrive. It didn't take long for a referral to come in the mail, telling us that our new daughter— a three-month-old named Huh Ok Kyung—was on her way. On the appointed day, we made our way to the airport and watched her plane come in from Seoul. (She was one of five babies arriving on the flight.) She disembarked in the arms of her escort, came down a long escalator, made her way through customs, emerged through double glass doors, and was handed over to us while I added up all the tiny twists of fortune that had resulted in this particular baby being ours: bureaucratic delays, financial shortcomings, breakneck technological progress, Bill Gates's and Paul Brainerd's ambitions, rapid obsolescence. . . . These and unnumbered other circumstances, insignificant in themselves, had conspired to assign us a baby no less arbitrarily and no less definitively than genetic fates assign you your birth children. Had we managed our money better, had Ok Kyung been born a day later, had an agency worker in Seoul typed up her stack of reports in a different order, had the sale of the machine not gotten our adoption moving again, had Bill Gates decided to stay in Albuquerque, or had any one of thousands of other imagined and unimagined things happened differently, we would have gotten a different baby, or possibly never adopted at all. Now, standing in the airport, surrounded by crying relatives and friends and other families taking in other babies, we knew unequivocally that fate had arranged everything perfectly so that Ok Kyung would be the baby we adopted. Any other baby among the hundreds that had arrived during our forced hiatus, I could now see, would have been the wrong one.

I came to feel infinitely blessed by virtue of living in Seattle. I started believing that Seattle in the latter half of the twentieth century was a nexus, a magic confluence of physical and temporal forces, a place and time where lives were changed more dramatically and more for the better than anywhere else on earth. The burgeoning boom going on around me, outside of my life, now seemed less alienating than affirming—like beautiful orchestral background music in tune with the musical magic sounding in my home, in my soul. The boom I'd been deriding for so long seemed like evidence of a blessing, and every time I ventured out of our house I would believe myself to be encountering further proof that Seattle was on a roll, both materially and morally. I felt like I was living through a latter-day Enlightenment, that everyone in Seattle was blundering into lives as blessed as mine simply because they were living in the right place at the right time.

Two years later, I would travel around the country with the Seattle Seahawks, along with a press contingent that included a Chinese-American photographer, Rod Mar, who took game pictures from the sidelines for the *Seattle Times*. Mar was an exuberant, sarcastic, energetic party animal just out of college, and everything he encountered—whether at work or elsewhere—struck him as further hilarious proof of endearing human idiocy. He was the kind of kid who could never manage to wipe the smirk off his face—an Asian Happy Gilmore. In Cleveland, fans shouted racial epithets and dumped beer on him. "I took one for the team!" he said afterward. In Kansas City, fans made machine-gun noises and shouted, "I got you, you gook!", and cries of "Gook! Gook!" trailed him in Boston, Atlanta, and San Diego. In every city, at every insult, he reacted with laughter. He turned around in Kansas City and mockingly challenged his tormenters to come down on the field and fight, "Right here! Right now!" Infuriated, they charged the field, were collared by security guards (sympathetic, black), and escorted from the stadium before the end of the game's first quarter. Their last vision inside the stadium was of Mar standing on the field, laughing at them.

I was astounded at how lightly he took the treatment. "These people," he said, with a classic Seattleite's condescension during one flight back, "they can't tell the difference between Japanese, Chinese, Vietnamese. . . . They just don't know—it's not like in *Seattle*."

Was Seattle different from the American urban norm in some admirable way I'd never noticed? Was it destined, as so many in the city seemed to believe, to show the rest of the country how to live a better life, both psychologically and morally? It was about to become the first predominately white city in the nation to elect an African-American mayor—Norm Rice—and our Chinese-American county executive, Gary Locke, was only a few years away from being elected governor. He would be succeeded as county executive by another African-American, Ron Sims. I was even thinking about all this in politically correct English. Did this apparent racial harmony signal that Seattle was undergoing a moral boom as well as a material one? Were we, after all, as different, as much better, as we thought ourselves to be? Or was I just giving in to Seattle's constant temperate emotional climate, its enduring contentment, its perennial self-satisfaction?

My lapse into uncritical love of Seattle was brought up short by another *Pacific* magazine assignment, this one about the prototype for a potential new restaurant chain called "Jose Pepper's Chicken and Ribs." Founded by the Sherwood Group, a commercial brokerage firm that included a former Nordstrom shoe salesman, Jose Pepper's was described by these gentlemen as being "as pure a Seattle play as you could get." Seattle, they said, was a place where people "have that fast-food mindset," yet want "a full-service-quality meal in a comfortable environment." People here, they insisted, "will trade up from the traditional hamburger experience—they respond to the upscale fast-food concept."

After researching Seattle tastes, values, and consumer attitudes, they had come up with an "adult fast-food" restaurant with wood furniture, soft music, real plants and art on the walls, and decorated in earth tones and muted brighter colors. It was a melding of fast-food and full-service restaurant ambience. Its signature drink was a wine-and-crushed-ice con-coction served in a frosted mug and called a "Mug-a-rita" (winner of the "Most Popular Drink" award at that year's Bite of Seattle festival). Cus-tomers read a giant menu board and placed their orders at the counter beneath it, as in fast-food places, then had the food delivered moments later to their table, as in traditional full-service restaurants. The menu, while more varied than a fast-food menu, consisted of foods that could be prepared in short order, yet still have the look, taste, and style of solid restaurant fare. The food, moreover, was served on china rather than plastic or cardboard, beer was served in a hefty frosted-glass mug, and patrons were given an almond-scented hot towel when their meals were finished.

I went to a lot of meetings of the Sherwood Group in 1986 and got a crash course both in marketspeak and in what these gentlemen insisted was the soul of Seattle. They were constantly throwing around phrases like "the chicken position in the fast-food market." "Seattle," they told me, "has more pizza restaurants per capita than any other city in the country." They explained that Seattle had given birth to adult fast food "with Red Robin, which in the mid-to-late seventies became identified with that market segment." Now it would seem that Seattle consumers were the New Hampshire voters of the fast-food marketplace, their reac-tion being a make-or-break proposition for a candidate with national-franchise ambitions. If it weren't for Seattleites' disdain, Jack-in-the-Box would be known today as Monterey Jack's. Skippers, Sea Galley, and Black Angus were tested in Seattle before going nationwide, and Godfather's Pizza went national with its pineapple–Canadian bacon pizza after succeeding with it in Seattle.

For all my emerging conviction that there was something unique about Seattle, something setting it apart from the rest of the United States, some of the best minds in the mass-market food business apparently believed the opposite: that Seattle was where the national middle could be found, fed, and best exploited. For every item of evidence I cited as proof positive that Seattle was enlightened, exceptional, they came up with more compelling evidence that it was middlebrow. The city, for example, was the third-most-tested product market in the country, after Orlando, Florida, and Columbus, Ohio—not particularly sophisticated company, to my way of thinking. "If you can make it in Seattle with a concept," one of them told me, "you'll make it even better in other parts of the country." "Welcome to Seattle," I thought, "where everybody is really, really, really average."

Greater Seattle certainly believed the best about the city—or believed, at any rate, that the opportunity had come at last to raise Seattle's national and international profile. Seattle in the late 1980s started garnering all kinds of national attention even without the strenuous efforts of city boosters. The resurgence of Boeing and the continued rapid growth in wealth, power, and size of Microsoft—which in 1985 announced that it was moving farther out of town to vast acreage in Redmond, where it would build a massive campus—had increasing numbers of Seattle-datelined news stories appearing worldwide. The sight of little groups clustered around tourist maps of downtown became common. Walking to the *Weekly* offices one morning, I was stopped by a group of Japanese girls, one of whom asked, in charmingly hesitant English, "Excuse me . . . can you tell us where is the Pioneer Square?" From the excitement in her voice, you would have thought she was asking directions to Mecca rather than Maynardtown, and her reverential excitement was particularly entertaining when measured against my memories of the district as a minefield of corpses and staggering and sleeping drunks and drug addicts.

Walking away, I realized that I saw similar groups almost every day now, all year round—from Tokyo, Los Angeles, Cleveland . . .

Greater Seattle was convinced that much of Seattle's emerging cachet had to do with its pro sports franchises. The Seattle Seahawks under Chuck Knox and the direct control of the Nordstroms had turned into a credible, competitive NFL franchise, carrying the Seattle name onto the covers of national magazines and into television-sports prime time, where cameras would adoringly pan over the Space Needle, Seattle skyline, and surrounding splendor during the lead-in from commercial breaks back to the game. Knox's first season had brought Seattle for the first time into the NFL playoffs, which they were to revisit for all but two of the next seven seasons. In 1986, the Seahawks overcame a 5–6 start to finish the season 10–6 and playing the best football in the league, only to fall one victory short of making the postseason tournament. *New York Times* columnist Dave Anderson, noting that his city's Jets were far less deserving of a playoff spot than the streaking Seahawks, suggested that the playoff-bound Jets swap their berth with the Seahawks for "an offense to be named later." (The *New York Times*! Writing about Seattle!) In 1987, Seattle signed celebrity college superstar linebacker Brian Bosworth, better known as "the Boz." Bosworth had a flashy, high-profile agent and a headline hunger seldom seen outside of professional wrestling—he was the most notorious football player in the country that year—and his arrival in Seattle not only signaled Knox's and the Nordstroms' determination to win a Super Bowl, but also a mammoth cultural shift: Seattle was embracing celebrity. Never before had the city dared to think of itself in the same sentence with aggressive, egomaniacal superstardom. With the arrival of the Boz, Seattle was trying to go Hollywood.

The event was odd enough to provoke the monthly *Washington* magazine to arrange for a cover picture of Bosworth and Bill Gates together. It was an act of perverse inspiration—a shot of "Bill and the Boz" at Seahawks headquarters—that illustrated in a single snap the essential weirdness of Seattle's stumble into the international spotlight. It also signaled the odd calculus of celebrity: Such was the public (and, even more to the point, the Gatesian) perception of the relative merits of these two that Gates came to Seahawks headquarters for the photo session so as not to inconvenience the better-known Boz.

A player strike in 1987 and injury in 1988 would limit Bosworth's NFL career to a single season, during which time he would publish a best-selling as-told-to autobiography, endorse an array of products from Gargoyle sunglasses to a mullet-enhancing hair pomade called Rad Crew Styling Wax (it appeared identical, save for its label, to the Butch Wax of my childhood), and flame out as a football player. 1988 was also the Seahawks' best season—the year Knox's rebuilding project, begun five years before, reached its pinnacle. The Seahawks advanced to the American Conference championship game—one game from the Super Bowl—before losing to the Cincinnati Bengals. Now a perennial playoff team, the franchise had become a massively visible Seattle promotional banner—particularly on television.

That, however, was as good as it got. The 1980s closed with the 1988 sales of the Seahawks and the Mariners to out-of-town owners with grandiose dreams for both of them. These sales were tremendously symbolic and eye-opening events. The teams had been acquired in the late 1970s and early 1980s for $16 million each. Now, the Seahawks were being sold for an eye-popping $100 million and the Mariners for an even more stunning—given their frightening box-office numbers—$80 million. The sales and the prices sent shock waves through Seattle, largely because they signaled that the city had taken on what Jonathan Raban called a "dangerous luster" in the eyes of the nation. Now, here was Indianapolis media mogul Jeff Smulyan, purchaser of the Mariners, talking excitedly about the size and rapid growth of the "Seattle market." And the relinquishment of the Seahawks by the sane, local, staid, reliable Nordstrom family to Ken Behring, a California real-estate developer with hilariously gross tastes for the gaudy and ostentatious, was Californication writ large. Behring lived on a $12 million northern California estate, with a koi-stocked man-made river running through his house; owned a Lear jet and a $112 million museum, named after himself, that showcased his 250-item antique car collection; and wanted everyone in the world to know all that about him. Worse, he bought the Seahawks because he wanted to spread his name around the Seattle area, which he saw as an emerging ideal place for doing what he did best: building lavish, massive golf-course communities.

The arrival of Behring and Smulyan and their money and dreams practically on the same day signaled that frighteningly big things lay ahead for Seattle. The two new owners were Godzilla and Rodan, descending enthusiastically on an utterly unprepared and naïve Tokyo.

There was no question in the minds of anyone taking in these spectacular franchise sales that Seattle was headed for unprecedented grandeur. The 1990s loomed as a decade of possibilities as exciting as they were alarming. You could see the beginnings of the ripple effect from Microsoft's outsized success, which appeared even in light of its multimillion-dollar dimensions to be only just beginning to get under way.

For all of my Lesser Seattle pretensions, I couldn't help but be excited by the city's spectacular future. As late as 1988, I had had magazine editors from elsewhere in the country asking me if Seattle was in California or Alaska. Now I could see the day coming when everyone could find Seattle on a map. I gave in to the excitement all at once, in that overdone way of the sudden convert, the redeemed skeptic.

I was so enthralled that I couldn't bring myself to pay proper attention to these kids I kept encountering in the lobby of the *Weekly*'s building and in the elevator I rode up to my fourth-floor office. "Dude," they would shout, taunting me as I got off the elevator, "you should be writing about *us*." The doors would close on them shouting, "Sub Pop! Upstairs on the tenth floor!" I ignored them, not recognizing that they were ragged little choristers shouting out at me from Maynardtown, trying to drown out the voice of the coming boom's Siren, which was already beginning to hold Seattle—and me—in thrall. Ahead lay a small recession that ultimately would prove nothing more than a speed bump in Seattle's Road Ahead. Boom times the likes of which no one in Seattle history had ever seen were coming, and no one—including me—had time to heed the cries of alarm being sung by the boomers' children.

Breaking Out

I was not the only one being hectored by the kids upstairs. On my infrequent days in the office, I shared a cubicle with Kathryn Robinson, an ebullient and brilliant young woman who was energetically chronicling Greater Seattle's emerging upscale retail and restaurant scene. (She was not, however, a Greater Seattle enthusiast, her coverage tending toward the sardonic. It was Robinson who dubbed the late eighties new-singles-bar scene at the south end of Lake Union the "Herpes Triangle.")

On her way in to work every morning, she would stop at an espresso stand in the Gravity Bar, a hipper-than-thou restaurant on the ground floor of our building, and buy a latte. The youngsters working the stand would regale her with their visions of future glory. "We're in a band that's going to be *huge....*" She would pat them on the head indulgently and come upstairs. "That Jeff Ament," she liked to say, "makes the *best* lattes ... but does he have to talk about his band *every single morning?*"

The late 1980s and early 1990s were incredibly busy years for Robinson. Until then, Seattle had had so few restaurants to be taken seriously that Brewster and his new managing editor, Katherine Koberg, used to sit in meetings every week in a panic because there were no restaurants to review. "Then," Koberg recalled years later, "there suddenly were ten new restaurants opening *every week*. It was like it changed overnight." Robinson, who had grown accustomed to working at leisure for weeks at a time on an occasional story about a new restaurant, store, or trend, now found herself cranking out copy at an almost suicidal pace. She was covering the rapid transformation of downtown Seattle—once a depressing mix of slums, low-rent office buildings, and out-of-scale new skyscrapers—into a Scene replete with national retailers (Ann Taylor, Abercrombie & Fitch, Barneys New York, Victoria's Secret), high-end downtown shopping malls (Westlake Center, Pacific First Centre, that spelling of "Center" being symptomatic of the city's grander turn toward pretension), and what came to be called "new downtown concept restaurants" (Palomino, Gravity Bar).

In 1989, Robinson wrote a *Weekly* cover story highlighting the degree to which the forces of Greater Seattle were winning the battle for control of the city's destiny. The story, about Starbucks as it was poised to leap from the regional to the national market, was filled with telling details—most of them supplied by a voluble Howard Schultz, who now is Starbucks's CEO and at the time was the company's marketing director—signaling the dramatic change both in Starbucks and the national definition of "Seattle."

When Gordon Bowker moved on from the defunct *Seattle* magazine in 1971 to co-found Starbucks with his friends Jerry Baldwin and Zev Siegl, Seattleites interested in good coffee were resigned to driving three hours north, to Vancouver, British Columbia, to buy coffee from Murchie's, a gourmet coffee and tea shop that enjoyed legendary status in Seattle. Bowker and his partners wanted to build a homegrown Murchie's. Their first store, on the edge of the Pike Place Market, sold tea, spices, catnip, and dark-roasted coffee beans that brewed a robust, black, thick beverage with a tremendous kick. They learned the technical arcana of roasting coffee—and a great deal of the marketing and mythology around it as well—from Alfred Peet, the Dutch-born founder and owner of Peet's Coffee in Berkeley, California, where all three apprenticed. Customers entering that first Starbucks store were served by salespeople steeped in coffee lore. Starbucks was as much an evangelist for good coffee as it was a retail operation; customers during the seventies, whether buying beans or ground coffee, often were treated to lectures that made them feel like they should be paying tuition. I took to drinking Starbucks almost immediately—even having it shipped to Ann Arbor during our years in exile—and knew full well what Robinson meant in her piece when she quoted an observer of Starbucks devotees as saying, "They're not just drinkers, they're disciples."

While Starbucks's three founders were entrepreneurs, they also were Lesser Seattleites, and they had relatively modest aspirations. They wanted to build their business into a regional enterprise that produced something they could be proud of, that would make them a reasonable amount of money, and that would save people the long drive north to Murchie's. It was a measure of their purity of heart that they named their company after one of Captain Ahab's crew in *Moby-Dick*, and adopted a company logo—a whimsical, Ivar-worthy drawing of a bare-breasted mermaid/siren, done by Seattle designer Terry Heckler—that was more silly than savvy. Moreover, they exerted almost no effort in coddling their customers—they worked hard at making perfect coffee and teaching people how to store and brew it properly. "Starbucks's whole angle," one of Robinson's interviewees said, "has always seemed to be, 'Are you good enough to drink our coffee?'"

It was not until 1984—two years after they hired Schultz as marketing director—that Starbucks opened its first coffee-by-the-cup outlet, at Fourth and University in downtown Seattle. When the doors opened on its first morning, a line extending around the corner half a block away had already formed. Bowker, for one, was stunned when he heard that news—at that point, he realized, the big-business potential of his company was beyond the scope of his imagination, and certainly beyond the scope of his interest.

By then, the visions of Schultz and the company founders were diverging drastically. Not only was Bowker dubious about serving milk-based coffee beverages, as Schultz insisted on doing, but he and his co-founders had little interest in turning Starbucks into a massive business, as Schultz was obsessed with doing. Schultz had visited Italy in 1983 and been stunned by what he saw there: The country had 200,000 coffee bars—social centers where people gathered, read newspapers, talked, and drank copious amounts of excellent coffee. Milan alone, he noticed, had 1,500. Why not do that in the U.S.?

Starbucks bought Peet's Coffee in 1984, and Schultz and the company founders went their separate ways two years later. Shultz founded a new company named Il Giornale (The Newspaper), a chain of upscale, high-concept, Italian-style coffee bars. The next year, Bowker left Starbucks to concentrate on a new venture, Redhook Ale, which sought to duplicate with beer the gourmet turn he'd executed in coffee, and Schultz bought Starbucks back with the idea that he would continue his Il Giornale vision under the already-established Starbucks name. He opened the company's first store outside the Northwest that year, in Chicago, which had long been the city with the most mail-order Starbucks customers. By 1989, there were thirty-eight Starbucks outlets—twenty-four in the Puget Sound region, five in Vancouver, and nine in Chicago. And Schultz was on the verge of taking over the country. The specialty-coffee business had grown from $50 million per year in 1983 to $500 million in 1988, and it had barely gotten started. Schultz saw it as a multibillion-dollar business in which Starbucks had an insurmountable head start.

By then, Schultz had reworked the founders' formula into . . . well, into as pure a Seattle play as you could get. Customers placed their orders at a counter with a menu board mounted on the wall behind it, then sat in stylish thematic splendor drinking coffee and eating pastries. The first time I walked into a post-Schultz Starbucks, I was so struck by the resemblance to Jose Pepper's that I was visited with a vision of the meeting in which Schultz, making his case for reinventing Starbucks to the three company founders, was surely describing to them "the coffee position in the beverage-by-the-drink market" and insisting that "people in Seattle are willing to trade up from the traditional coffee experience."

With his adult fast-coffee concept refined enough for national expansion, Schultz knew he also had a spiritual ace in the hole for marketing it: Seattle. He had seen how Nordstrom invoked the city's name constantly in its recent, tremendously successful national expansion. The Nordstroms had made the Seattle of the country's imagination synonymous with quality, integrity, *authenticity*. They understood that the city either was already viewed as an unspoiled paradise inhabited by the pre-corrupt or at the very least could be marketed as such to Americans who knew nothing about the place. In the eyes of the rest of the country, Seattleites were practically the next best thing to Native Americans. "There is name recognition with Seattle," Schultz told Robinson. "People associate it with softness, sensitivity, honesty, good food, fresh products. The Nordstroms made sure when they went national that people knew they were from Seattle; that's what we're trying to do with Starbucks."

It was an astonishing moment, reading that quote—almost the direct opposite sensation from that vertiginous moment I had experienced among the Hmong six years before. I executed a dizzying, sickening spiral spin down into a depressing rabbit hole, where Seattle looked like a theme park. The indefinable, near-infinite series of small and large accidents in Seattle that conspired by happenstance to create a psychological state equivalent to the surrounding water, mountains, and oyster light—perfect peace, perfect joy—had now been distilled by a marketing mind into a "concept."

Schultz's cynicism was depressing enough; more depressing was the implication that the raw material he used to refine his concept—the difference I had long felt defined Seattle and set it apart from the rest of the world—was a deluded notion, an adman's fiction.

Most depressing of all was the way the rise of Starbucks made it so undeniably clear that Lesser Seattle could never keep the city from becoming a wholly owned subsidiary of Greater Seattle. Anything Lesser Seattle did, Greater Seattle could do up grander. Even the very raison d'être of Lesser Seattle—preservation of the Northwest from the corruption that overtook older, more populated, ambition-poisoned American cities—had been turned by Greater Seattle into its most powerful, corrupting promotional weapon.

As part of his Greater Seattle cooptation of Lesser Seattle's Starbucks, Schultz made a tremendously symbolic strategic decision before launching his behemoth: He moved the tresses on the company logo's sea siren just enough to cover her breasts. It was as if he had moved Starbucks across Yesler Avenue, out of Maynardtown, and cleaned it up before opening its doors to the national public.

There was no question that Schultz was right in noting that Seattle was now viewed by the nation as an alternative to the American urban norm. National magazine stories invariably mentioned Seattle's opera- and theater-goers wearing blue jeans and parkas to performances, and stuffing their backpacks under their seats. This was mentioned so often in the press that it became a virtual defining image of Seattle. And it was beginning to seem that every local-business story was an alternative-business story. By 1989, Starbucks was competing with eleven Seattle-area specialty coffee roasters, some of whom were already being cited around town as hipper purveyors of a better product. Gordon Bowker, a board member of the *Weekly*, had left his alternative-coffee company to concentrate on his alternative-beer company, Redhook. His new venture was very much like the old Starbucks, with the same trappings of old-fashioned, pre-commercial authenticity: a whimsical, retrograde logo—this one a grandiosely mustachioed "trolley man" and the slogan, "Ya sure, ya betcha!"—and evocations in every way possible of a mythic, pre-commercial past, back when quality was a beverage purveyor's sole concern. Just as Starbucks had first been headquartered in the storied Public Market, now Redhook was headquartered in the storied Fremont District. It operated out of a converted trolley barn—the name "Redhook" referred to the red hook used to pull trolleys into the barn for repairs—and adhered to time-honored "craft beer" production principles. Disdaining the swill that mass-market beer had become—a light, flavorless, bland, distasteful lager—Redhook brought back the traditional full-flavored English ale, a robust, hoppy beverage carefully crafted according to time-honored traditions, etc., etc., etc. . . . , served and distributed by salespeople steeped in etc., etc., etc. . . .

Redhook was one of three craft beer companies to take off in the late eighties Northwest, the other two being Grant's and Pyramid. All three produced beer as phenomenal (and as story-rich) as the original Starbucks coffees. Between Starbucks, its eleven competitors, and these three craft-beer companies, Seattle was a veritable alternative hothouse.

It also was paradise rendered as a rollercoaster: Between my craft coffee days and my craft beer nights, I was alternately jabbering frantically and mumbling somnolently with incomprehensible joy. I was to spend the nineties largely avoiding the boring middle ground of coherence.

It was hard not to fear for the future, though, no matter how much coffee and beer I drank. The Starbucks bowdlerization had me wondering how long it would be before alternative statement after alternative statement surrendered its all to Greater Seattle and the mainstream market. The Sub Pop kids upstairs from the *Weekly*—who, unbeknownst to me, were madly crafting a powerful alternative to mainstream rock, which during the 1980s had devolved into a product utterly devoid of art, wit, or genuine emotion—would have looked, had I cared to notice, to be headed for a fate at least as bad as Starbucks's. In 1989, having already produced regionally successful records by Mudhoney, Tad, the Walkabouts, Cat Butt—all bands sustained by Seattle's thriving new club scene—Sub Pop had come up with a national underground hit album that cost only $600 to produce. Called *Bleach*, by Nirvana, a band from Aberdeen—a hard-scrabble town 100 miles south of Seattle—with a drummer, Chad Channing, from Bainbridge Island, the CD sold 35,000 copies in less than a year, its fame spreading by word of mouth and college-radio stations. Had I known what was going on up there, I couldn't have helped but wonder what sort of devoured-by-the-mainstream fate awaited Sub Pop, Nirvana, and their purity of (he)art.

I spent 1990 absorbed in Seattle's struggle over the worth of hosting the Goodwill Games—an alternative athletic extravaganza that, as far as I could tell, had been invented by Ted Turner, under the pretext of fostering world peace, in order to provide his cable superstation with the kind of content that would give him a better chance at competing head-to-head with the three established TV networks. Since the networks had all the mainstream big-ticket athletic events (Olympic Games, Super Bowl, World Series, and various other professional and college playoffs and tournaments) wrapped up, Turner was intent on creating an alternative for his enterprise.

Turner's grander pretension—that the Games could grow into a means of breaking the Cold War impasse between the United States and the Soviet Union and lead the world into a new era of peace and love—was classic Ted Turner eccentricity. It was so preposterous that it was almost endearing. It was also the sort of notion that only a city with Seattle's peculiar delusions of alternative grandeur could buy into. Greater Seattle's rubelike eagerness to host the Games, which no other American city wanted to take on, was borne largely of the city's starting to believe too much of its own hype. For at least the past fifteen years, the image of Seattle—as Raban had described, and as Howard Schultz had pointed out—as a locus of softness, sensitivity, and authenticity, a Shangri-La of civility, a city that had found an alternative way of life, had taken on the dimensions of self-delusion in Seattle itself. More and more, you read and heard Seattle commentators, editorialists, Chamber of Commerce flacks, and politicians proclaiming Seattle as an exemplar of an alternative way of life—a place where consensus and decency rather than greed and competitive rage thrived, and where people had found a more peaceful way to advance as a civilization without fighting for advantage over one another. Inevitably, the notion grew to the point where you started hearing promoters advance the proposition that Seattle could show the rest of the world how to coexist in harmony, that all we had to do was export our civility and behavior along with our coffee, beer, customer service, and software.

Everyone, save for a few chronically disgruntled journalists and Lesser Seattleites who saw every bid for attention as another step toward civic self-destruction, got on the Goodwill bandwagon. Brewster and his friend Paul Schell—the Seattle 2000 vision guy and failed mayoral candidate—the Chamber of Commerce, the Sports and Events Council of Seattle/King County, downtown businesses, hotels and restaurants, and all the usual suspects hyped the Games as a combined second coming of the World's Fair and opportunity for Seattle to lead the rest of the world to enlightenment.

Brewster, to his credit, gave me free editorial reign to lament and lambaste the event promoters, but the city unaccountably went ahead with its plans anyway, and the Games went off as scheduled. Out of a sense of duty, I attended a series of world-class track and field, basketball, and other sporting events, often staged before empty houses. And all through the weeks-long gala, the debate raged: Were the Games a success or a failure?

People covering the events and taking in the empty venues, people checking the Turner Network's dismal ratings, and people keeping track of the Cold War knew full well that the Games were a flop. But the promoters both of the Games and of Greater Seattle faced the press day after day, night after night, proclaiming the Games a colossal success. By the time of the closing ceremonies, the relationship between reporters and the Games personnel forced to deal with them were frayed to the point where a hot war was about to break out. My most memorable Games experience—aside from watching the Brazilian women's basketball team—was watching a confrontation between the Games' Barbara Smith and two local reporters at the closing ceremonies, which were held in mid-downtown, at Westlake Center—an indoor mall with an outdoor town square attached to it—early one beautiful summer evening.

The crowd was sparse. Reporters, trying to get a crowd count from Smith, finally cornered her, with KIRO Radio's Frank Abe asking repeatedly, "Barbara, can you give us a crowd count?"

"Fifteen thousand," Smith replied.

Abe was stunned. "Impossible!" he shrieked.

"Fifteen thousand," Smith repeated, her jawline hardening.

"Where'd you get that?" Abe asked.

"From the police major."

At which point the *Tacoma News Tribune's* Rob Carson intervened. "I just talked with the police major," he said, "and he said it was more like six thousand."

I didn't know at first whether to be heartened by the low attendance—proof that Seattleites in general had refused to buy into this meretricious event—or to be disheartened by the establishment's disingenuous power over the city. Standing there, I looked back over the 1980s and saw them as a decade of gradual conquest of Lesser Seattle by Greater Seattle, a relentless march toward the same civic misadventures that had eventually either ruined or signaled the ruin of pretty much every other American city. Increasing portions of Seattle's money and energy were being invested in lavish and worthless displays of "prestige" that amounted to little more than Roman circuses. Why couldn't Seattle be different? It was allowing itself to be turned into a cliché: the city intent on establishing that it has achieved "major league" status, desperate to be perceived as the next "New-York-Pretty-Soon," hosting games that savvier cities didn't want, and either trying to steal professional sports franchises from other cities or spending whatever it took to keep the ones it managed to get. Now Seattle, in hosting the Games, had spent millions on a lavish athletic extravaganza that the rest of the nation, if not the world, saw as silly. All three Seattle professional sports franchises—basketball's Sonics, baseball's Mariners, and football's Seahawks—were demanding greater civic investment, either in the form of better stadium leases or taxpayer-financed new stadiums, if Seattle didn't want to lose them to other cities. The Sonics were threatening to move across Lake Washington to Belle-vue; new Seahawks owner Ken Behring was threatening to move his franchise to California; new Mariners owner Jeff Smulyan was insisting that his team could not survive in Seattle without more substantial taxpayer investment; and Seattle's business community was overtly and covertly pressuring city and county politicians to give in to all of those demands.

Somehow, you just knew that the city ultimately would capitulate. Seattle, for all its pretensions to alternativeness, was shaping up as just another urban American wannabe, a Kansas City, a Cleveland, deter-mined to be "major league" as defined by the kind of mind everyone in Seattle had moved here—or so I thought—to avoid.

As if I weren't despondent enough, the closing ceremonies offered up this musical image of Seattle in the form of a saccharine Games theme song, sung over and over and over and over by children in Seattle and Moscow, linked by satellite, full of lines like this:

> *And if everyone lit just one little candle,*
> *What a bright world this would be.*

Then the ceremony finally closed with Seattle's children, clustered just below center stage, waving ersatz phosphorescent "candles" under the glare of television lights so intense that they washed out the glow from the children's little props.

Depressed, I walked back to the *Weekly* office to write and file my story. I got in the elevator with a kid from Sub Pop. He was wearing a plain white T-shirt with a single word printed on its chest, in big, bold, black type. I recognized the font as Helvetica. The word was "Loser." I decided he was wearing the shirt solely for my benefit. He was rebuking me for spending my working life the way I did, chronicling the ridiculous exploits of Greater Seattle. The real Seattle story, he was trying to let me know (that part of his message was falling on blind eyes), was going on upstairs.

It came as a considerable shock in October 1991 when my *New Yorker* arrived one day with the first of a two-part series in it on James Acord, a Seattle sculptor who had left Seattle for Barre, Vermont, in 1979. The story, by Philip Schuyler, exhaustively detailed how Acord had begun work in Barre on a masterpiece entitled *Monstrance for a Grey Horse*, returned to Seattle in 1986, worked alternately on the sculpture and various other projects, and by 1991 had nearly finished *Monstrance*. In 1989, he moved to Richland, Washington, in the eastern part of the state, near the Hanford Nuclear Reservation, because he wanted to work with live nuclear material in his sculpture. *Monstrance*, in fact, was supposed to have a canister of the stuff embedded in it—although Acord had run into some amusing trouble trying to acquire nuclear waste for that purpose.

Almost as amazed to see a Seattle artist in the *New Yorker* as I was by the story of the sculpture, I tracked Acord down over in the Fremont District and went out there to visit him. Now fifty, and having worked at his craft for thirty-three years, almost entirely without recognition or remuneration, he looked the way Samuel Beckett would have looked had Becket been born an optimist. Acord sported pretty much the same face as Beckett, along with the same backswept, spiky plume of hair, the same round spectacles, and the same inward-directed look in his eyes. What distinguished him from Beckett was the utter lack of sobriety in his face, as if it was all he could do to keep himself from breaking out laughing—particularly when he talked about his career. Over his thirty-three years as a working sculptor, he had held, by his count, forty-six jobs, among them logger, carpenter, monument carver, plater of high-voltage conductors, pipe welder, ship fitter, and forklift operator. He had sold virtually no work—largely because he never tried, but also because a great deal of it was tremendously odd. One of his pieces, for example, *The Fiesta Home Reactor*, was an aquarium-like contraption that, Acord insisted, produced radioactive material—right there on your kitchen table! He did not have an agent or gallery to represent him and he avoided publicity the way vampires avoid daylight. Whenever anyone wanted to interview him—particularly writers from art magazines—he would practically cringe in fear, and talk incessantly about how he wasn't sure he could "handle" that kind of conversation. He consented to the *New Yorker* profile only because when he met the writer, by accident, they hit it off. Three months after it was published, he still had not read the piece—"because," he said, "it freaks me out to read about myself." And he consented to talk with me only because I was excited about seeing *Monstrance for a Grey Horse*.

We met at a Fremont tavern and chatted over beer before he walked with me over to the Fremont Fine Arts Foundry—a place where artists could rent studio space built around a large, factory-like floor for working on large pieces of sculpture—to see *Monstrance*, which was stored there so Acord could put the finishing touches on it.

Acord first began conceiving and making sketches for *Monstrance* in 1977. He had grown preoccupied with nuclear technology, which he regarded as the central and most alarmingly unexamined problem of our age, and as this sculpture took form in his imagination it turned into both a monument designed to last as long as nuclear waste did—so that earth-lings 30,000 years or so from now, not understanding human language, would somehow be warned away from waste sites by these sculptures— and as an artistic examination of the meaning and impact on humans of nuclear technology. In a sense, *Monstrance for a Grey Horse* was to be a religious monument in the grand tradition of religious artwork from the Middle Ages. In the Catholic Church, the monstrance is the ornate, gold- and-glass, cruciform vessel in which the Eucharist is placed during the interim between the crucifixion on Good Friday and the resurrection on Easter Sunday. In this *Monstrance*, the Eucharist would be live nuclear material—the dubious "sacred substance" of our dubious age.

After two years of thinking and composing, Acord commenced a near- lifetime of obsessive and highly impractical career decisions when he decided the only way to make *Monstrance* properly was to move to Barre, Vermont, where he could "stand next to a seventy-three-year-old tooth- less Italian carver who came up in Cabrera, and have the opportunity to listen to his approach to chisel work." Barre has some of the best granite in the world, and is renowned for its stone-carvers—men who spend their working lives carving monuments, most of which adorn graves. Before Acord could begin hands-on work on his piece, he wanted to study stone- carving techniques from the masters, and he wanted to work with the best material possible. "Of the old, traditional materials for art sculpture in the stone family," he told me, "only granite really is holding up well in today's polluted, corrosive environment." He had observed in the 1970s that most outdoor sculpture began deteriorating within a few years of installation—the legacy, he believed, of an increasingly polluted environ- ment and the budget-driven decisions of sculptors doing publicly funded art projects to use the least expensive materials possible, in order to turn a profit on their work. And since Acord wanted *Monstrance* to last for 30,000 years or so, he would need exceptionally durable material.

Arriving in Barre, Acord immediately rented a small, unheated studio-and-living space and took a job at a gravestone-manufacturing company, learning and working by day and working on *Monstrance* by night. He worked in this fashion from 1979 until 1986, then shipped himself and the half-finished *Montrance* back to Seattle, with the delivery address for the sculpture being a vacant lot. Acord was too broke to pay the C.O.D. cost and he knew that the shipping company, Burlington Northern, would impound the sculpture until he could raise enough money to "bail it out." He felt that *Monstrance* could come to no harm sitting on a Burlington Northern loading dock, since there was little the shipper could do by way of disposing of a one-ton granite package. After spending the summer fishing in Alaska, he retrieved his masterpiece and got set up again in Fremont. By 1989, when the sculpture was finished save for a titanium mask, the embedding in it of its canister of live nuclear material, and its installation, it had cost Acord two fingers, innumerable relationships, half his career, $12,000 to $14,000 in "receipt costs" for stone and tools, with another $8,000 still to be spent casting and adding the titanium hood. (Later, he would abandon the idea of encasing the sculpture's head in the hood.) The costs in years, dollars, and quality of life were so high that Acord never thought in terms of selling the sculpture to recoup his investment. Instead, he talked of selling it for the cost of finishing it and moving it to its permanent home. "If I could find a site for it," he says, "and have enough money to get the sculpture there and get the site prepped and everything, jeez, you know, I'd practically give it away."

With that, we walked over to the foundry to see *Monstrance for a Grey Horse*. We walked down a small flight of stairs and turned a corner into a little storage space next to the stairs. There the sculpture stood, in profile. And there I stood, suddenly helpless, awestruck, stunned. The encounter sent me spinning off and up into a revisitation of my experience among the Hmong, that same exquisite sensation in the soul, the feeling that it is being flooded with light, celestial light, the light of Truth. I understood what had happened to Philip Schuyler, why he shadowed Acord for nearly two years, and why he had gotten the *New Yorker* to devote nearly an entire issue's worth of space to an unknown artist. Acord had taken a cold hard chunk of stone and imbued it with mysterious power. How on earth had he done it?

To hear him tell it, he had done it with obsessive, hands-on technical work, eschewing the use of power saws and tools so as to work the stone the way it had been worked in medieval times. *Monstrance for a Grey Horse* is composed of a granite base on which stands a five-foot trapezoidal granite column, eighteen by thirty-one inches at the bottom tapering to eleven by twenty-four inches at the top, then giving way to an incurved portion out of which rises the granite carving of a horse's skull. Two cylindrical holes, one drilled in the top of the base and the other in the bottom of the column, line up to form a receptacle for a stainless-steel canister containing the live nuclear material.

Acord sculpted the entire work himself with hand tools. There is a mathematical exactitude to the symmetry of the piece, to the trapezoidal shape of the column, to the beveled edges of the column and the base beneath it, that seem impossible when you realize it was all done essentially by eye. And the variety of textures on *Monstrance*'s surfaces display, in Acord's words, "the full vocabulary" of techniques for stonework listed in the *Stoneworker's Manual.* Acord used a variety of chiseling techniques—including a particularly magical one called "bluing"—that cause light to play variously and spectacularly off the carving's surfaces.

With Acord talking technical arcana in the background, I started laying my hands on the sculpture. I couldn't help myself—the thing practically hypnotizes you into fondling it. Made of one of the hardest substances in the universe, it was both soft to the touch and impossibly variegated in texture. Parts of it were rough and sharp enough to cut my hands; others harshly smooth; another section was weirdly pebbled; and the mouth, eye sockets, and teeth were polished to a texture so smooth that it didn't feel like stone at all. Many of the textural differences were invisible—I could only perceive them by running my hands over the stone.

I stepped back to focus on the skull—an intricate fusion of the abstract with the anatomically correct. The skull was such a careful study that veterinarians who'd seen it correctly identified the breed of horse Acord used as a model; yet it also had breathtaking abstract designs carved into it that turned it from a purely naturalistic rendition into an inarticulable and eloquent artistic declaration. "The shapes are so varied and so complex," Schuyler had written in his *New Yorker* opus, "that the slightest change in angle alters your entire impression of the work."

I kept looking at Acord, who is the definition of homespun, and looking at his sculpture, trying to figure out how this masterpiece had come out of Seattle—and particularly out of this Seattleite.

I also was baffled by the fact that the sculpture was sitting in this basement storage room—that Acord hadn't sold it yet. But the more I talked with him, the more I could see that he had no capacity for interest in the commercial potential of his work. He couldn't conceive of translating it into money. He would become seized with an idea, do whatever it took to realize it, then would be seized anew, with a new idea, before he could figure out how to get rid of his finished work.

Once he had sculpted *Monstrance for a Grey Horse*, he spent years trying to get nuclear waste for it. The quest for live nuclear material became an art form in itself, Acord involuntarily and enthusiastically turning his life into a quest for his Grail. He secured a nuclear handling permit—at one point, utterly frustrated in his attempts at laying his hands on some nuclear waste, he had tattooed his permit number on the back of his neck—and turned federal and state bureaucracies inside out in his attempt to fill *Monstrance*'s void. Now, the quest had turned into grist for the endless-story mill that Acord liked to grind. "I called the Trojan Nuclear Power Plant down in Oregon one day," he told me, "and I said, 'I was wondering if I could get some nuclear waste from you people. I'm a responsible guy—I'll keep it tightly sealed in plastic bags and everything! I'll even come down in my pickup and get it!'" They didn't follow up on his request. "It turns out that you're either in the club or you're not," he said, laughing.

Finally, he hit upon an ingenious solution: He set up a little mining operation in his Fremont studio and started mining the uranium off orange Fiesta Ware plates. He had collected quite an impressive pile of the stuff until someone in Fremont got wind of what he was doing, dropped by with a Geiger counter, and panicked at the reading he got, which indicated a rather high level of radioactivity. The next thing Acord knew, the Fremont Community Council declared the area a "nuclear-free zone," and his mine was shut down.

Now, Acord had moved on to grander obsessions. He wanted to use a nuclear reactor to "transmute" nuclear waste into a form of platinum and use the transmuted material in a sculpture. To that end, he had moved to Richland—from Seattle's point of view, a redneck-infested backwater—begun taking physics classes at the community college there, and talked his way into the local community of nuclear engineers. Acord is incredibly charming, and before long he had quite a coterie of nuclear scientists trying to help him realize his dream. They formed a group, named by Acord the "Fine Art Flux Technical Advisory Committee" (FAFTAC), chaired by Dr. Robert Schenter, who was developing medical nuclear isotopes at the Hanford Nuclear Reservation's Fast Flux Test Facility (FFTF). The team held monthly meetings at Acord's house, where he and his long-suffering wife Margaret (who eventually would leave him) served lemonade and pie "with a little Rutherford atom [the universal symbol of atomic energy] in the crust—you know, they get such a kick out of that."

Acord had spent the previous three years in this fashion, learning nuclear technology and finding ways to use it in his art. He had designed, then decided not to try making, sculptures that would be misshapen by a nuclear reactor, and sculptures so radioactive they would have to be buried deep within the earth and viewed by means of remote-controlled cameras. He also had designed nuclear-heated soup spoons, radioactive-jewelry-and-lead-blouse ensembles, the desktop nuclear reactor, a radioactive codpiece, and "Artheads" (replacing nuclear warheads on multiple-warhead missiles, Artheads could be launched at a moment's notice and dropped by parachute around a nuclear-disaster site, surrounding it with granite-and-titanium sculptures that would serve both as warning signs and as works of art).

Now, he was fixated on his goal of getting access to a nuclear reactor for a project that would involve coating granite and stainless steel with an atom-thin layer of ruthenium-100, a non-radioactive element that Acord intended to transmute from technetium, a form of nuclear waste, by means of neutron bombardment in the FFTF's nuclear reactor. "This is the best of all possible worlds!" he said excitedly. "I get to use the nuclear process to create art. I get this dynamite material that I can lay down in a layer one atom thick right across stone and stainless steel, and—without giving myself any undeserved credit here—I've raised the interest level in technetium transmutation as a way to burn nuclear waste."

Acord was fixated on this project for all manner of reasons. "As a sculptor," he said, "I want to have access to the best techniques and materials that we have. And no sculptor has ever tried to express what it means for human beings to have their hands on the nuclear process. There's never been an opportunity for art to address this, our being in the nuclear age. Why should this vastly important problem be dominated, entirely monopolized, by people with Department of Defense contracts? The scientific community is poorer without the input of the artist, and the rest of society is poorer when science predominates." He also wanted to find the best materials possible with which to realize his artistic visions, and felt that he had found them in Hanford. "From the Stone Age on, artists have always worked with the best materials and technology."

It was getting harder and harder to tell, the more I talked with Acord, where his art left off and his life as an artist began. It seemed to me that his quest was turning into an art form in itself. For example, he was putting together a show of sorts at the Fremont Fine Arts Foundry, and his promotion for it was as interesting as the show. Acord was billing it as a fund-raiser to save the FFTF, which was slated to be closed down by federal budget-cutters. "We're hoping to collect $8 million at the door," he said.

Now I felt my attention drawn irresistibly across Lake Washington, where the Microsoft story had grown—to a Seattle-bred mind, at any rate—into something incomprehensibly huge. In April 1990, *Forbes* magazine published a picture of Bill Gates on its cover, with the caption, "Can He Be Stopped?" The story inside described Gates as a Titan who had maneuvered his company into a position of such power that it was, in effect, bigger than its own industry. Microsoft's operating system was running on more than 80 percent of the world's personal computers, Microsoft applications were proliferating madly and threatening to dominate nearly every applications market the company entered, competition was dying off, the company was growing at a far faster rate than the computer industry itself, and everyone in the industry professed to be terrified of Gates. He was viewed by his competitors as ruthless, intent on totalitarian rule over the world of computers, thoroughly untrustworthy, and unstoppable. The occasional lawsuit or alliance among competitors would surface from time to time as a "threat" to the company's growing indomitability, but would offer only brief hope of slowing Gates down. In 1988, to cite one of the most attention-getting examples, Apple Computer sued Microsoft over computer-interface copyright and licensing issues, and, in 1990, Novell and Lotus 1,2,3 announced their intention to merge and form a company nearly as large as Microsoft to protect their shrinking leads in networking and applications. But as Gates and his company grew in wealth and power, those moves looked more like desperation than sound strategy.

The change in his image was jarring. When I last had been paying attention, Gates—if he was noticed at all—was perceived largely as a charming eccentric with a gift for business, a mysterious boy genius who was converting his arcane computer knowledge into millions of dollars. He was the oddest Local Boy Makes Good story in Seattle history—a mad scientist who just happened to make money at his hobbies. Not many people in Seattle even knew what exactly his company did; most Seattleites in 1986, as Ann Senechal discovered, would have been hard-pressed to define the word "software." Now, four years later, the computer industry was the most glamorous in the world, generating billions in sales and wages and stock earnings every year, taking over the universe to the accompaniment of earth's press trumpeting the planet's entry into the "Information Age." Leading the way, Gates was half Moses, half Godzilla. Not only had his chosen business arena grown into one of the world's leading industries, but Gates had managed to seize almost complete control over it. Now, to judge from press descriptions, it was as if he had been a monster all along, disguised as a nerd, and the world had woken up to what he really was too late to do anything about it.

The idea that a Seattle kid, while still essentially a kid—Gates in 1990 was only 34—was among the richest, most powerful, and most feared men in the world just didn't compute. How had he taken the extremely unbusiness-like company I saw only a few years before and turned it into such an indomitable power? And how on earth could anything as terrifying as Gates—and as infinitely ambitious—have come out of Seattle?

Microsoft's numbers were staggering in 1990—particularly when measured in a Seattle context. In 1983, company revenues of $55 million had seemed outsized to locals, not the sort of thing that could possibly be generated out of Seattle. The next year, revenues nearly doubled, to $95 million, three years later they came in at $345.9 million, and in 1990 Microsoft made $1.47 billion. Nothing else in Seattle was making money that fast, and certainly nothing else in Seattle history had ever grown that fast. In 1981, there had been 106 employees at Microsoft; 10 years later, there were 8,100, and 2 years after that there would be 12,000.

Then there was Microsoft's stock price, which hit $125 per share in 1991. With stock splits factored in, the value of the stock had been approximately doubling in value every year since the company's 1986 IPO. The *New York Times* estimated in 1991 that Microsoft had spawned 2,000 millionaires. By my reckoning, one of them was soon to be Jan Allister, whose holdings—assuming she still had them—became something of an obsession with me. Whenever I did the math ($40,000 × 2, $80,000 × 2 . . .), my head would spin out of control before I could get up to 1991. I had more or less lost touch with her except for one visit of hers back to the Northwest in 1989, when she showed me a picture of a house in the Minnesota woods. Laughing—she could never get over the weird good fortune brought her by her short, timely stint at Microsoft—she described her home as "the house that Bill Gates built."

I kept reading about and running into stock-market analysts who insisted that Microsoft's stock price could not keep doubling and tripling in value year after year forever. One Paine Webber analyst in New York told the *Seattle Post-Intelligencer* in 1990 that he stopped recommending the stock because the company faced too many challenges, chief among them the Apple lawsuit. But the stock kept defying history, reason, and expert analysis, and it was getting harder to believe that the end would ever come.

Outside Seattle, the Gates/Microsoft story was the story of the birth of an industry and the nouveau Rockefeller who midwifed it. Inside Seattle, the Gates/Microsoft story was one of outsized personal wealth. In 1989, the Seattle papers breathlessly noted that Gates had just become the world's youngest billionaire, and Paul Allen—who by then had retired from Microsoft, although he remained a member of its board—was turning up in local papers more and more often in stories about lavish expenditures. He built a massive mansion with an array of outsized features, including a spa, sound studio, full-sized basketball court, etc., etc., etc.; he bought the NBA's Portland Trailblazers . . .

Gates's wealth became the object of intense citywide fascination. Stories frequently would appear in the local papers detailing how much he made in a single day because of a rise in Microsoft's stock price. You would read and hear constant rebukes directed at him for not donating more of his fortune to charities. Local commentators on every Seattle problem would eventually get around to suggesting that Gates solve the problem with his money. During the two troubled years Jeff Smulyan was to own the Seattle Mariners—years in which he tried desperately to make the franchise solvent either with local tax revenues or by winning the right to move it elsewhere—requests were floated almost constantly, in radio call-in shows, letters to newspaper editors, countless conversations, and letters to Gates himself, asking him to buy the Mariners franchise and turn it into a contender. People would say to me all the time when talking about the Mariners, "Why doesn't Bill Gates just buy them?" as if doing so was Gates's civic duty.

I was taking all this in when I looked ahead to 1992 and saw the January day when Microsoft's market capitalization reached $21.9 billion, putting it past both Boeing and General Motors. Nationwide, this would be seen as a tremendously symbolic milestone, the supplanting of traditional American nuts-and-bolts industry by New Age industry. Locally, the symbolism would be far more resonant, for Boeing had forever owned the local economy outright, and to have a company still in its infancy soar past it in value would be one of the most telling incidents in Seattle history, proof that the city was no longer a company town.

It seemed to me, reading national stories about Gates, that all of them missed the essential point about him. None of them understood or even saw the Seattleite in him. From my perspective, Microsoft was an alternative corporation, a classic Seattle product. It struck me as far more a Seattle phenomenon than a national, international, or computer-industry phenomenon. At the same time, its chairman was goosed with a form of ambition so extreme as to be unthinkable in any kind of Seattleite. Gates was a paradox waiting to be solved.

I was mulling all this over with a memoirist's exquisite timing when the *New York Times* called to ask if I were willing to write a magazine story about Gates. And within a few days, I found myself at the gates of the Microsoft castle.

There was a good deal of personal-computer history that was not widely known at the time, as the durability of the Apple lawsuit, which was not to be settled until 1992, attested. Popular received wisdom had it that the "graphical user interface," or GUI, was an Apple invention that Microsoft "stole" in stages, introducing Apple's overlapping windows to the MS-DOS world with Windows 2.03 in 1988, and a full-blown knock-off of Apple's Macintosh interface with the full-color Windows 3.0 in 1990.

What really happened, as Gates and his Microsoft allies kept insisting in deposition after deposition, was that Microsoft and Apple both stole the GUI from Xerox. Xerox, in fact, had built the first GUI computer back in 1972, after nearly a decade's research in its now-famous Palo Alto Research Center (PARC). Xerox executives in the 1960s, foreseeing that their stranglehold on the office copier market was destined to end, assembled a team of brilliant researchers and told them to work on developing the "office of the future." The group built a small desktop computer with a mouse (the first mouse, built by Douglas Engelbart, was a piece of two-by-four with some hardware embedded in it), keyboard, bitmapped screen, and network connection allowing the computers to communicate with one another over what the researchers dubbed an "Ethernet." Naming their new machine the Alto, they excitedly demonstrated it to Xerox bosses in 1972—and were almost immediately deemed insane.

Undaunted, the team kept working and refining its concept. One member, Charles Simonyi, built a word-processing program, called Bravo, that made the screen look white with black characters (until then, screens always were black, with phosphorescent characters). The idea was to give it the familiar real-world look of a sheet of typing paper with characters like those imprinted by a typewriter. It was the world's first GUI word processor. But corporate support for the team's work was waning to nonexistence, and Simonyi and other disillusioned researchers started peeling off from the company. By the early 1980s, all were gone. (There is a great book on this colossal boner: *Fumbling the Future*, by Douglas K. Smith and Robert C. Alexander.)

In 1980, Simonyi, following up on a suggestion from a friend, came to Seattle to meet Gates. Microsoft at the time was working madly on an operating system for IBM, which was anxious to break into the emerging personal computer market. As Apple Computer had already proven, this was not only a potentially huge market, but one that threatened to break IBM's near-monopoly hold on computer processing power. Simonyi showed Gates what he had been doing, and Gates, as Simonyi told me later, "got it immediately!"

Similar revelations were being visited upon Steve Jobs at Apple, and he put a team to work in 1981 on what would emerge in 1983 as the Macintosh. By then, Apple was losing market share to IBM, and Jobs decided to compete with an entirely new, easier-to-use interface that would move computers beyond the hobbyist market to what Apple called in its ads a market "for the rest of us." The Mac was essentially the commercial version of the Alto, developed by many of the same people—including Simonyi, who eventually would write a substantial portion of Microsoft's first versions of Word for the Macintosh. (Simonyi, in fact, claims that Microsoft was responsible in the early going for "50 percent of the development of the Macintosh.") The decision was a controversial one inside Apple, with those who had developed the Apple I and II deriding the notion that anyone would ever switch from a traditional alphanumeric computer interface to one where you pointed at and clicked on little pictures, or "icons." But there was no question in the mind of either Jobs or Gates where the future of computing lay, and when the Macintosh appeared in 1983, the war was on between the GUI people and the DOS, or alphanumeric, people—with no one on the alphanumeric side understanding that the only one among them whose opinion mattered, Gates, had already bet on the GUI.

IBM in particular was skeptical about the GUI—partly because the company had a huge alphanumeric installed base, including mainframes and minicomputers, to protect—and Gates's development of Windows went on for years in the face of IBM's active resistance. Microsoft had a huge and growing installed base of MS-DOS customers, and Gates spent eight years executing an amazing balancing act, both growing that market and developing the product that would destroy it.

This all came to a head in 1990, with the unveiling of Windows 3.0. IBM, which had bet its future on a next-generation DOS dubbed OS/2, developed by Microsoft, eventually took over the OS/2 effort and was now competing directly with the company that had made it a personal-computer power. It was only with the unveiling of Windows 3.0 that the world in general first began to see in its full flower Gates's strategic brilliance: Where most owners of a billion-dollar enterprise would do everything in their power to protect it from innovators, Gates understood that progress on that front could never be stopped. So he made sure that when the time came to wreck the MS-DOS franchise, he would be the one wielding the wrecking ball.

There is no question that what set Gates most dramatically apart from his competitors was his vision from the beginning of where computing was headed as a *business*. Most of the pioneers in the personal computer industry were technology buffs with little interest in anything other than computer science. They were not particularly interested in building big companies and managing large businesses. And those, like Apple's Steve Jobs, who *were* interested did not see, as clearly or as early as Gates did, that prices would have to be driven down dramatically on the hardware side of the business, where profit margins would always be thin, and that the real money was to be made selling software to all the hardware competitors—and, by extension, to everyone who bought a computer. Gates also understood better than most of his contemporaries that eventually a single software standard would have to emerge—one that would run on hardware made by virtually every manufacturer. In the personal-computer industry's beginning, competitors all offered complete, proprietary hardware/software solutions the way Apple still does: They built their own operating systems, the hardware that ran it, and either built or supplied the applications that ran on it. Just as had been done in the mainframe and minicomputer businesses, so was it done at first in the microcomputer business: You bought everything—hardware, operating system, and applications software—from the same manufacturer. Gates—and, for that matter, Andrew Grove at Intel—understood that as computers moved onto every office desktop and from there into American homes, they would do so as cheap appliances. The key to outsized success was to own the microprocessor standard, as Intel eventually would do, or the operating-system standard, as Microsoft eventually would do. Only through intense hardware competition driving prices down and the emergence of a single computing standard driving ease of use up would the machines gain the mass acceptance necessary to make the industry succeed. Both by virtue of understanding that and by betting on Intel's microprocessor, Gates fought his way to the top of his industry in the beginning, and has skillfully fought to stay there ever since.

Early on at Microsoft, Gates and his cohorts made thousands of decisions that contributed to his eventual power and success. But by far the two most important were his decision in 1975 to reserve the right to sell Microsoft BASIC, written for the Altair 8800—a computer kit, manufactured by MITS, that came out that year and set off the personal-computer revolution—to other hardware vendors; and his decision to do the same with MS-DOS when he negotiated Microsoft's contract with IBM. Gates was a teenager the first time around, and only twenty-three when he stood toe-to-toe with IBM, one of the most powerful corporations in the world. Had he not had both the proper vision of the future and the courage in his youth to stand up to far more powerful foes— MITS, for example, sued Microsoft over that contract clause, and Microsoft was driven to the brink of bankruptcy before an arbitrator ruled in its favor—I would not be writing about Gates and Microsoft now.

I met Charles Simonyi in 1991, as part of my get-to-know-Gates exercise for the *New York Times*, when I was ushered by Microsoft's public-relations guru, Pam Edstrom, into a nearly pitch-dark office on the company campus. The only light there was that given off by a blue computer screen. Simonyi was sitting in the middle of the room, in an office chair with no desk, staring off into space. He was the most disheveled human being I had ever seen—and I had been to Berkeley and Haight-Ashbury in the 1960s. He did not seem aware that we had entered, and when he noticed us at last he jumped up, startled. Edstrom introduced me, and Simonyi started chattering—"gushing," as he put it—immediately:

> And a person like Bill that is both a technical genius and a big businessman is just . . . Technically, I would say that that's like probably the equivalent of P-squared, you know, if you have to look at probability, a probability of one in 1,000 of having one property, and you have a probability of one in 1,000 of having another property, then having both properties is one in a million. Well, I think that Bill is probably one in 100,000 and one in a million in each of those two . . . no, I couldn't say that. Say, one in 10,000 . . . OK. So, one in 10,000, one in 10,000, say, would be one in ten to the tenth. Would be Bill. Which is pretty close. Let's see . . . world population is five times ten to the ninth, now we

have to fudge the figures in some other way. . . . We have to come out with a probability that is less than the reciprocal of the world population. So I think that he is about one in . . . am I right? No, no, I'm sorry, I was wrong. Ten thousand is ten to the fourth. Yeah, OK, so he's one in 10,000 in both. That makes him one in ten to the eighth, right? Which would be one in 100 million. Right. Which means there is about three of them . . . no, two of them, two-and-a-half of them in the United States, and there are, you know, fifty of them in the whole world. If you . . . if they are distributed evenly, which I don't think they are. And so there you go! Three in the United States! One out of three! Well, I think . . . let's see . . . but, look, we just pulled the 10,000 out of a hat, so this is not a valid calculation. I just did the calculation to see if the numbers are plausible.

It took a while, but I was eventually able to interject questions into Simonyi's monologue—although they didn't often lead me anywhere other than into entertaining digressions. When I asked about his days at Xerox, he said only, "I made a lot of mistakes at Xerox, but fortunately they were all proprietary mistakes, so under penalty of law I must never make them again!"

I did finally manage to redirect the flow of his thinking just enough to give me something coherent to pass on about Gates. At one point, Simonyi made an extravagant comparison that actually holds up well now that you can look back from sufficient temporal distance at the role Gates played in the early days of the industry. The PC industry, Simonyi says, floundered at first—and by "at first" he was including his days at Xerox—because "the technical knowledge was there, but the connection of the technical knowledge to the business sense was completely lacking. Because there was no person who had both, and there were no two persons like General Groves and Oppenheimer [Groves was the military officer who built the Manhattan Project infrastructure and kept the project on schedule; Oppenheimer was the physicist who led the scientific effort], who had one *and* the other, and would be very close to each other. But Bill is both of these guys in the same person!"

The Daimonian

I was warned about Bill Gates. Warned repeatedly. "Bill has *no* patience for interviewers who don't know anything," Pam Edstrom said on the way to his office for our first meeting. "Don't ask Bill about his wealth—he hates talking about that. *Hates* it. And don't ask him about his house . . ." On and on she went: Bill hates this, has no patience for that, can't stand it when you ask about this . . . The portrait that emerged as I stood on the threshold of his office was that of a martinet on a microfuse. One blundering question, one hesitation, and he would explode in my face.

And this was the portrait painted by his PR person. What horrors would I hear from his enemies?

Edstrom was helpful there, too. "If you want some good anti-Bill quotes," she was saying, "call Philippe Kahn at Borland, Mitch Kapor at Lotus, Jim Manzi at IBM . . ."

Thoroughly unnerved, thoroughly paranoid, I stood in Gates's office waiting for him to enter. When he walked in and we were introduced, he turned out to be relaxed and affable. Wearing a striped shirt and tan slacks, he looked like a low-level office worker out for a lunchtime stroll.

Almost immediately, he started peppering me with questions. When I told him I'd written a book on the Seattle Seahawks, he asked question after question about the book market: "What's an example of a really successful sports book? There's no runaway best-seller in that category? None that's ever risen up to the point where people say, 'Hey, you ought to read this stuff?' There's no Jabbar book, no Russell book, that is really thoughtful?"

I told him that one of the best-selling books I knew of was Brian Bosworth's *The Boz*. "Yeah," Gates answered, "because it was positioned in sort of a unique way. That was what . . . '*An Antihero*' or something? This magazine decided once to put us both on the cover. And I was stunned that his scale and mine were *not the same*. His hands were just . . . *bigger than mine*! Hunh-hunh-hunh . . . I thought, 'Maybe I should start using steroids!' Now they say he's trying to be a movie star. But I've seen a lot of movies, and I haven't run into him."

We went on in this fashion for some time, with me mostly answering his questions and wondering who was supposed to be interviewing whom. I had heard that Gates turned virtually every minute of his life into an opportunity to take in information, and now I was seeing firsthand what that meant.

Then I mentioned that I'd written about the Nordstroms in the past. "Well," he said, "the press has been so nice to them for so long. And everybody loves Nordstrom. The buying of the Seahawks, being involved in that, did kind of put them out in the open, where they were attacked a lot, it sort of changed their status. In retrospect, I don't think they ever would have bought a sports team, and they've backed off a lot from that. Actually, they've backed off extremely. Now, they're not on any boards, although they do give generously; timewise they're very focused on their business. Although they have this new structure that leaves me a little confused." He laughed. "You've got three chairmen and three presidents . . . an unusual structure. Actually I have a summer place next to theirs, right next to the Nordstrom compound. Jim Nordstrom has his place here, their father here . . . anyways, their family comes up there, and we have . . . kind of an imitation of their place. My sister has a cabin, I have a cabin . . ."

Suddenly I saw the secret of Microsoft's success revealed in a vision of little Billy Gates sitting on family patriarch Elmer Nordstrom's knee, taking in American business lessons while everyone else was playing on the beach. Good God, I thought, is there nothing in Seattle that can't be traced back to the Nordstrom influence?

Finally I was able to get Gates focused on the day's agenda. I told him I wanted to hear him talk about the present state of the industry, how it got there, and what role he had played in getting it there. Once the topic was raised, his manner changed markedly. He leaned forward, putting an elbow on each leg and crossing his arms, and began rocking back and forth in a terribly distracting and disquieting way. I was to read perfect descriptions of this habit years later, in an article about autism.

No sooner was the suggestion out of my mouth than I could see clearly how intensely Gates loved talking about the PC business. He delivered himself of a long monologue that remains, more than ten years later, a revealing look into his mind and heart:

> There's a couple of ways to look at it, and you have to look at it in each of these ways to kind of make sense. One way is to look at the supply side, the supply of computing power. And this is the miracle story of the microprocessor, where every year and a half they can make a chip that's twice as fast. And if you look at an industry where you have such rapid increase in supply, usually it's pretty bad, I mean, like the price of wheat goes down because there's too much wheat, or like when radial tires were invented, people didn't start driving their cars a lot more, and so that means the need for production capacity went way down, and things got all messed up. So the tire industry's still messed up. It's a decade now with that increase in supply without increase in demand. In our case, it's just such a lot of things, that these machines keep getting faster and faster and faster . . .

As he switched topics in mid-sentence, I gave myself a second to see the industry the way he did: not as a "computer" industry, or even as a "software" or "hardware" industry, but as an industry whose product is computer-processing power. Gordon Moore, one of the founders of Intel, had propounded what became known as Moore's Law back in 1965: that microprocessors would double in speed every eighteen months indefinitely. The challenge to hardware and software companies was to come up with compelling uses for this product—uses that at first would drive people to buy computer hardware and software, then eventually would drive them to buy new, improved machines again and again, so that the computer industry would not go the way of the tire industry.

. . . and at the same time you have this structural change, where all these companies used to make their own computers. In fact, they'd literally start with making little components and boards and writing operating systems and languages and the whole thing. . . . They had it from here to here. So they'd go to a customer and give 'em a DEC system . . . although software through the use of high-level languages had some portability, whenever you get into issues of interface and databases, basically software was pretty stuck on one machine, and wouldn't move around. And IBM with its 360 family, that became the 370, started to get more and more of the applications in that mainframe area, and it was kind of obvious they were just gonna beat everybody. It took a long time for it to play out, but they got more applications, more trust, and then actually the compatible machines came along, and gave you choice within that environment, and so, you know, the feeling of choice and yet the solid nature of it, basically wiped out all the other mainframe companies. And so, even that hasn't totally played itself out. NCR has gotten out of the mainframe business, Unisys is blowing up, Unisys is really the last non-Japanese, non-IBM noncompatible mainframe company . . .

Back in the mainframe computer days, IBM owned nearly all the computing power in the United States, if not the world. Customers not only bought their hardware from IBM—they also bought their software and their service from Big Blue. Even spare parts for everything from mainframe computers to electric typewriters were owned and sold by IBM. It was in large part a reaction to the company's monopoly that the personal-computer revolution took place at all. By building inexpensive machines that you could put on your own desktop and use yourself, PC hardware and software companies wrested computing power out of the hands of the IBMs of the world and gave it directly to the citizen. In that respect, the invention of the microprocessor was a revolutionary act. By 1991, when Gates and I met, the desktop machine you could buy for your home had as much computing power as an IBM mainframe from the late 1960s.

. . . But anyway, the structural changes that, um . . . now, let's take the computing problems that Intel microprocessors can solve. And that's not a fixed thing, remember, because there's that, every time it gets twice as powerful, okay, we used to say, we can't do our payroll on it. Well, at some point you can. We can't do our documentation on it, we can't do our customer database . . . anyway, at some point, heeey, I'll just . . . give me the application, I'll name the year, a very very high percentage can today, because of course we're as powerful as mainframes were. And so anything people bothered to create back then now can be done on this microprocessor. Anyway, these structural changes that . . . Intel makes that chip, and now there's a lot of people cloning them, because there's so much capital costs involved in sort of chemical magic, even with people cloning their chip they'll still probably have a good position. Then we make software, and so what's left? Well, you have to take a hard disk, and screen-in graphics, there's still parts to do, but . . . there's . . . you could measure the engineering time in a small number of man-years to go from that to build state-of-the-art machines like the 486 machine.

In other words, Intel on the hardware side and Microsoft on the software side had virtually unassailable positions. But innumerable companies can take Intel's microprocessor and Microsoft's operating system, build machines around them, and make considerable amounts of money. They will have to compete frenziedly, and will struggle constantly to survive, but the demand for computing power is strong enough to sustain a huge competitive arena.

And so you have—well, we have over three hundred licensees who take our software and put it in machines and . . . um . . . so you actually look at who sells PCs, there's been this shift away from the top ten to the mid-tier in the last year, which is rather stunning. It's partly because the top guys have high overhead, and they were overcharging, it's partly due to the specific mistakes these people made, it's partly due to a change in distribution channels, where there were these deals, these stores that you would go to. Well, a couple new things came out: One is direct selling, where you just call up a phone number and the computer shows up. Dell is mostly associated with that. I mean, we can pat ourselves on the back a tiny bit, because we . . . Anyway, besides direct selling, you also have the broadening of distribution. You want to buy a 386 machine, you say to me, "Hey, where should I—what should I do?" I say, "Go to Price Club, or Costco or wherever, where the low-cost distribution is found, and get a 386, four-megabyte machine, pay nineteen hundred bucks, an incredible deal." And those machines really do work, and they have good warranties and everything like that. So you've got people recognizing that these machines are compatible, buying them through different distribution channels. . . . You know, from nineteen . . . from like eighty-three, early eighty-three, people's willingness to say, "Yes, these things really are the same [as IBM]" has just increased, and it's undergone . . . just in the last year, an acceleration where even large companies think that way. Well, there were some misgivings, but more and more large companies think that way. So structurally, it's extremely competitive. And the supply is unbelievable. Now, it's complicated, because the demand is also unbelievable. They say that this is the Information Age, I don't know who said that first, but somebody said that quite some time ago. When did they say the Information Age started? I don't know, fifties, sixties, ah, and, and . . . how can you be in the information age? I mean, to be in the steel age, it means you learn how to forge steel and refine coke and coal and all those things, and you build products out of them. What does it mean? It doesn't mean we're gonna evolve and read faster or have big file drawers or something, it means using electronic forms of the information . . . uh . . . to deal with information effectively. And that means computer hardware and computer software. So you have the technical change and the structural change. You also have this scale change, where computers are now sort of individual things. And even the computers that aren't individual things. . . . I mean, if you use your little computer and you ask questions, it may go out to your company mainframe, or it may go to Lexis to get some law case or Dow Jones to get some stock prices, and all that. But you're supposed to use a single interface. This is not true today, but it's the way it's supposed to work. And you just are always going to browse and be looking at information. And you don't know, I mean, you may have a sense, because it's very ephemeral data or something, or it's very big data, but you don't really know what phone number, which microwave or in what protocol or anything that's used to get that data. So those back-end computers are servers. They're just providing capabilities.

And they're no longer the place you're writing all sorts of software. There's different services they can provide, like databases is a big one, but document libraries is another form of that. So now computers are just a very individual thing. Even to the point of a little Sharp organizer, or the notebook thing we're gonna handwrite onto, or plug a CD in and look at the encyclopedia.

Before personal computing could get anywhere near that point, of course, computers would have to become ubiquitous. And in order for them to become ubiquitous, all manner of reasons *not* to buy PCs had to be overcome. Computers would have to become more useful, far easier to use, and secure enough to protect everything from private personal information sent over networks to credit-card numbers and other valuable financial data.

It means that the buying decision is based on being comfortable with the thing, and people really wanting to use it as a tool. Of course, then the infrastructure building up to those networks so you can get all that information, that's more of a corporate, I call it top-down kind of decision. So you have this interesting clash, between individual choice of software and machines, and yeah, it can help me get stuff done . . . and then you have people thinking about security and standards and . . . perhaps conservative in their view, because they've been involved in the older style of data-processing. And that's a big change, bringing it down to the individual level.

Moore's Law, meanwhile, was moving personal computers from simple data processing machines into combination productivity and entertainment machines, as hardware and software makers tried to figure out what to do with all that extra computing power. All sorts of information, in all sorts of media, was moving to the digital platform so quickly that the emerging new digital entertainment technology was a classic solution in search of a problem.

Um, and we have this coming thing, called consumer electronics, which is also becoming digital, and the differences between what's a computer and what's a TV or what's the differ-ence between a disc and a videocassette, what's the difference between a camera and a scanner, ah, what's the difference between a fax and a PC or a copier and a PC printer? And all these things will be the same, once we get into digital form. When things get into digital form, the flexibility and the interconnectability and all that gets to be really good. It's not trivial, you know, you think even of the . . . ah . . . still camera, making that digital, the number of bits that are in a picture, the equivalent of a halide or seventy-millimeter slide is very large. And so we're not to the point of direct replacement. It's interesting that music is the only place where digital technology prevails now. Because the number of bits and the speed at which you need the bits in music is very small. In fact, TV technology is actually pretty obsolete stuff. They can put ten times as much stuff on those disks, using new technology. But then you'd have to create a new standard. Also, who wants ten hours on a single disk? So you see a proliferation of smaller disks, and maybe putting on some other kinds of information.

Gates seemed to see digital technology as a force moving into being on its own, and the early progenitors and profiteers as more fortunate than ingenious, being carried along on this tide of ineluctable progress, more passive recipients of technology's grace than brilliant tacticians forcing technological advances along. He and Allen had launched Microsoft at a propitious time, and by dint of tactical brilliance and astounding good fortune had lived through and helped create a new para-digm: The paradigm of the *startup*, where the storyline was short and sweet: A, B, C, D . . . rich. Within a few years, it would be viewed in Seat-tle not as an anomaly but as the norm.

Um, so all this turmoil, where these companies have a hard time making profits, it's all happened with the invention of the microprocessor and the recognition of how quickly the micropro-cessor would get better. And to me, myself, were among that group, a fairly small group. I mean, this is . . . Intel first came out with the 8008 in 1971, and Paul and I were the first ones in this area to go out and buy one and use it. It was a very crummy little microprocessor. You couldn't do much with it. The 8080—which is where you get the first kit PC, this Altair that was on the cover of the January seventy-five *Popular Electronics* . . . that's the 8080 that they first issued back in late seventy-three, and started putting the kit, started offering it in September of seventy-four . . . But Paul and . . . some issue of *Electronic* magazine, deep in it, like page seventy or something, where he was reading about the 8008, and that would have been seventy-two, sometime. And he came and showed that to me. Anyway, everything—in my nice, simple view—is just what had to happen after that kit came out. Now, there were some other pieces, like how are you going to get standards? There were many people with chips, which chips would be . . . would there be a lot of chips, and where would the software come from, and would there be applications that would make these things interesting on an individual level, and there's some pretty interesting twists and turns that could have prevented us from getting where we are. But we emerged as the primary people designing the software, Intel emerged as the primary people providing the chip, not solely because they did a better technical job, but because of this notion of compatibility, you know, that once one thing gets ahead then everybody works on stuff for that, and because people work on stuff for that then it gets ahead more, and so for something new to come in, when this something's going through this positive feedback loop, which sort of DOS with Intel processors did in the early eighties, Mac did a little bit in the mid-eighties, and we are right now with Windows. It takes something really revolutionary to come along and get any attention.

Now he was ready to take questions. And he sat, patiently rocking, waiting for me to gather my wits.

The more time I spent with Gates, the more interesting and confusing he became. It wasn't hard to see what made him successful; his power as a strategic thinker was obvious, and the historical record in the computer industry was taking coherent enough shape for people like me to look back and glean from it the events, decisions, strengths, and weaknesses that had proved pivotal in his meteoric rise. What *was* hard to see was the reason he wanted not only the success he had already attained but at least as much more—maybe even infinitely more. Whenever I asked him to articulate or define his goals, he would simply say, "I want to win." Whenever I asked him to define "winning," he would lapse into talking about something else—the nature of competition, how being second in a software category nearly always meant being too distant a second, and so on.

To me, the most vivid illustration of how far Gates would go for the sake of winning was the house he had under construction when we met. A complex of eleven structures totaling 37,000 square feet and originally budgeted at $10 million, it was two years into construction, and its budget, depending on who was citing a figure, had at least doubled, and possibly tripled. Yet the physical size of the project was unchanged; the lion's share of the expense was due to the technology, much of it experimental, that Gates wanted built into it. It was not enough for him to bring work home—he was essentially making work his home by erecting another Microsoft building to live in. "Everything in this house is a new invention," an exhausted James Cutler, one of the two lead architects on the project, said to me one day. "We're inventing it all as we go along. Bill really has a very high aspiration level on the technology."

When I talked with Gates about the house, he described it almost entirely as if it were a work project. He had formed another company, Interactive Home Systems, to develop software systems for the house's various features and to work at commercializing some of the discoveries they made along the way. "When I started thinking about building a house," Gates said, "I listed the things that were important to me. I wanted it to be closer to work; I wanted to be able to have work functions and events at it; and I wanted to try out some new things."

Chief among those were large flat-screen displays distributed throughout the complex. Gates had seen these screens under development in Japanese laboratories, and as he always did when confronted with new technology, he started trying to think about what would make people buy them once they were commercially available. "Consumer electronics companies, most of whom are in Japan, are building these big flat screens, and then the hardware to store the data, that just keeps getting cheaper and cheaper. So knowing this hardware's going to deliver that, then you say, 'What is interesting? What will it create demand for?'" Gates decided it was likely to create demand for "high-quality still images that you can access in an easy way. It certainly creates my interest in having that. Now, my bet there is that I'm only unusual in the ability to afford it now, and other people, as it becomes more reasonable because the hardware price comes down, will also want the same thing."

These large screens were going to be in some fourteen of the complex's rooms, and residents and visitors could control the screen displays with a "cordless mouse." The images would be accessible either via the Internet—Gates described a scenario to me in which someone in his home could take a kind of "walking tour" of the Le Mans racetrack, accessed over the Internet—or from the databank of CD-ROMs built into the house. Cutler was working on a system, which he called the "Wurlitzer," that allowed users to call for images or other information that would be retrieved by a robot fetching CDs from the collection. Gates was busily buying up digital reproduction rights for the world's art and photography so as to build databanks of images for this sort of use. "You can say," Gates said to me, " 'What artists were in France during this time period? Was there any sculpture done in Italy before this date?' It will have all the information it needs to show you pictures. Viewers will want a fairly deep set of information web even beyond the pictures themselves. So you can call things up by name and by grouping, you can say, 'Show me all the pictures that will have yellow birds in them.' And then you'll see if it's a picture in Rome or something painted a thousand years ago. So we go fairly deep in terms of imagery information."

He had no idea whether he was exploring the right path of commercial potential, and it was testament to his care for Microsoft's financial resources that he was spending his own rather than his company's money on something with such an uncertain financial return. "What I'm doing with the screens there," he said, "in terms of seeing how that can display art or spark people's curiosity or create kind of this dynamic environment, is an experiment. And I think it'll be very interesting and fun, and how well will it work, well, we'll see. Are those screens turned on all the time, or are they sequencing interesting stuff, or is it like some game you buy, and it just sits there? I'm pretty sure it's the former—I mean, it's certainly more expensive than a game, and I'm putting some thought into it."

He also was putting a good deal of feeling into it. I sat in on a meeting one evening between Gates, his architects (Cutler and project co-director Peter Bohlin), and an employee from Interactive Home Systems. Cutler was breaking the news, as gently as he could, that it was not technically feasible to install one of the screens in the swimming-pool room because it was impossible to protect the screen's wiring from the effects of the pool's evaporation. This outraged the IHS employee, who shouted, "We're down to ten screens!" Gates jumped up, alarmed. "Is that true?" he asked, his voice rising. "No, no," Cutler assured him. "We still have fourteen." Mollified for the moment, Gates relaxed.

The oddest and most remarkable thing about the house was its Seattleness. For all the expense Gates was putting into it, he was lavishing little money on outright self-indulgence and none of it on ostentation. A great deal of the size of the place was attributable either to his desire to have large work-related events at the complex or to experiment with technological applications. It was an oddly unpretentious home, with its most expensive touches being far more work- than pleasure- or status-related.

Particularly untycoon-like was the expense being devoted to making the house less visible and less environmentally objectionable. Seen from the lake, the complex was to look more like a neighborhood of small homes than an estate. There were eleven separate components, terraced into a steep hill, connected by covered passageways. Included in the complex were a reception hall, the indoor swimming pool and spa, a twenty-car underground garage, a children's wing, caretaker's quarters, guest house, Gates's own home, and a few other scattered buildings.

One of the requirements Gates had written down when first thinking about the house was that it look like a Northwest home. "I knew I wanted a wood house that was kind of hidden in the trees a little, that wasn't supposed to look like a big house or feel like a big house," he said. He rejected one design because it was "too ostentatious," and another because it "felt like a museum." As part of an experiment urged upon him by Cutler and Bohlin, the complex was being built almost entirely from recycled wood. Gates bought and had dismantled an old lumber mill from southwest Washington, shipped it north in pieces, and had all its timber remilled. Also at his architects' urging, he was restoring one-third of his shoreline to natural habitat, installing a 100,000-gallon cistern under his garage to collect groundwater for reuse, and had gone to considerable expense to avoid cutting down several trees on the construction site. "I just admire him to the nth degree for the different things he's allowed us to do in this place," said Cutler. "All the environmental stuff, which is definitely costing more money, the tree-saving, buying into the notion that in the future resources are going to be more scarce and that it's not right for a building of this size necessarily to be drawing a lot out of the resource base of everybody else."

Gates was somewhat more succinct. "He's really hardcore," he said of Cutler, shaking his head in amazement. "There are a couple of trees out there whose valuation is in the hundreds of thousands of dollars."

I toured the construction site one day with Cutler, who took me down an extremely long set of ladders to the floor of the garage. Concrete for the floor and the arches holding up the roof were already in place. The arches were the most magnificent things I'd ever seen outside a Gothic cathedral. When finished, the garage would have a forest growing on top of it, and sunlight would filter down into the structure through skylights. Even Cutler was astounded by the hidden magnificence of the structure, telling me, "This is the coolest thing I've ever worked on." Gates was no less enthralled, having brought his mother out one day to see the garage going up. "This is a fun project," he said to me. "It's a weird thing, where you get a house that's kind of unusual, and it's going to pioneer some new things, and . . . just take that garage. Jeez! Man, that's an unusual garage. Like a *monument* the guy's building out there for those *cars* or something!"

That may have been the only time anyone at Microsoft expressed unease about grandeur. The rest of the time, Gates and everyone else I encountered sketched dreams for Microsoft so grandiose that the company in its highly successful 1991 state was risible by comparison. The defining moment for me—the moment when I finally saw where Gates was trying to take Microsoft—came during a conversation with Rob Glaser, director at the time of the company's Multimedia Systems division. Glaser had just shown me a personal computer displaying a little one-inch-square video window. This was 1991—the video, playing at only fifteen frames per second, was slow and jerky, but nonetheless remarkable: I had never seen anything like it displayed on a personal computer. Glaser explained that coming hardware advances—Moore's Law, again—would allow for high-quality video display in ten years or so, and that Microsoft was now working on video applications. He saw personal computers eventually taking on many of the functions of a television, just as it already had taken over for the calculator, spreadsheet, fax machine, and typewriter (and, alas, phototypesetting machine). Then, brushing aside my comment that Microsoft had already "won" the battle for ownership of the PC market, he said, "Our competitors aren't companies like IBM that sell three million computers a year. They are Japanese consumer-electronics companies whose volumes are far higher than IBM's. On the worldwide market to date, 100 million CD players have been sold, 250 million VCRs, probably over half a billion televisions. That's the league we're focusing on, and when you're in that league—I mean, we're just pipsqueaks."

That was hardly the word Microsoft's current and former competitors were using. Microsoft at the time was under investigation by the Federal Trade Commission, which was trying to determine if Gates & Co. were abusing their de facto monopoly in the operating-systems market by giving themselves an unfair advantage in the market for applications that ran on Windows. There was certainly no question in the minds of competitors—all of whom were fighting ferociously either for their lives or his death—that Gates did not play fair. When I called around about him, his rivals—those, that is, who were willing to comment on him at all—most often referred to Microsoft as the "evil empire," and to Gates himself, variously, as Rockefeller, Henry Ford, Edison, Putsy Hanfstangel, Goliath, Hitler, Darth Vader, and Satan. Not, for the most part, an admirable lineup.

Gates himself felt that his rivals both overestimated and underestimated him. He saw himself not as a Goliath in the personal-computer industry but as a David in the consumer-electronics industry. It was a difference of vision: Others were trying to win the battle for control of personal computing, or simply to maintain a foothold in it, while Gates was looking beyond the narrow confines of the PC and trying to grow the industry itself from a niche in the world appliance market into the winner in that infinitely larger arena. As Glaser pointed out, Microsoft was not competing against other software companies; it was competing against established consumer-market giants.

Now my years among the Russians came circling back into my brain. I started thinking about Joseph Stalin—given the league Gates's competitors were putting him in, this made sense at first. But then I found my mind drifting not toward comparisons of Gates with Stalin but to contrasts between them. The Stalinist-era writer Evgeny Zamyatin—whose classic novel, *We*, depicts a totalitarian horror of a dystopia in ways that both anticipated and outperformed George Orwell's *1984*—wrote an essay, entitled "On Revolution, Entropy, Dogma and Heresy," that took Stalin to task for misunderstanding the nature of revolution. A true revolution, Zamyatin wrote, "is everywhere, in everything; it is infinite, there is no final revolution, no final number." Only by constantly overthrowing the established order—even the order the revolution itself establishes—can a revolution both retain its integrity and continue to improve the world. Otherwise, it ossifies, grows corrupt, and turns into a totalitarian effort to preserve the new status quo and keep itself in power. Once a revolution becomes reactionary, it seeks only to preserve its position of power no matter what the cost to its own ideals or the lives of its citizens. "When the flaming, boiling sphere (in science, religion, social life, art) cools," Zamyatin wrote, "the fiery magma becomes covered with dogma—a hard, ossified, immovable crust."

That, I decided, was more a motive force for Gates than personal wealth or corporate power. He never allowed Microsoft to settle for the status quo. He had forced his company out of the hobbyist market it dominated and into the IBM and Apple-driven mainstream market. Then he remade his MS-DOS company into a GUI company rather than take a defensive position in a market he dominated against the inexorability of Moore's Law. Now he was reinventing the term "application" by forcing his company to expand into multimedia. And every year he reorganized his entire company, destroying some divisions outright, blending others, creating new ones, and moving everyone around among buildings and slots on the company organization chart in order to spread computing power and Microsoft software into new markets. The revolutionary in Gates drove him to deliver computing power to the maximum number of people in the shortest amount of time, and the wealth and power it brought him personally was incidental—a mere side effect—in comparison with this grandiose vision.

It was safe to say even in 1991 that no one who started out in the PC industry with Gates had anywhere near his ambition for it. Nearly all the pioneers had reaped their rewards and stepped aside—not always voluntarily, true, but with at least an eventual understanding that the industry had passed them by—and turned the building of the personal computing industry over to people with more of a business bent. There came a time when the industry was no longer just about technology—and technology was all these early competitors knew. Gates spoke with some regret over the loss of those comrades from his salad days. "It was almost like we were all part of the same engineering team back then," he said. "So that was really fun. But you know, it was a small industry then. I mean, every year up until seventy-eight, I can list a hundred people and that was the industry. But I guess we just had a broader view of where the industry could go than other people did."

Gates believed that his coevals had dropped out mostly because they had neither the ability to run a big business nor the taste for it. "Partly they chose not to keep going," he said. "Like Mitch [Kapor, developer of Lotus 1,2,3, and one of the people who declined comment to me about Gates] didn't want to learn about management, the trade-offs that come in, and some of the inefficiency that comes in with a large organization. Gary Kildahl [founder of Digital Research and developer of DR-DOS, the operating system IBM nearly chose over MS-DOS] really didn't have the drive or the commitment to either building the company or leading himself. There's so many early guys who did so much good stuff in this industry that that's true of. I mean, Mitch did what he wanted to do. So is he better off or am I better off? Well, we're each doing what we want to do. He's a happy guy. So to some degree what I'm saying is that I wanted to do this. I wanted to learn, I wanted to hire in businesspeople, I wanted to pursue this vision, and I got involved in competition."

His zest for competition led Microsoft into an almost surreal version of it. Microsoft was engaged in so many battles, alliances, and relation-ships that were both battles *and* alliances that it was hard to sort it all out. Whenever Microsoft sent a Windows software development kit out to an applications company, it was most likely competing against itself by giv-ing a boost to a competitor in the applications market. Since competitors' applications sales helped sell copies of Windows, however, the company was also giving its system software sales a boost whenever it cooperated with an applications competitor. During my visit, I watched Gates tell a group of computer salespeople that the Apple/IBM alliance, forged solely to slow Microsoft down, would be "good for the industry." These two competitors hell-bent on stopping him also were in extremely lucrative partnerships with him in a battle against each other. Microsoft was devel-oping both OS/2, at IBM's behest, and Windows, against IBM's wishes. The products were in direct competition with each other. Microsoft was also leading the industry in production of Apple Macintosh applications software—in direct competition with its own Windows applications and with IBM., which also was trying frantically to stop the widespread adop-tion of Windows. "We still have lots of cooperation with IBM," Gates said to me, "but we are absolutely in competition with them on this Windows-OS/2 thing."

You could only marvel at the scale and purity of Gates' ambition. If he were to walk away from the game at this point, with his company in one of the most dominating positions in the history of industry, he would have been viewed by everyone on earth save for himself as a tremendous winner. But he did not see himself as a particularly remarkable success— in fact, he all but refused to allow people even to think about Microsoft's successes. I used the s-word in one conversation and he immediately replied, "We're not known for reflecting back on the things we did well. We're always trying to figure things out, look at our mistakes, give our-selves a hard time." He did not attribute his dominant position to his own abilities as much as to fate: "Everybody should be pretty modest," he said, "because it took a lot of pieces." And he rather wittily brushed aside sug-gestions that he was a visionary, or that the future had moved along according to his predictions: "We wouldn't have made our mark as a market-research company."

He was particularly wary of complacency, convinced that it would lead his company to collapse: "I certainly have been fairly hardcore about looking at what we did wrong." And when I asked some questions about Microsoft Word, which at the time was the leading application on the Macintosh and second in the MS-DOS/Windows world, fast moving into top position there as well, Gates said glumly, "We didn't have enough focus on ease of use."

I finally decided that his competitive instincts were essentially primal—both too powerful and too much a part of his wiring, his unconscious, for him to be able to articulate them. I wondered if his vision of paradise was a game in which he was competing only with himself—that, at any rate, seemed to be where he was heading. I saw him as an obsessed kid playing a video game. The key to those games' maddening allure is the reward they offer for winning: When you win at any level, the only "prize" you win is the right to compete at a more difficult level. There is never any opportunity in those games to relax, to savor the joys of victory, every win being simply a way of forcing you to move happily on to a harder battle.

Thus had it been for Microsoft. In the early days of the industry, companies were making little machines, for hobbyists, that ran the BASIC programming language. Microsoft BASIC eventually ended up on 98 percent of those machines. Next came the full-blown personal computer, with MS-DOS. Microsoft began competing in a far larger, more volatile, and more complicated market with other operating-systems companies until eventually 80 percent of the machines in that world ran MS-DOS, with only 10 percent running other DOS systems, and another 10 percent running Apple's OS in what was essentially a losing battle against Microsoft to get the world to adopt a different interface standard. Turning its attention next to MS-DOS applications—Microsoft already was the runaway market leader in Macintosh applications—Gates by 1991 had Microsoft solidly entrenched at No. 2 in word-processing and spreadsheet applications, behind WordPerfect and Lotus 1,2,3, and he was closing fast in both markets. He also was looking for ways to make the overall personal-computer market grow bigger and faster, since he believed the PC industry had to grow out of the corporate market in order to survive. Eventually, every office desktop in the world would have a computer on it, and if the market were to continue to grow, it was going to have to grow new users. To that end, five years earlier, Gates had set up an entire division at Microsoft to develop multimedia systems and applications so that people would start buying computers not just for offices and work but for home and entertainment. Even in 1990, when Microsoft's plans became widely public, the move was greeted with fairly widespread skepticism among industry observers, one market analyst asking rhetorically, "Who the hell wants a talking spreadsheet?"

I was most struck during my time with Gates by the mix of compulsion and self-effacement in him. I had been told that he ate nothing but Japanese food for two years once, just to see if he could do it. And he had become a vegetarian for a time because he fell in love with a woman who was vegetarian. The relationship ended a few months later, but Gates kept up that regimen for another three years, finally abandoning it because he felt it drew too much attention to him at social gatherings, and risked inconveniencing and offending other people. "I said to people, 'Hey, I'm not eating meat,'" he told me. "And so then if I was sitting at one meal saying, 'Oh, gosh, maybe I'll just have a hamburger,' then you know, it's kind of . . . people say, 'Oh . . . what's this?' So it was *awful*. It was actually kind of embarrassing, because people would go out of their *way* . . . And then say it was something where they would serve you meat, and then it . . . half the people know that you don't eat it, and the other half don't, and then they're acting like, 'Oh, no!' I mean, what a pain: Should I say something, or just act like I'm not hungry, or . . . you know, anything that's abnormal like that causes disruption."

This gave rise to visions in my mind of people swarming around Bill Gates, Boy Legend, anxiously trying to keep him happy, while the inner Bill Gates was consumed with worry about putting people to too much trouble.

I also was taken with Gates's willingness to talk about things I was warned not to discuss with him. Eventually, I got around to raising every topic his PR people had told me to avoid, and every time, Gates talked about it affably and at length. "Sure!" he said when I asked if we could discuss his philanthropic responsibilities now that he was a multimillionaire. "There's a question of . . . in your thirties, how big a focus is that? And particularly where ninety-five percent of my asset is ownership in this company, and although I've sold five percent of what I own, I want to retain most of that, because that's what I do, and it makes sense to hold on to it. So I'm not in some super-liquid position. My focus of my life is my work. Certainly in my thirties and probably in my forties as well, so I don't have the time to figure out what things make sense. And to the degree Microsoft can do well, it's just that much more to give later. I think a lot of that stuff people do particularly well late in their life."

This struck me as uncommonly wise for someone still in his early thirties. Gates seemed to understand that his wealth brought with it a tremendous responsibility to do as much good with it as possible even if that meant—as it did at the time—that he would endure a fair amount of criticism for not being more generous in the short term.

The industry-wide view of Gates was far less complicated than the more privileged memoirist's view, benefiting as it does from 20-20 foresight, that I was afforded during my week with him. The prevailing belief held that he was a devious, greedy, power-hungry businessman who disguised himself as a harmless eccentric in order to trick naïve technologists into signing away their crown jewels to him. "I've always wondered how much Bill calculated that nerd image," Philippe Kahn told me, "because he is so sharp on contracts. He's really not a technical guy—it's an image he's trying to put out."

In one respect—although not the respect he intended—Kahn was right: The Bill Gates who emerged at the top of his industry was not at all like the Bill Gates he had seemed to be in the early days of computing. But it was less a matter of Gates's intentionally assuming a disguise than it was a matter of people misreading his Seattleness. All those associations with the name "Seattle" that Howard Schultz had invoked—softness, sensitivity, laid-back attitudes, low ambition, tolerance, and so on—had contributed to the first impression Gates made among his peers. That impression, which lulled partners and competitors alike, was deepened by Gates's Seattle-born lack of pretension: his casual wardrobe, insistence on flying coach rather than first class, disinterest in drawing attention to himself, distaste for limousines and other perks of corporate power . . . He was a cultural descendant of the Nordstroms, who obsessively eschewed the spotlight while driving themselves and their company to the top of their business. Just as one morning Americans woke up to find a store run by the shy Scandinavians on every streetcorner in the country, so too did they find themselves blindsided by the sudden dominance of a software company run by a shy Seattle kid. Nordstrom, Starbucks, and Microsoft all had presented themselves to the nation as soft-spoken, sensitive alternatives to the American corporate norm, then had gone out and crushed their competition the same old-fashioned way it had always been done.

Gates, of course, was in a newer, more turbulent, and vastly bigger industry than were Howard Schultz and the Nordstroms. The stakes were higher, the payoff immensely bigger, and the scale of Gates's ambition for himself immeasurably greater. My visit ending, I fell to wondering where that outsized ambition had come from—how it possibly could have grown in the heart of a Seattle native. I tried imagining growing up surrounded by acres of clams, among people content to dwell on their happy condition, and being cursed with little Billy Gates's outsized intelligence and the tremendous energy that comes with it. He must have felt positively freakish, crackling with a discontent and drive he could find nowhere else in the sea of complacency around him.

A kid like that would be driven to find an outlet for that intelligence, on the one hand, but on the other would be driven by his Seattle cultural traditions to disdain personal ambition and greed and the appearance and symbols that come with American success. I found it impossible not to picture the young Gates as someone feeling so out of place that his estrangement would eventually drive him to feel chosen, or destined, to pursue outsized success almost against his will.

I came to believe that this accounted for the obsessive focus Gates now had on his vision of spreading computer power to everyone on the planet. It was almost as if he were consumed by an abstraction. He was not driven by personal greed for money or power so much as by his conviction that he and he alone understood how to improve the world through the power of personal computing—the engine of change available to the ambitious of his generation. He was a zealot, a revolutionary, rather than a mere Midas, and his competitive greed was no more than a means of helping him achieve the vision he felt destined to fulfill. The sense of destiny that drove him, I decided, was almost purely because of his Seattle roots: Here in the Northwest, ambitious energy like his would be so anomalous, seem so strange, that it could only be understood by the one possessed by it as an affliction—a function of destiny.

From Here to Infinity

I came back from my week at Microsoft to a Seattle that looked like a small old town—faded, dated, outmoded, befuddled. It was like coming back to your childhood home, in adulthood, after having matured elsewhere, in a real city, and marveling at how much smaller and more drab it looks than you remembered. After all the energy I'd encountered at Microsoft, Seattle felt like Mayberry, R.F.D. I suddenly fell prey again to that same disgruntled restlessness that had driven me out of Seattle in the 1970s. Having seen the energy and excitement at Microsoft, and the conviction—which, as far as I could tell, was more than justified—that people there were changing the world, I found it impossible to settle back into the complacent slough I'd been inhabiting for the past ten years. Everything looked provincial now, benighted; I'd been to the Center of the Emerging Universe, the coming century's Big Bang, and writing about local sports, politics, urban self-image debates, and Seattle's purportedly emerging arts scene was no longer psychologically tenable. I had seen color personal-computer screens, I'd seen computers displaying video, and the whole technological spectacle turned me instantly into a True Believer: I decided that Microsoft was going to change the way we did everything—including the way we composed and viewed art—and I wanted to watch it happen from up close.

It was amazing the way a single week in that place made me lose all patience with Seattle's charm. It turned me into a completely different person. A week before, the thing I had loved most about the city was its resolute backwardness. Now I hated it, viewing it as willful ignorance about the inevitable. Here in our own backyard this burgeoning progress was taking form, and because it was Seattle-generated, it was different, more enlightened, promising splendor rather than ruin, offering progress toward a life both spiritually and materially better rather than the dubious tradeoff ordinary material progress always pushes on the hinterland and its settlers. Suddenly it was stunning to me how little notice Seattleites were taking of Microsoft, not only as a business success story but also as a harbinger of what life in the near future—the wired life, the enlightened life—would be.

I couldn't help notice, too, that Seattle was mired in another one of its periodic recessions even as Microsoft was generating mountains of cash by the minute over on its campus. Juxtaposed with the city's downturn, Microsoft's prosperity looked like all the more dramatic a sign that the future belonged to it, while Seattle—along with my employer—was mired in the past. For the first time in its history, the *Weekly* had to lay off employees as yet another Boeing downsizing brought on yet another recession, sending Seattle into yet another company-town decline. The fading city, with its reliance on old-fashioned heavy industry, looked in 1992 like the discarded chrysalis of the butterfly spreading its spectacular wings on the other side of the lake.

Now my carefully cultivated disdain for ambition felt cranky and pretentious. I decided I had wasted the best years of my life trying to turn myself into a young fogy, a curmudgeon. Ignoring Microsoft for all those years had been like turning my eyes from enlightenment. I saw myself as one of the yokels hanging around the Wright brothers' bicycle shop laughing at them for thinking their invention would ever get off the ground. How could I not have seen what was coming at Microsoft? How could I not have seen that it was defining the future of the world?

This sudden, uncharacteristic, irresistible urge to be where the action is took on the proportions of a complete personality change, a midlife crisis. Disgusted with myself for having disdained ambition and settled for contentment, I sat down and wrote out two proposals—one, to Microsoft, asking permission to move into an office on its campus and follow along with a product team from beginning to end of a project, writing a book about its quest; and the other, to a publisher, asking for an advance to fund my research and writing. Snuggled into this remote corner of the country, living a life as temperate as the climate, hiding with my family among fellow dropouts, people in retreat, now struck me as an extravagant waste, an opting out of the excitement taking form only a few miles outside town.

As if to reinforce my new conviction that the future, not only of the world but also of Seattle, belonged to the technology sector, a new group of wealthy tech-industrialists suddenly announced its intention to buy the Seattle Mariners and make the team a success in Seattle. Led by Japanese citizen and resident Hiroshi Yamauchi, the owner of Nintendo (the company's American subsidiary was located just down the street from Microsoft), the group—which also included several Microsoft executives—declared its eagerness to pay $100 million for the moribund franchise and turn it into a title contender no matter what the cost.

For a number of reasons, this was a Seattle historical first. It was the first time owners moneyed enough to compete with big-market teams like the New York Yankees declared themselves willing to invest in Seattle baseball; it was the first time local fans, more excited by the announcement than about anything the Mariners had ever done on the ballfield, reacted with anything other than weary cynicism to the news that new team owners promised to spend at legitimately competitive levels; it was the first time the local technology sector bought into a Seattle pro sports franchise; and it was the first time a Japanese businessman tried to buy an American Major League Baseball team.

The press conference announcing the intended purchase sent the strongest signal to date that Seattle was fast becoming a tech-industry town. Present at the conference was Slade Gorton, the longtime U.S. Senator from Washington who as Washington State Attorney General in the 1970s had successfully sued Major League Baseball over the theft of the Seattle Pilots, winning a settlement that included placement of an expansion franchise—the Mariners—in Seattle. Gorton was part of the senatorial generation succeeding Senators for Life Warren Magnuson and Henry "Scoop" Jackson, the latter known throughout his tenure as the "Senator from Boeing," and Gorton, now serving the technology sector as assiduously as his elders had served the aerospace sector, was doing what senators had always done: Follow the money.

It turned out that Nintendo's Yamauchi was putting up 80 percent of the purchase price of the Mariners at Gorton's request; the senator had inserted an extremely lucrative-for-Nintendo amendment in a tax bill a few years before, and Yamauchi now was more than happy to return the favor.

There followed months of what looked from Seattle's point of view like a backward United States trying to come to terms with the future Seattle had already embraced. Major League Baseball refused to approve the sale of one of its franchises to a Japanese owner, a stance leading Seattle commentators to lecture the national establishment over everything from the city's self-styled enlightened racial attitudes to the existence of Asia as an untapped source of talent, fans, and money for the American pro baseball industry. Baseball finally relented, but only after Yamauchi agreed to a Nordstromesque arrangement in which he would fund the purchase of the ball club but cede control of it to less wealthy members of the Seattle establishment.

Outside Seattle many saw the purchase as either strange or dangerous—the handing over of something as iconic as a Major League Baseball franchise to a Japanese owner seemed to bear terrible symbolism to Americans living east of the Pacific-coast states. But inside Seattle the sale was symbolically perfect, not only because Washington State had always been Asia-looking, but because the sale signaled the passage of Seattle from a one-company town dependent on an outmoded industry to a knowledge-worker town dependent on the far healthier and more diverse emerging software industry. Both Nintendo and Microsoft, being software companies, represented a future in which a "clean" industry producing the fruits of mental labor took over from a "dirty" industry producing the fruits of physical labor. Who wouldn't want to turn a chronically losing baseball franchise over to this vanguard? Even I, who had long since given up on the notion that major-league baseball was worth the trouble and money Seattle kept pouring into it, couldn't keep myself from believing that this ownership—enlightened, demonstrably smart, Asian—could redeem baseball from its hidebound, good-old-boy-constricted past and give Seattle endless World Series championships in the bargain. Seattle, I thought, was now ready to show the world what twenty-first-century baseball would—and should—look like.

For some reason, it never occurred to me that I was asking the impossible of Microsoft when I requested unfettered access to its campus. I called Pam Edstrom and told her I wanted to write a book about the development of a Microsoft multimedia product. Instead of turning me away, Edstrom acted as an agent and advisor for me, explaining what it would take to get inside Microsoft's world and arguing on my behalf with company executives. She set up interviews with possible book subjects and lobbied tirelessly on my behalf. The key, she said, was to get one of

Microsoft's four senior vice presidents to allow me into his or her division. As for Gates, she said, "Once one of his senior vice presidents signs off on this, Bill will, too. As long as they're comfortable, he won't even ask any questions about it."

For the next three months, I waited for someone at Microsoft to react with enthusiasm to the idea of being a book subject. The problem turned out not to be what I expected—fear that the company's image would be damaged by revelations about its inner workings—so much as worry either that I would reveal trade secrets to a competitor or that my presence would cause a product to fall behind schedule.

The first concern was easily dismissed. I explained to one of the Microsoft public-relations people deputed to talk with me that I was not interested in company trade secrets—all I wanted was to study company culture—and that in any event I worked so slowly that by the time I got my manuscript finished and my book on store shelves, technology would have advanced far beyond the technology in my book.

Her eyes lit up. "That's a good data point!" she said. Two days later, I was on the Microsoft campus getting ready to talk directly with potential subjects. I may be the only person in history with something to sell to Microsoft whose pitch succeeded because of the seller's *lack* of ambition.

I finally managed to hook onto a product team that had just finished the first version of Microsoft Encarta, a multimedia encyclopedia on CD-ROM based on the *Funk & Wagnalls New World Encyclopedia*. The Encarta group, one of four multimedia product groups at Microsoft, was about to begin development of a multimedia children's encyclopedia on CD-ROM. The group's manager, Craig Bartholomew, had earned a bachelor's degree in Russian from Dartmouth before getting an MBA from the University of Washington. In a weird retwist of fate, Bartholomew turned out to be intrigued at the news that I knew Joseph Brodsky, and suddenly I had an in at Microsoft.

The informal ease with which Bartholomew and his troops decided to let me into their domain was almost as stunning as the way Brodsky kept surfacing at critical junctures in my life. I met with the group once and briefly declared my intentions. Like adolescents, they looked around at one another in confusion when I was finished talking, then shrugged and mumbled something barely coherent about how it was all right with them if I wanted to sit in on their meetings and record everything they did. "All right, then!" Bartholomew said briskly. "We have a meeting after this right here, and you can start right in if you like."

The meeting turned out to be an eye-opener. In an experience I was to repeat constantly for the next two years, I sat there marveling at the youth of the other people in the room—none save for Bartholomew was over thirty, and he was scarcely older than that. I was to meet only two people on the Microsoft campus during my time there who were older than forty-five—my age. I walked the halls day after day feeling like Rip van Winkle—old, confused, largely ignored—and sat in on meeting after meeting in which twenty-some-year-olds debated how to deplete multimillion-dollar budgets on projects that were half business, half research-and-development.

I was struck too by the mixture of confidence and exuberant uncertainty in the kids around the table. They spoke briskly and efficiently, with proper corporate determination to keep moving forward in line with their strategic vision, and they displayed the impatience of people who knew they were on the right track and wanted to get the meeting dispensed with as efficiently as possible. They looked like children earnestly playing at being corporate bigwigs. The impression that they were kids playing a game was heightened by their tendency to lapse into childlike hesitancy whenever—as was often the case—they were suddenly confronted with a question they couldn't answer. One minute, you would hear a young woman say, "I envision this to be something that's extremely deep, and not just deep in the sense that there's a lot of content in one area." Then when someone would ask her to explain what she meant, she would say, "Um . . ."

The group was charged with having to define a completely new product, design it, make sure it would work properly on a near-infinite array of personal computer brands and configurations, make a business case for it, get Gates's endorsement, then get it developed, marketed, and out the door in eighteen months. Theirs would have been a difficult task even in a well-defined market with a history to guide them. To create and dominate an entirely new market was a far more daunting challenge—particularly for people with as little experience as these people had.

Bartholomew, who had spent several previous years overseeing production of Microsoft's first version of Encarta, had at least some experience in conceiving of and designing for a multimedia CD-ROM market. And three of the people in this meeting had worked for him on that project. But none of them had any idea at all about how to design a children's product. They had looked at children's computer games and children's encyclopedias, and decided from that cursory research that they knew they wanted to create something informative that had a gamelike element to it, so that kids could enjoy navigating around in it as much for sheer pleasure as from the desire to find information. Beyond that, they seemed helpless, adrift, vacillating constantly between bluster and fear. One minute Carolyn Bjerke, who had designed the user interface for Encarta and would be leading the interface-design team for this project, would be saying, "We always blow competition away"; the next, she would be voicing fear that Disney would suddenly enter the multimedia business and blow Microsoft away. They could compete with Disney on technology, at least for a time; but could they ever compete in aesthetics or content? One moment Sara Fox, a young woman who had studied early childhood development at Stanford, then worked for Broderbund Software, a children's educational software company, before coming to Microsoft as an editorial lead for children's titles, would say confidently, "We just have to make a plan and get done what we need to do"; the next, she would wonder if anything they were planning was feasible.

After a while, Bartholomew left the meeting, leaving Bjerke and Fox alone to brainstorm. The two decided to convene an "education summit," bringing some of the nation's top experts on early childhood education into Microsoft for consultations on the design of Sendak—their code name for the product. The summit would help iron out their own theories on what form the encyclopedia would take, and would give them solid, expert, credentialed evidence to present to Gates. The only problem with their plan for the summit, Bjerke pointed out, was the timing. They were late in getting under way and it was unlikely that they could make the necessary arrangements for such an event far enough in advance of the presentation to Gates for it to do them any good. "What's your strategy," Bjerke asked Fox, "for getting these people in here on such short notice?"

The two women stared thoughtfully across the table at one another. For a few moments, neither spoke. Finally, Fox, said, with a laugh, "I'm just going to call them up and scream, 'I have a Bill meeting!'"

During the first weeks of my stay at Microsoft, I watched the Sendak team work at putting together a product development schedule. The schedule was built entirely around rehearsals for Bill meetings, leading up to the actual meeting with the actual Bill. Interface design, art, content, and development ("development" being coding, the computer programming that would realize the designers' visions) all worked in parallel, building a series of prototypes, schedules, product specifications, marketing plans, and product versions that were to be presented or described at a given month's "dry run for the dry run of the Bill meeting," which would lead to revisions upon revisions leading in turn to the "dry run of the Bill meeting," which eventually would help the team prepare for the

Bill meeting three months hence. At the dry runs, more experienced employees from other product teams would sit in and play the role of "Bill," peppering the presenters with rude questions, hammering away at them on detail after detail after detail. Whenever a Bill surrogate took an adverse stance or uttered a criticism, it was taken on faith, without objection, as a pronouncement from On High, and the team would accordingly revise its plans and presentation to eliminate the problem, address the issues raised by the objection. Anyone seeing what I was seeing could be forgiven for thinking that the business of Microsoft was simply dreaming up products and strategies that were pleasing to Bill.

This was not only a matter of getting the chairman's imprimatur; it was a matter of competing with other product teams for it. Microsoft was organized into hundreds of small teams, all in competition with other teams for head count, money, and Gates's endorsement of their vision. Multimedia Publishing had four product units, each free to pursue its own vision. Each had sketched out three- or four-year plans that were considerably different from one another's. Each wanted to be the most successful of the four product units, to prove that its vision was the wisest and most deserving of more money and personnel. "A couple of years from now," said one of the Sendak team members, "the four multimedia units will be fiercely and closely comparing profit-and-loss statements. Those with the most profit will get the most resources and the best hearing for new ideas."

Bartholomew had taken a beating from Gates when the first version of Encarta missed its deadline. A year later, he was still brooding over it. "You guys cannot convince me that you can make a business of this until you can ship products on time," Gates had written, "because every day you don't ship once you've announced a product, your competitor knows what your features are, and your competitor's out there getting the sales that you aren't. Let's say we sell 10,000 units a month of Encarta. We just lost four months of sales. So we just lost 40,000 units."

It may have been later than its competition, but Encarta was also the best in its market. Whatever advantage Grolier's and Compton's encyclopedia products gained by coming out a few months ahead of Microsoft's offering was more than offset by Encarta's infinitely better interface, far better performance, and far superior multimedia elements. Encarta fell short only in portions of its textual content because it was based on the Funk & Wagnalls text, and the company was hard at work closing that sole disadvantageous gap for Version 2. There was no question back in 1992 that Microsoft was well on its way to obliterating the competition in this category. Encarta was as much a breakthrough onto the multimedia platform as Microsoft's first versions of Word and Excel for the Macintosh had been breakthroughs onto the GUI platform. You could look ahead and see the day when Encarta would be pretty much the only multimedia encyclopedia on the market.

Gates, apparently, did not agree. A few months after Encarta came out, he sat down and examined it in detail, then sent this e-mail to the multimedia group:

> I used this product more today than I ever had before. Maybe it's because I am used to a higher level of quality now . . . but I just thought it was good not great.
>
> The speed is the weakest part. There is something really WRONG with the speed of this thing. For example before you start it is so slow to show sample images—a taste of what is to come. . . . When it shows a small image and you ask for the big image WHAT IS IT DOING?? There is something wrong wrong wrong with this . . . Multimedia elements should not be the slow part of a CD title . . .
>
> You want slow—try to use MINDMAZE—that is the slowest thing I have ever seen. . . .
>
> The UI is weird in too many places. A weird setup. Weird dialog boxes . . . Lots of weird UI things. . . .

Even though they received this message months after Encarta was released, months after it had received reams of computer-press reviews rating it the best of the three encyclopedias on the market, and months after it was clear that Encarta would be the runaway market leader—none of the team bridled at the criticism. Jabe Blumenthal, the Multimedia Publishing product unit manager with the closest relationship to Gates, offered Bartholomew advice based on his thirteen years at the company. "You have to understand," he said of Gates, "that he is beset with constant angst that someone will catch Microsoft. He's worried about the tendency of people to relax, to stay on a plateau."

Everyone I met who had worked on Encarta came away feeling responsible for their team's perceived failure rather than resentful at Gates. They were determined to do better on the next project—it had turned, in fact, into a quest of redemption. In e-mail to Gates and in a subsequent "postmortem report"—every Microsoft team filed such a report after its product's release—Bartholomew exhaustively detailed Encarta's failings, the decisions leading to them, and a plan for eliminating the errors on the next version. The "What went wrong" list was endless: "Specification not complete . . . Keyboard equivalents an afterthought . . . Too much of a 'can-do' attitude . . . Tons of redundant code . . . Not even close to zero-defect . . ." and on and on and on.

I had a great, if gruesome, time at Microsoft reading postmortem reports. More than anything else at the company, they highlighted Gates' fixation on mistakes. Not once among these reports did I come across a success story. Products—Word for Windows, for example—on their way to virtually 100 percent market penetration were viewed as disasters in the eyes of their creators. I read reports of managers being hospitalized from exhaustion, stress, frustration, of team members disappearing or going mad, of errors compounded by errors compounded by errors. Only once did I encounter something akin to a boast, and it was followed immediately by an implied apology: "What Worked Well and How We Will Improve on It."

I was relatively amazed at all this self-abnegation and agony—particularly since most of the people in question no longer needed to work for a living. With their ceaseless ambition and conviction that work mattered more than anything in the world, they were the antithesis of what I and my fellow Seattle youngsters had been in the sixties and seventies. I had to keep biting my tongue around them for fear of sounding like an old fogy fondly berating them with recollections of his better-misspent youth: "Why, in my day, we never even thought about work . . . When I was your age, I was sitting around getting stoned all the time . . . We would never have sold out to the Man like this!"

I watched over the course of two years as the relentlessness of the company wore away at the youth and vigor of the people I was following. I noticed that the end came for many employees in a sudden burnout manifested either in physical ailments or the inability to work any longer. I watched one four-year veteran suddenly start spending all his days in his building's company kitchen, trying to strike up conversations with everyone who entered. Another came down with carpal tunnel syndrome in both arms. Yet another was hospitalized for exhaustion; and one unfortunate woman started screaming angrily in the middle of a meeting and finally was taken away by Microsoft security personnel. In nearly all the cases I knew of, the company, as if understanding that industry conditions were to blame for the employee's sudden collapse, offered each one tremendously generous severance packages.

I was talking with Sendak lead software developer Kevin Gammill one day about programming when we fell to talking about a computing phenomenon known as the "infinite loop": a piece of miswritten code that causes a computer to keep performing the same function over and over again until it finally crashes. We were laughing over the instructions on a bottle of shampoo—"Lather. Rinse. Repeat"—because in the computer software world such an instruction would be a fatal mistake. A few days later, talking as we often did about the travails of the Sendak team, which were considerable, and about how typical their frustrations, disagreements, unhappiness, misdirection, redirection, false starts, and renewed starts were, Gammill said, "Our product cycles are so . . . *cyclic.*" I found myself thinking then about the Moore's Law–driven, and Bill Gates–driven, pace of progress in the computing industry. Employees at Microsoft were doomed to develop a product, regard it as a failure, develop a new product with the intent of atoning for the previous effort, regard it as a failure, and so on, constantly repeating their experience by developing new software for what they called a "moving platform"— perpetually evolving computer hardware. They always ended up back where they started relative to the industry and the state of the art in computer hardware. They were trapped in an infinite loop.

The average career tenure at Microsoft, I learned, was seven years— three product cycles at the most—and after seeing up close the psychological conditions there, I could see why people found it so hard to stay on longer than that. The more ambitious they were, the more they learned that all ambition is futile. I came to see Microsoft employees as people trapped in a modern, perverse version of the Hmong's consoling circle of time, their devastating loop a progressive circling toward despair rather than the contented resignation of the pre-modern. Working there was like being a kid on an out-of-control carousel: It just kept spinning faster and faster and faster, the nauseated kids being flung off one by one as they lost their grip.

My favorite moment at Microsoft, as it happened, involved the concept of infinity. I spent a great deal of time sitting through dry runs of one sort or another of various teams' Bill meetings (one of the dress rehearsals took place at 7 A.M. on the day of the real meeting), and I followed along to two different presentations to the chairman himself. Since both Bill meetings involved pitches by Multimedia Publishing, a great deal of the discussion with Gates had to do with the publishing industry. Although by then I was used to his incomparable ability to become an expert on virtually any subject, I was nonetheless surprised at how much he had taught himself about publishing. He knew the ins and outs of everything: distribution, backlists, profit margins, copyright, how to avoid paying royalties . . .

Since Microsoft's multimedia titles were essentially electronic books, Gates correctly saw his main competition as being both printed versions of the titles he wanted to do and future multimedia titles published by book publishers—who, he reasoned, would be getting into CD-ROM publishing in a big way. He was particularly worried about the advantage publishers enjoyed by virtue of owning so much content in advance. They did not, as Microsoft did, have to go out and buy electronic rights to titles or sign authors to create new works. "What's their sustained competitive advantage?" he asked rhetorically at one meeting. "They own titles!" He was fearful that publisher/partners with Microsoft would learn technology from his company, then turn into formidable competitors. "I just feel like we're babes in the woods with these people," he fretted.

He was terrified of locking Microsoft into a licensing deal that would lead to trouble down the road. Technology might take an unforeseen turn, leading to development of a platform that Microsoft couldn't control. "If you do deals where the content guy owns you," he said, "I just don't see where you can make money. The content guy always gets to do whatever he wants in the long run. If you do deals where you just do the content on a finite number of platforms, that's just a windfall for the content guy. You prove out the title and the concept on a few platforms, and you don't get to do the big platforms, then you're just totally creating a windfall for the guy who owns that content. We could find ourselves in that position on a lot of these things." He wanted contracts with publishers that locked up all future digital platforms, even those not yet discovered. "So from the beginning we wanted to go after anything that moves, basically. It's just completely unfair to have somebody say you have limited platforms! That's *just not fair*! Because you can clearly create the image of what the product can be and come up with the design and popularize it and it's totally a windfall for them to be able to go tuck in on those other platforms! The default position is that it should be broad platforms! If we can't get that, fuck 'em! I mean, it's just *not fair*!"

Gates could never discuss the publishing industry without using the word "greed." He liked the idea of dealing directly with authors rather than publishers because "the least greed is down at that author level." And his conviction that all publishing was headed to the digital-platform world was so intense that he was thoroughly confused by the apparent lack of greed and aggression among book publishers in moving their titles into the multimedia CD-ROM world. At a meeting in which he gave Multimedia Publishing the go-ahead on the full range of titles proposed to him, Gates fulminated at some length on the vast money-making opportunities he saw in multimedia, and the blindness of publishers. "What are they sitting there *thinking*?" he blurted out at one point.

"Well," someone answered, "they're conservative companies, privately held companies, uptight about doing development . . ."

Gates's eyes lit up. It was as if he had been circling these hybrid partners/competitors warily, trying to figure out what sort of creatures they were, when he suddenly realized that he would enjoy a tremendous emotional advantage in his dealings with these people. It was a "Eureka!" moment. Excited, he interrupted his subordinate in mid-sentence: "So they have finite greed," he said.

Kidsplace

My fixation on them notwithstanding, exhaustion and despair were by no means the norm at Microsoft. It was only at the end of their careers that employees there would give in to them, overwhelmed at last not so much by Gates's demands as by their ceaselessness. The more you strived at Microsoft, and the greater your success, the more Gates demanded of you.

This had two effects that I found strange. One was that employees were energized rather than demoralized by the company's voraciousness. They got high from it, coming to work under the most stressful of conditions visibly alive with a fierce joy, and leaving late at night feeling, at worst, blissfully tired. The other was that I was just as energized as they were. You could feel electric life in the air. Something in the atmosphere of that place took away my need for sleep, rest, television, and purposelessness. I turned into an aging juggernaut, a knowledge worker without portfolio. For more than a year, I would rise at 4:00 A.M. every weekday and catch a 4:45 bus that got me to the ferry terminal in time for the 5:35 sailing, the first one of the day. At 6:10, the ferry would land in Seattle and I would join the parade of longshoremen, Boeing workers, attorneys, and stockbrokers walking off the boat. I would walk six blocks to the corner of Fourth and Union and board an express bus full of food-service workers, hotel maids, and software engineers that would deposit me on

the Microsoft campus a few minutes before 7:00. There I would tran-
scribe tapes, read e-mail, and watch the team members I was following
arrive one by one, all of them well before 9:00. Then I would begin a day
of attending meetings, doing interviews, and typing transcriptions, notes,
impressions, and e-mail. I would leave at 5:30, make my way by bus, ferry,
and bus back home, arriving at 7:15. I spent all my commuting time in
both directions reading company documents just like all the attorneys and
technologists around me—real adults with real jobs, deadlines, obligations, and ambitions.

Life outside Microsoft was barely noticeable, so wrapped up was I in
the struggles and lives of the people I was stalking and in the problems
posed by Sendak's development. Seattle, the city I would pass through
from my home in the sound to my work on the other side of the lake, was
a barely noticeable blur. My family faded into the background. I took on
the preoccupation—and the preoccupied air—of the people around me at
Microsoft. It was as if I had been sucked into a parallel universe. I was
aware that there was another, more real universe around me, one that
evoked fond and distracting memories, but I could not bring myself to
turn my attention to it for as long as I was v-fredm@microsoft.com, a
card-carrying citizen of the Microsoft Empire.

Most of my days were spent in the office I shared with Kevin Gammill, a twenty-five-year-old programmer who had been working at
Microsoft first as a contractor, then as a full-time employee, for seven
years. Gammill had grown up in Gig Harbor, a small town southwest of
Seattle, worked as a counterman at Kentucky Fried Chicken, delivered
pizza and worked as night manager for a Gig Harbor Pietro's Pizza outlet,
worked one summer for United Parcel Service, been a student assistant in
the University of Washington computer lab, and signed on at age eighteen as a software developer for Microsoft. He worked as much as 120
hours per week while carrying a full academic load, majoring in computer
science. He was shifted from contractor to employee when he was
twenty-one, during an IRS crackdown on Microsoft's use of temporary
workers. He married another Microsoft employee, Nicole Mitskog, that
year, and the two bought a home in Kirkland, ten minutes by car from
work. Within a year, their daughter, Cassidy, was born, and they settled
into life as an upwardly mobile Microsoft couple.

Mitskog had grown up in North Dakota, then gone to the University
of Texas at Austin, and, like Gammill, started working for Microsoft
while still in college. She had been at Microsoft longer than Gammill and
now was one of the company's "technical evangelists"—people who go

out to hardware and software companies and attempt to persuade them to develop products taking advantage of coming new Microsoft operating-system features, like those supporting display and manipulation of multimedia elements. Both she and her husband were reputed to be among Microsoft's brightest employees, and both had earned substantial bonuses, raises, and stock grants every year they had worked at the company.

In many ways, Gammill was the consummate 1990s Organization Man. He was on an established career track at Microsoft, earning generous raises and bonuses every six months and moving up the salary ladder as quickly as company custom allowed. He and his wife had a large investment portfolio that they managed carefully, and had opened a coffee house, called Seattle Bean, in New York City. They were stolid, politically conservative, extremely wealthy twenty-somethings with an unwavering devotion to their employer and lives that were extremely conventional and staid by any standards I could imagine. To be twenty-five years old with a house in the suburbs and more than a $1 million in a diversified asset portfolio was, from my perspective, to be tragically, prematurely adult.

For all their seriousness and level of achievement, though, Gammill and Mitskog were still like kids. Adult behavior looked funny on them. Gammill wore a T-shirt, shorts, and boat shoes without socks nearly every day to work. I was at their house for dinner one night when I came upon Mitskog standing helplessly in the kitchen, carefully reading cookbook instructions on how to boil asparagus. She read the beginning of the instructions, turned to the stove, carefully turned on the burner under the pan of water she had placed there, and turned back to the book. She looked as if she had never before set foot in a grown-up's kitchen.

Gammill, too, came across as a brash and irreverent kid rather than a prematurely serious adult. His favorite quote about Seattle came from a *Beavis and Butt-head* episode: "Seattle, yeah . . . that's that country where everybody's cool." His hardest habit to break after getting married was sleeping with the radio turned up loud all night long. "Nikki didn't care much for that," he told me. Once a month or more, he would walk from his home down to a nearby video arcade, called Quarters, and play games for hours at a time. His favorite game was Total Carnage. His favorite word was "sucks." He drank Redhook beer with Rabelaisian fervor. He was an avid sports fan and even more avid fan of rock music. He faithfully attended as many shows as he could, whether they were held in outdoor arenas on the other side of the state or in downtown Seattle bars and clubs. The schedule he kept on his computer at Microsoft might have recorded, on any given day, a business matter, two or three meetings, and a rock show: "9:00 Mail stock to broker! 10:30 New palette meeting. 2:00 Technology update. 5:00 BOC and Bathtub Jin," this last appointment being in a downtown Seattle tavern.

The most paradoxical thing about Gammill was the way he combined zest for upward mobility with tremendous devotion to hopelessness. While his career and wealth were soaring into the stratosphere, his mind and heart were fixated on death, depression, futility, the struggle to endure being human, the horrors of American family life, the inevitably bad ending all relationships have, and the essential ridiculousness of human expression and achievement. I read him a quote from Samuel Beckett one day—"The sun shone, having no alternative, on the nothing new"—and his eyes lit up the way my oldest daughter's had the first time she tasted chocolate. He became enthralled to the point of demanding readings almost daily. I would open one Beckett book or another and select a quote at random. "And backsliding has always depressed me," I read to him one day, "but life seems made up of backsliding, and death itself must be a kind of backsliding, I wouldn't be surprised." "I wouldn't either!" he exclaimed, delighted. "It is lying down," I read another time, "in the warmth, in the gloom, that I best pierce the outer turmoil's veil, discern my quarry, sense what course to follow, find peace in another's ludicrous distress." "That's what you're doing here," he said, laughing. "Every word I write is an unnecessary stain on silence and nothingness," I intoned. "OK . . . *that's* what you're doing here."

This inner darkness struck me as more or less typical of Northwesterners (certainly more typical than Gammill's drive to succeed), but Gammill's capacity for appreciating great artistic expression of it was unusual—particularly in someone whose reading tastes ran mostly to thrillers. ("Tom Clancy," he told me once, "is the only author who I've read all of his books.") His sensibilities led him to spend his college/Microsoft years alternately sitting at his computer and taking in rock acts from local bands whose work during that time was rising to the level of literature, including Biblical literature. For years in the late eighties and early nineties, scarcely a weekend went by without a trip downtown to hear shows by Nirvana, Alice in Chains, Mother Love Bone, Tad, Soundgarden, Screaming Trees, Mudhoney, and countless other local acts, many of which would suddenly be launched into international fame and fortune after the overnight success in 1991 of Nirvana's *Nevermind* album. Taking part in what came to be known against its will as the grunge scene before any of these bands had hit it big was among Gammill's most treasured memories now. He listened to grunge records all day long in his office, on an entertainment system he had cobbled together with some cables, a computer that served as his "$3,000 CD player," and two gigantic speakers he had propped up in opposite corners of the room.

Gammill was highly amused by my backwardness in virtually all areas of modern life. When he saw how inept I was at using a computer, he derisively dubbed me a "Mac user"—his favorite insult. He disdained my old-fashioned reverence for the English language, which he deemed inconsistent because "it was all evolved over the years and all fucked up." Far better was the language of mathematics and computer programming—straightforward, consistent, reliable. When I told him I didn't own a CD player but instead still listened to music on a stereo turntable playing vinyl records, he snorted in disbelief, then decided to subject me constantly to the digitally stored music he had grown up with. "I just can't *believe* you don't own a CD player," he said the first time he slipped a disc into his machine and hit the play button. It was the Alice in Chains *Facelift* album.

The room instantly was filled with a rich, mournful, energetic sound that I recognized immediately without ever having heard it before. It was the translation into music of the dimness-driven mood every Northwesterner contends with, every day—rage subsumed by exhausting gloom. (Years later, a young friend of mine, Patrick Duhon, who settled here in the mid-1990s after growing up in Cleveland, would say in amazement, "I never *got* Alice in Chains until I moved here.") All the dubious dark charm of a heavy-lidded Northwest day, tempting you to luxuriate in despair, is encapsulated in *Facelift*, particularly in the opening thundering thumping instrumental lead-in to lead singer Layne Staley's lamentations in "Man in the Box."

I spent the rest of the day (and, for that matter, the better part of the next two years) listening raptly to record after record—Nirvana's *Bleach* and *Nevermind*, Soundgarden's *Superunknown* and *Badmotorfinger*, Alice in Chains' *Facelift* and *Dirt*, Screaming Trees' *Sweet Oblivion*, and earlier records by Green River, Mother Love Bone/Pearl Jam. . . . I couldn't believe that I had spent years condescendingly ignoring those kids upstairs from the *Weekly* while they were cranking out what sounded now like the best rock I'd ever heard.

This was in 1993, when grunge—a label indelibly tattooed on the Seattle music community by British rock critic Everett True in 1989— was at the apex of its fame outside Seattle. The first known use of the term in connection with Seattle rock, according to Invisible Seattleite Clark Humphrey in his incomparable *Loser: The Real Seattle Music Story*, was in a letter to the alternative rock 'zine *Desperate Times* in 1982. The letter was written by Mark Arm, later of Mudhoney, generally regarded as the seminal Seattle grunge band, and it read in part: "I hate Mr. Epp and the Calculations! Pure grunge! Pure noise! Pure shit!" Arm was a member of the band at the time.

By 1992, grunge's Seattle devotees had already declared it dead, killed by international acclaim. The shocking success of Nirvana's *Nevermind* album was seen by everyone in the Seattle music community—particularly Nirvana lead singer/songwriter Kurt Cobain—as a disaster. By the spring of '92, when Seattle bands were selling out arenas all over the world, appearing regularly on MTV, *Saturday Night Live*, and the cover of *Rolling Stone* magazine, longtime local fans of the music were walking around Seattle in "grunge is dead" T-shirts. A famous photograph of the time shows a girl at a Seattle rock show, staring coldly at the camera, wearing a tattered white T-shirt on which she has crudely hand-lettered the slogan, "You trendy grunge people SUCK."

The best-known and most compelling figure of the grunge era was Cobain, who had come north to Seattle from Olympia with his band in 1988—by which time the Seattle scene was already well established. By 1993, he had withdrawn into physical and psychological seclusion, either hidden in a home he bought with his wife, singer Courtney Love, or lost in the relatively comforting fog of heroin addiction, which was complicating the band's touring and recording efforts.

Having grown up in a hardscrabble town, Aberdeen, in southwestern Washington, Cobain lived in virtually unrelieved misery for most of his life. His parents divorced when he was nine, and he spent his teenage years drifting among friends' homes, overstaying his welcome with family after family. He had seen the brother of a friend commit suicide by hanging himself outside Aberdeen's elementary school, had an uncle who drank himself to death and a great-uncle who shot himself to death. He talked frequently of his own impending suicide from the time he was fourteen years old, telling various friends that he had "suicide genes." He was afflicted with chronic, often crippling stomach pain that reminded me of that stomach pain suffered by Hmong refugees, which eventually was diagnosed as a symptom of depression. Cobain spoke quite freely of his misery from the time he was first being interviewed by the press. In a 1989 interview with the University of Washington's student paper, the *Daily*, he described Nirvana's music as having "a gloomy, vengeful element based on hatred." He was twenty-one years old. At about the same time, he wrote in his journal, "I mean to be passionate and sincere, but I also like to have fun and act like a dork."

Eventually, I would divine that the sound later to be called grunge began taking form in the late 1970s—the heyday of Red Dress, whose echoes could be heard clearly in the sound and the lyrics of these bands that hit it big years later. By 1979, there was enough of a Seattle music population to support the launching of *The Rocket*, a rock tabloid edited by an Invisible Seattleite named Charles Cross. In the early 1980s more hardcore alternative publications like *Desperate Times* and *Punk Lust* were cropping up, their exuberantly inflammatory copy testament both to the scope of the emerging alternative-music community and the level of anger among its adepts. While older-generation Seattle (including its baby boomers, who now were entering middle age) was settling happily into traditional Northwest complacency, very much in tune with the in-thrall-to-Ronald-Reagan rest of the country, its children were forming bands with names like Danger Bunny, Popdefect, the Fartz, Cat Butt, and the Refuzors, and gathering after dark in tattered old downtown buildings to scream out their rage.

Like matter drawn toward a center to form a spectacular new galaxy, musicians from the suburbs and small towns throughout the Northwest began coalescing around Seattle clubs, principally the Gorilla Gardens, Metropolis, the Fabulous Rainbow Tavern, Squid Row, Ditto, and the Central Tavern. Their numbers were augmented by kids from around the country drifting Seattleward as the word spread that something "cool" was going on there. By the late eighties, hundreds of musicians were playing Seattle venues—a second generation, including the OK Hotel, Crocodile, RKNDY, and the Off Ramp, had sprung up—drawing kids in ever-greater numbers to music that offered a bracing alternative to the horrors of mainstream radio.

In the 1980s, the only thing in America worse than its politics was its radio. Having emerged from the dreadful disco years, commercial radio settled on bloat rather than redemption, playing nothing but oldies, heavy metal, and bubble gum reprise acts like New Kids on the Block. The present time excepted, it is hard to remember or even imagine a less creative and vibrant period in the history of American popular music. The eighties are memorable now mostly for a dreary and deafening succession of male rock groups more noted for big hair, spandex, and dick jokes than musicianship or songwriting. Kids interested in rock as an art form had nowhere in the mainstream to turn.

While Top-40 radio was playing Poison, Whitesnake, and Bon Jovi for legions of minds at rest, restless youngsters all over the country were turning to small, punk-descended "alternative" rock labels like SST in Los Angeles, Twin/Tone in Minneapolis, and—as of 1987—Sub Pop in Seattle. These labels had grown out of an underground movement called "DIY" ("Do It Yourself") rock, through which musicians turned off by the mainstream music industry made their own cassette tapes and circulated their work among like-minded audiences. Two DIY bands from elsewhere in the country who eventually were accorded mainstream stardom earlier in the 1980s were the B-52s, from Athens, Georgia, and R.E.M., from Austin, Texas, both of which started out peddling homemade cassette tapes and self-financed seven-inch singles.

Demand for DIY recordings was considerable—testament to the degree to which American kids were turned off by the culture that claimed to have nurtured them. Eventually, I would track down my favorite of the grunge bands, Screaming Trees, and see from its experience how considerable that demand was, and what a powerful alternative it offered aspiring serious musicians in the 1980s.

The four original Trees (the band would change drummers in 1991) grew up in Ellensburg, ninety minutes east of Seattle, on the other side of the Cascade Mountains, playing and listening voraciously to music from early grade school on. Their high school years consisted largely of "always, like, driving somewhere to buy records all the time," in bass guitarist/songwriter Van Conner's words, and fooling around with the idea of forming a band. When the youngest members—Conner and lead singer/songwriter Mark Lanegan—were high school juniors, they contacted a local record producer, Steve Fisk, who had founded a studio, named Velvetone, after graduating from college in Ellensburg. After Fisk heard the Screaming Trees play once, he asked if he could make a recording of their music.

This proposition was greeted with some surprise by the band. "We never realized we could just put something out ourselves," Conner told me later. "But then we started finding out about cassettes, how people would just put them out and distribute them themselves, and we had a couple hundred bucks, so we went in and recorded five or six songs, called it 'Other Worlds,' and put it out." After making that cassette, the band borrowed money from friends and parents and made a vinyl record entitled *Clairvoyance*. It promptly sold 2,500 copies, which struck both Fisk—who originally pressed only 1,000 discs—and the band members as astounding. Fisk put together a "tour" in which the band members traveled by van to a succession of clubs, dives, and college-kid apartments along the West Coast, culminating in a series of performances in Los Angeles, where they were heard by an SST Records executive who offered them a recording contract.

Similar stories were popping up everywhere around Seattle, where DIY had an important outlet in the form of the University of Washington's student radio station, KCMU. The station was both a showcase for Seattle music and a nexus for many of grunge's early leading lights. Mark Arm; Kim Thayil, later of Soundgarden; Charles Peterson, whose photographs now stand as the definitive record of grunge's pre-discovery heyday in Seattle; Jack Endino, a legendary Seattle record producer; and Bruce Pavitt and Jonathan Poneman, founders of Sub Pop, were among many eventual grunge figures who worked as volunteer disc jockeys there.

By 1987, Pavitt and Poneman decided there was enough product and demand for them to turn the fanzine they were publishing, *Sub Pop*, into a record company. Sub Pop's first release, in 1987, was a cassette compilation of bands, entitled *Sub Pop 100*; its first vinyl release, issued later that year, was Green River's *Dry as a Bone*, Green River being made up of musicians who would go on to form Mudhoney and Mother Love Bone, which would turn into Pearl Jam after the death of lead singer Andrew Wood and his succession by Eddie Vedder. By the end of 1988, Sub Pop had released records by Soundgarden, Mudhoney, Tad, the Fluid, Blood Circus, Beat Happening, Screaming Trees, the Walkabouts, and Nirvana, and had issued a second compilation—this one a grunge landmark—entitled *Sub Pop 200*.

In 1988 and 1989, grunge started to break out into the mainstream. Corporate record companies were descending on Seattle; like IBM in 1980, they were worried about losing their franchise to the underground. Polygram signed Mother Love Bone, A&M signed Soundgarden, and Columbia signed Alice in Chains. Screaming Trees' fourth album, *Buzz Factory*, and Nirvana's first, *Bleach*, each sold 30,000 copies—an unimaginably high number for independent labels, the previous high-sales mark being around 10,000. (By 1991, Screaming Trees would be signed by Epic and Nirvana by David Geffen.) Pavitt and Poneman flew a group of British rock critics to Seattle in 1989 and the critics went back home to write raves about the Seattle scene. College radio stations around the country started playing Seattle music constantly, and many bands' tours now consisted of occasional stops in large cities interspersed among numerous shows in college towns.

Technology's advance, it is clear now, played a pivotal role in the grunge explosion. The invention of the compact disc allowed Sub Pop to begin making records for a fraction of the cost of only a few years before. In 1983, Screaming Trees had made a vinyl record for $2,500; in 1989, Nirvana recorded *Bleach* on compact disc for $600. And the presence of Microsoft and its hordes of young programmers lent Sub Pop and its bands a large audience with bankloads of disposable income to plunk down in bars and clubs all over town. Kevin Gammill and his co-workers spent enough money during their rare off hours in the late 1980s to pay grunge legions a living wage for years for working on nothing but their music.

Sub Pop's marketing was reminiscent of the subglorious tradition of Ivar Haglund. It was short on sophistication and long on self-deprecation. The company's most visible promotional artifact was that T-shirt I'd seen, emblazoned "Loser." Sub Pop described Mudhoney in one promotional piece as "masters of disease and grunge," Nirvana in another as young people who "own their own van," and Cat Butt as "this derelict clan of hillbilly raunch . . . totally subhuman." In 1989, Sub Pop showcased its best bands—Nirvana, Tad, and Mudhoney—at Seattle's historic Moore Theater, advertising the event as "Seattle's lamest bands in a one-night orgy of sweat and insanity." The event, called Lamefest, was a classic display of Seattle's reflexive loathing for ambition and self-promotion. "Yes," implied the event's promoters and participants on the one hand, "what we are doing here is worth putting up on a marquee and charging people money to see," while on the other they were saying, "but, alas, everything we're doing in here is *lame*, staged by losers for losers." The show itself was similarly ambivalent, the bands simultaneously playing their hearts out and drawing attention away from their music with behavior intended to set their fans to rioting. *Seattle Times* critic Paul de Barros noted with clucking disapproval the bands' unease with the idea that they should strive for stardom by showcasing their musical gifts: "Beyond extra-musical distractions," he wrote, "the whole point of this show seemed to be based on the perverse, reverse notion that grungy, foul-mouthed, self-despising meatheads who grind out undifferentiated noise and swing around their long hair are good—and 'honest'—by virtue of their not being 'rock stars.' How confounded this primitivism is, which defines bands in the reverse image of someone else's market position, rather than music."

In retrospect, even after studying the intricacies (and the beauty) of grunge with a singlemindedness that was at best bewildering to my family, it is easy to see why de Barros was too rattled by Lamefest to actually hear the music. Like everyone else his (and my) age, he had long since bought into the image of the Northwest as a place of peace, relaxation, tolerance, and tranquility. Small wonder that he was profoundly shocked—here were our own children rising up in rage and striking a powerful responsive chord in the heart of Northwest adolescents by giving the lie to their parents' storied "happy condition."

From the beginning, grunge—a synthesis of punk with the more melodic music of the 1960s—was determinedly dark, turning Ivar's "Keep clam" into something along the lines of "Keep clam, asshole!" The music is at once rude, beautiful, depressing, and uplifting. Van Conner, in describing his band's music to me, got at the heart of grunge in general when he said that the intent with every song "is to have a really nice melody within a song and keep it dark at the same time. 'Dark pop' is what we like to call it."

The result for all of these bands was the antithesis not only of happiness and hope but also of anger and rebellion. Grunge is the most consistently lugubrious sound in rock history. The classic themes of rock—adolescent rage, alienation, rebellion, hopelessness, and anger—are subsumed in the plodding, overwhelming cloud cover of sound that grunge sends swelling over the strenuous efforts of its lead singers. The best grunge songs begin with an overwhelming buildup of sonic fog, from which eventually emerges the singer's voice. From somewhere in that ear-blinding mist, the singer growls, moans, screams, and mumbles as if trying to escape to the light, only to acquiesce at song's end to the mood and power of the swirling music.

Grunge seemed remarkably different to me from garden-variety musical trends. It was defined less by the storms and stresses of adolescence than by the prevailing temper of its region. It was the most undeniably "Northwest" of all Northwest exports—a psychological manifestation of our meteorological condition.

Four bands in particular—Screaming Trees, which came first and had a profound influence on the bands that came after, Nirvana, Alice in Chains, and Soundgarden—perfected this Northwestness of sound. Nirvana's Cobain would mumble melodically in his songs, burst into screams, then lapse again into murmuring, then silence. The entire *oeuvre* of Alice in Chains' Layne Staley was a gradual descent from dark screams to long, mournful, sometimes barely audible muttering on his later albums. And Screaming Trees' Mark Lanegan sang languidly in a deep, rich, husky voice of the quest for "sweet oblivion," the fruitless search for "a reason to carry on," and the refusal of life ever to change for the better.

The paradoxical element running through the songs of all four of these bands is the way their gloom, resignation, and mournfulness is laid over with extremely pleasant melodies. It makes for an ingenious rendition of the Northwest condition: Set in ideal natural surroundings and a comforting climate, we find to our horror that we are still *us*—lame, lonely, losing. "My pain is self chosen/At least I believe it to be," drones Layne Staley in "River of Deceit" to an almost relaxing tune that pleases the ear as much as the lyrics disturb the mind. And one of Cobain's lightest and most pleasant melodies accompanies a local tale of horror and violence. In "Frances Farmer Will Have Her Revenge on Seattle," he croons about the Seattle film star who was lobotomized at nearby Western State Hospital.

The more I listened to these records, the more I wondered why the music ever caught on outside the Northwest. It sounds so *regional*. The emotional condition of these songs—torpid rage—is that of the Northwesterner thoroughly conditioned by endless dimness, damp, maddeningly moderate temperatures, and a spectacular landscape that makes human achievement look laughably puny. These singers were showing us again and again that the weather, having seeped into our souls, had reduced us all to a constant state of near-sleep, subverting ambition and replacing it either with complacency, low-grade self-loathing . . . or both.

Which made it impossibly odd for me to have encountered and been subsumed by it at *Microsoft*, of all places.

I went on in this fashion—commuting to Microsoft, working and studying there to the constant accompaniment of Seattle's grunge music—into early 1994. It felt like the hardest work I'd ever done, the constant traveling, meeting, observing, thinking, reading, writing, trying to keep up with Gammill's pace of work and beer consumption, and madly typing transcripts of taped interviews. I began cultivating—or so I thought—the constantly purposeful and productive manner of the Microsoft employee. Occasionally, others at Microsoft would look up from their work long enough to notice that Gammill was sharing his office with someone outside the norm. Near the end of one particularly exhausting day, I came back to our office to see Gammill looking up at me and laughing. "What's so funny?" I asked.

"Someone was just in here asking me, 'Who's that guy in your office who's never doing any work?'"

On and on I commuted and worked and watched, the background music often chiming in with the perfect word at the perfect time as if the singer were watching and commenting on the spectacle around me. I was sitting off in a corner one day watching Gammill interview a job applicant while his favorite radio station, KISW ("Solid rock. No useless talk."), played in the background. Gammill had put a chunk of programming code on his white board and asked the applicant to tell him what was wrong with it. The code was an infinite loop. The applicant—a newly minted Ph.D.—stood staring at the board, his shoulders sagging, the spirit seeping out of him. He was helpless. And on the radio I heard Cobain mumbling the famous intonation from "In Bloom," about the kid who has no idea what it means.

I emerged from Microsoft early in 1994 to find an entirely different Seattle from the one I had left two years before. Optimism and money were everywhere. Instead of seeing old Volvos and Dodge Darts on the roads, I saw BMWs and Mercedes. Everyone on the streets looked as young and purposeful as the people working at Microsoft. There were disturbing new faces at the *Weekly*—kids who had come west to Seattle "because it's cool," and, more disturbing, because they saw the city as a place to make their fortunes rather than drop out. Downtown was packed at night with young, moneyed people instead of the derelicts who had ruled the streets for the better part of the last century. And the grunge kids with their loser message were fading away. The music I had fallen in love with in Gammill's office was effectively dead. Writing in the *Weekly*, Robert Myers took note of how record-industry money, promotion, and stardom had leached all the inspiration out of grunge, leaving most of its musicians in psychological tatters. He saw the rise and fall of grunge as a classic American rags-to-riches-to-ruin story, an object lesson in how the larger culture eats its young. "You don't tap into the Zeitgeist," Myers wrote, "the Zeitgeist taps into you."

Talking with Myers, Sub Pop cofounder Jonathan Poneman sounded like a bitter, disillusioned old man presiding over the ruins of a dream. "I am a businessperson of sorts, I guess," he said, "but it's really troubling how I read in rock-band interviews a lot of discussion about deals and such. I did not get into this business to discuss deals." I was convinced I could hear a dire warning in his words: Beware the blandishments of ambition. They never lead you anywhere worth going.

Dark Pop

How can I explain how shocking it was to come back to Seattle again? I had been to the frontier at Microsoft, the edge of the universe, my spaceship the frantic manic madcap nonstop whirling center of the Silicon Rush. I'd been surrounded by unfolding tales of wealth and high drama and insanity. I'd seen Microsoft discoveries under way that were going to change the world. Work and life and art would never be the same again because of what I'd witnessed out on the cutting edge. By the time I came back to earthbound Seattle in 1994, struggling to ratchet back to my normal sleepy pace, the world's media had glommed onto the Microsoft story and were madly speculating about the miracles to be wrought by the coming release of Windows 95—the operating system that would take us all where no man had gone before. And I'd been there! I'd felt the excitement, drunk in the glamour. I'd lived in Bill Gates's mining camp—the land of lore and lucre. All you had to do was dip your fingers into the stream of bits there and you'd come up with a fistful of gold . . . Hell, a man could get rich at Microsoft, be set for life, after working for only a year!

Settling in again at the *Weekly*, all I could think about was what it would have been like for Doc Maynard to go back to Ohio after taking in the splendor and potential of the Pacific Northwest. Everything at the *Weekly* looked faded, tired, outdated, out of touch. The alphanumeric interface on my computer made me feel like I was wearing green eye-shades and sleeve garters, working for a bank that forced its employees to use adding machines while all the gleaming new banks in town had installed calculators. We didn't even have e-mail! And the paper was still mulling over Seattle's identity, values, traditions, downtown conditions, and the same old lackluster prospects for the Seahawks and Mariners. I'd been gone for two years, watching a revolution unfold, and came back home to find not only that nothing had changed but that everyone around me was oblivious to the world-changing events exploding just outside the door. I would sit, stunned, in my cubicle, feeling like the only person in all of Rome who sees the Visigoths massing on the hills outside the city.

I found myself fixating against my will on the notion that the massive flow of money into the software industry was somehow legitimizing—a blessing conferred on it and its participants because of the revolution's inherent goodness. Money, which I had always affected to disdain, now looked like a measure of moral worth, and my lifelong indifference to it looked to me like the emptiest of pretensions—the principled rejection of the unattainable.

Now when I thought of software's nouveaux riches, I didn't picture programmers and other exotic fauna so much as I pictured people like me—English majors—who had gravitated to the right place at the right time while I was indulging in my poorer-than-thou hauteur, my Seat-tleite's affected purity of heart. I thought again of Jan Allister, whose 1,600 Microsoft shares, by my increasingly frenzied calculations, must have bal-looned in worth to somewhere in the neighborhood of $2 million—assuming, as I tended to assume in mid-fantasy, that she hadn't blown it all back when the windfall was small enough to spend.

I was brooding about all this when it was announced that Adobe Sys-tems was buying Aldus in a transaction that would convert all Aldus stock shares into Adobe shares and make early Aldus shareholders—particularly, to my ever-more-envious mind, Ann Senechal—rich in the process. Press accounts of the merger were filled with expansive visions of a digital future. Phrases like "$2 billion desktop publishing industry" and "the breadth of new market opportunities offered by the digital revolution" littered the local papers when the deal was announced in mid-1994, as did visions of a near future when everyone would be wired up to a digital grid. "A driving force behind the deal," reported the *Seattle Times*, "is expected to result in a new software product, called an 'authoring tool' in industry lingo, that will help people create an electronic document out of video, sound and data received over fiber-optic cables expected to be fed into many homes and offices in the not-too-distant future."

I sat in my grimy cubicle the afternoon of the announcement and wondered how far the software wealth, no longer confined to Microsoft, was destined to spread.

Would the last person clinging to Seattle's past please get with the program?

When I wasn't feeling sorry for myself, mourning the financial opportunities I'd missed, the security I could have bought for my family with very little effort, and regarding the infusion of software wealth into Seattle as something benevolent, I was lamenting the money-driven material progress and moral regress I saw threatening the city at every turn. It was as if my mind saw marvelous progress and prosperity on the horizon while my heart saw only software-wealth-driven danger. Was Seattle being redeemed or destroyed? For every Jan Allister, Ann Senechal, and Kevin Gammill I saw out there, I decided there were thousands of less admirable good-fortune cases.

There was, for example, Paul Allen, who seemed intent on razing and rebuilding the city as a monument to himself. While he came across largely as a harmless, shy, awkward, but well-intentioned kid who ended up with $13 billion in the bank, he also appeared to have a profound Edifice Complex. Allen had retired from Microsoft in 1983 (although he remained a board member), when he was diagnosed with Hodgkins Disease, and settled into a life far less frantic than Gates's. He started a modest new venture, Asymetrix, to make software authoring tools; he founded another company, Vulcan Ventures, in 1986, to invest in new businesses; and in 1987 he bought the Portland Trailblazers. In 1992, he established Interval Research in Palo Alto with the mandate that it do the kind of pure research-and-development that Xerox PARC had done, and that had largely faded away as American corporations both in and out of the personal-computer industry focused increasingly on research promising short-term returns. Only in a pure research environment, Allen reasoned, free of the pressure to placate shareholders, could the next Alto be discovered.

All of this was relatively harmless—some of it even admirable. But Allen also started buying up land all over the Pacific Northwest, particularly in Seattle, and spinning out grotesquely grand visions for it. Two of his most noticeable and controversial initiatives were the Jimi Hendrix Museum, a high-tech rock-and-roll entertainment venue he wanted to build on the hallowed Seattle Center grounds, and the Seattle Commons, a planned transformation of the south shore of Lake Union into a Utopian mixed-use neighborhood centered on a park. To that end, Allen "loaned" $20 million in 1992 to the group seeking to build the Commons, with the understanding that if Seattle citizens did not vote to levy $50 million in property taxes to fund the vision, Allen would take 11.5 acres of south Lake Union land—bought by the Commons with his loan—in exchange for the money.

The debate over the Commons highlighted the shift in Seattle's self-image and dreams for itself. Now there was no longer any question at all that we lived in, and defined ourselves as, a technology town. Just as more and more employees and tradespeople had been flowing toward technology companies and out of resource-based and traditional manufacturing industries, so too now were more and more of the city's politics and urban development flowing techward. City Hall under Mayor Norm Rice was solidly behind the Commons project, which amounted to a massive urban-renewal tax plan, seed-funded with tech-sector money, for turning one of the most symbolic sections of the city into a high-tech business park. Seattle Commons was promoted as the wave of the future, an inspired means of accommodating rapid population growth and making way for the "clean" industries of the post-industrial age—software, biotechnology, and other nonpolluting industries whose primary factory assets were the brains of their employees.

From 1992 into 1995 the debate raged, with battle lines being drawn not only between those in thrall to technology's money and those who held to a more traditional and less greedy view of Seattle, but also along socioeconomic lines: Polls conducted by research firms found that enthusiasm for the Commons came largely from Seattleites with incomes higher than $60,000 per year. But Commons promoters tried to define the divide differently—as one between forward-thinking people with a clear vision of the future and backward people clinging to outmoded views, jobs, and traditions.

Lost in the overarching philosophical debate was the reality that ninety-five businesses would be displaced by the Commons. I went over one day and walked through the south Lake Union neighborhood, noting the distinctive lack of glamour there. It was the Seattle Jonathan Raban—who I heard had returned here to settle down—had invoked so fondly in 1989. I walked past a scrap-iron yard, antique and secondhand-furniture warehouses, a bike shop, used-car lots, an appliance store, a sewing-machine shop, a trophy shop, and various other small enterprises, all in rundown buildings, many with anti-Commons signs in their windows, and none destined to take over the world or the city or even the neighborhood. No one here was intent on defining the future. These were just little family operations trying to get by as I had with my typesetting business so long ago. Walking these streets now, newly back from my frenzied sojourn at Microsoft, I waded through the same emotional slough I'd traversed years before during that depressing walk around Lake Union. Why, I wondered, is this city constantly turning against itself?

Ultimately, the *Weekly* wrote extensively against the plan—an editorial position that Seattle Commons promoters, who tended toward righteousness, viewed as outright betrayal. Project director Joel Horn repeatedly called Brewster, me, and anyone else who questioned the Commons project and excoriated us for our shortsightedness. He always sounded baffled and hurt, it being a given in his mind that the *Weekly*, with its moneyed, baby-boom readership and love of "progressive" initiatives, would line up along with the rest of nouveau-genteel Seattle behind a project with such a clear vision and glamorous demographic. The *Weekly* all but owned the new-restaurant and high-culture franchises, after all, and nothing seemed to fit more into that Seattle dimension than the moderne, civilized Commons, with its Harvard Yard-esque name, its carefully planned gentility, and its embrace of the city's tech-industry future.

But Seattle had always grudgingly allowed rather than enthusiastically embraced progress, permitting industrialists and other overly ambitious people to locate on the fringes here and use the region's charms as a recruiting tool. When an industrialist's visions of grandeur spilled over into the city itself, Seattle tended to react in horror, wanting the jobs and money that ambition brought without having to take on any of the airs that came with it. It was one thing to have professional aspirations—it was another to take on the look and feel of people who had them, and far worse to take on the look and feel of people who had achieved them.

When the Commons came up for vote in 1995, with the full support of City Hall, the downtown establishment, the *Seattle Times*, and Paul Schell—who always was connected in one way or another with grand Seattle development visions—it was narrowly voted down. Commons boosters reacted in stunned disbelief, turning around and putting it on the ballot again, this time spending more than $500,000 promoting it. The campaign backfired—news stories about the budget disparities between promoters and opponents, who were able to raise only $91,000 in opposition, highlighted the elitist nature of the Commons campaign, and many voters were outraged that their No votes were condescendingly ignored. In May 1996, the Commons went down to defeat again, and this time Allen accepted the results, taking control of the 11.5 acres of prime real estate he had secured with his $20 million, and settling down to wait for more ambition-friendly times.

A different battle between the same forces was taking place on the other side of downtown, where the Seattle Mariners ownership was once again threatening to sell the team to someone who would move it elsewhere unless the city built them a new stadium. By 1994, the vaunted 1992 salvation of the Mariners franchise by local high-tech millionaires and billionaires had turned into the same shakedown Seattle politicians and taxpayers had been enduring since 1977. The Mariners had persistently failed to field a competitive major-league team and just as persistently blamed city and county politicians for not investing enough taxpayer money in the franchise to enable it to compete for talent. The argument from Mariner owners had always been that they could not afford to field a competitive team at a financial loss, and that only heavily taxpayer-subsidized teams had a chance to compete for the World Series championship; the rejoinder from skeptical Seattleites held that baseball owners always recouped their "losses" and more when they resold their franchises. No major-league owner anywhere—including Seattle—had ever sold a franchise at a loss. Why, sensible Seattleites reasoned, should taxpayers subsidize a business owned by obscenely wealthy men when the subsidy only helps make them even more obscenely wealthy?

Whatever cachet the Nintendo-led owners had gained by being local was lost in the intense feelings of betrayal among Seattleites when they saw their local saviors behaving exactly as their out-of-town predecessors had. But then, in July 1994, tiles from the interior of the Kingdome roof fell onto some seats before the start of a Mariners game, with the result that the rest of the season had to be played on the road. Roof repairs originally estimated at $4 million ended up costing $50 million, and the Mariners had a powerful argument for replacing the Kingdome: Not only are its revenue streams inadequate for *us*, the team argued, but they can't even cover the repair and maintenance costs of the building.

There still remained the argument over who would pay for the new stadium. Mariner owners insisted both that it be "state of the art"—that is, that it be an outdoor stadium evocative of old-time baseball but packed with modern amenities, particularly luxury suites, high-priced box seats that would appeal to moneyed fans, and a retractable roof. In today's entertainment market, the team argued, ballparks had to offer a "fan experience" that amounted to far more than the simple enjoyment of a baseball game. Team executives promised that such a stadium could be built for between $200 million and $250 million, the bulk of which could be raised through a modest tax increase.

Politicians in Washington and its cities and counties had long been loath to raise taxes for anything, however, because doing so was politically suicidal. I spent a lot of time in late 1994 and early 1995 in King County councilman Ron Sims's office, listening to him lament the insidious blackmail Seattle businesspeople were visiting on him. A Democrat, Sims knew that supporters of baseball subsidies, being largely conservative, Republican, tax-loathing businesspeople, would be nowhere in sight when he needed support for reelection. And he knew that the same people who were clamoring at his door insisting that he raise taxes to build a baseball stadium would be calling for his head in the next election because he had raised their taxes. He'd been through that drill before, when he ran for a United States Senate seat against Slade Gorton, an indefatigable supporter of baseball and a rabid antitax campaigner. The Gorton ad that had done Sims in had the tagline, "Ron Sims voted to raise your taxes 19 times." Left unsaid was that seventeen of those votes had been for tax packages already approved by voters.

There followed a quasi-comedic round of buck-passing as state and local politicians looked for ways to "save" Seattle baseball without having to take on the tax-hike taint. In its 1995 session, the state legislature declined the opportunity to pass a stadium-construction funding package, but bravely voted to authorize the King County Council to raise the county sales tax for that purpose. The county council, crying foul, decided instead to put the issue directly to the voters, asking them to vote in September 1995 on a tenth-of-a-cent increase in the county sales tax to fund debt service on new stadium construction. In May 1995, the Mariners unveiled plans for the stadium they would build if given the money. Now pegged at $278 million, the ballpark was to combine nostalgia with cutting-edge technology, including a retractable roof that would bring open-air baseball to Seattle while ensuring that no Mariners game would ever be rained out.

The campaign proved to be a referendum less on the tax itself than on Seattle's self-image. The Kingdome's lack of pretension had always been seen by many citizens as its primary virtue—symbolic proof that Seattleites were not like the dimwitted citizens of Cleveland, Baltimore, Anaheim, and other typical American cities with the kind of misguided priorities that lead to taxpayer money being lavished on luxury boxes and caterers for wealthy people while more pressing needs like schools, highways, and medical care for the poor go unfunded. The Kingdome proved that Seattleites choose to spend their money on more important, less status-symbolic things than pleasure palaces, that Northwest citizens reluctantly allow pro sports to trade in their hallowed land rather than pay them astronomically for the privilege, and that in any event Northwest-erners prefer not to call attention to Seattle's arrival among the major cities of the nation. The less attention Seattle calls to itself, the better. Lesser and Invisible Seattleites in particular saw the stadium vote as a vote on whether Seattle would remain Seattle or would turn into just another Houston, Tampa Bay, or Anaheim. To these citizens, nothing could be a more alarming signal of the decline of Seattle than the erection of one of these monstrosities.

The pro-stadium forces, realizing that an opportunity of this magni-tude would never come again, played up the fear that Seattle would lose its baseball team, forever this time, if voters didn't approve a new stadium. As the election neared, polls showed that the large lead held by anti-stadium-tax forces was shrinking fast. But when the September election day came round at last, and the Mariners were in their customary place in the standings, a full thirteen games behind the division-leading Anaheim Angels, the measure went down in defeat by a microprocessor-thin 1,082-vote margin.

It felt at first like the forces of pretension had finally been van-quished—that Seattle could jettison its major-league franchise and settle back into the disgruntled tranquility that sustained it through all its recorded and unrecorded history. Nothing would have been more true to the Seattle of Doc Maynard and Ivar Haglund than to declare the citi-zenry's happy condition off-limits to baseball and all its shams. But when team owners said they would put the franchise up for sale on October 30 unless plans for a stadium subsidy had been approved by someone, some-where, Washington governor Mike Lowry called the state legislature into special session to come up with a funding package. Lowry's idea was to cobble together a combination of state and county funding that would call on the legislature to approve the state's portion of the funding and the King County Council to approve county-only taxes that would cover its "responsibility." The central element of the strategy was to invoke the Mariners' deadline as an excuse to bypass the voters; the deadline created a "crisis" that called for bold, determined action by the region's political leadership.

In a stunning—and, ultimately, critical—development, the Mariners suddenly woke up and started winning game after game after game in

September. From thirteen games behind American League West division leader Anaheim at the end of August, they roared through September virtually undefeated while the obliging Angels went into a free-fall. The two teams finishing the season tied for first place in the American League West, and Seattle won the one-game playoff between the two, held the day after the last day of the season. It was one of the biggest and least likely comebacks in Major League Baseball history. The Mariners would go on that year to beat the New York Yankees in a thrilling five-game division championship series before losing the American League pennant to the Cleveland Indians, who would go on to lose the World Series to the National League's Atlanta Braves.

What was most galling about the sudden Mariners winning streak was that theirs was a battle not for a championship but for a fourth-place finish in the fourteen-team American League. Major League Baseball, desperate to revive interest in a sport suffering rapidly declining popularity, had divided its two-division National and American Leagues into three-division leagues in 1994. The idea was to involve more teams in a race for a post-season playoff spot, thus fostering the illusion in more cities for more weeks that their teams had a chance at a World Series championship. For Seattle, the month-long sprint to catch Anaheim was a quest to finish first in a division race involving only four mediocre teams who would have finished out of the running in a traditional American League. Had the stadium vote been held two years earlier, the Mariners would have been mathematically eliminated from division title contention by September 1, and their September winning streak would have been essentially meaningless.

But Major League Baseball and Mariner ownership were playing Seattle for rubes, and Seattle happily played along. As win after win mounted up for the Mariners, and as they crept ever closer to the suddenly collapsing Angels and what local papers were now calling a "pennant" (a word formerly reserved for championship of the entire American or National League), local passion for the team was aroused for the first time in franchise history. Now, every home game was a sellout, and the Mariners began advertising their plan for playoff ticket sales (given the team's sad-sack history, this was like hearing they were selling the Holy Grail). The politically dead tax package was suddenly inevitable. I was visiting with Sims again near the end of the Mariners' amazing run, and he was glumly running through the scenarios that he knew would lead to the county council vote in favor of the new taxes. He was about to witness the twenty-year mortgaging of King County in a fervid playoff atmosphere that made reasoned debate impossible. "We wouldn't even be having this conversation," he said at one point, more dispirited than I'd ever seen him, "if the Mariners weren't winning like this."

Two weeks later, on October 14, the legislature approved a joint state/county fee-and-tax package to raise money for what now was to be a $320 million stadium. On October 23, the county council approved the measure, passing new taxes on restaurant and tavern meals and auto rentals. Although council members voting in favor of the measure insisted that this was a "different funding package" from that rejected by their constituents, the vote was seen by many—myself included—as an act that should have been impossible in the world's leading democracy: the overturning by elected officials of a popular vote.

While adult Seattle was assiduously pursuing big-league status and attention, its children were collapsing under the weight of national attention. Grunge musicians, having been thrown without warning onto the world's center stage, almost immediately fled to the wings, or to the deeper, more reliable darkness beyond.

By far the most dramatic collapse was that of Nirvana lead singer Kurt Cobain, who was grunge's most celebrated and most tormented figure. Almost from the day *Nevermind* made him famous, Cobain withdrew into heroin addiction, where he remained in what one of his doctors told him was a slow suicidal spiral until finally he committed suicide with a shotgun in April 1994. Cobain had nearly died of a heroin overdose a year before, attempted suicide with drugs and alcohol earlier in 1994 while on tour in Italy, and barricaded himself, threatening suicide, in a room with several guns during another 1994 incident in which the police were called to his home and confiscated his firearms. Each time, his wife intervened to save his life.

This last time he made sure no one could intervene. Just before he was to leave for Los Angeles to enter a drug rehabilitation facility, Cobain took his friend Dylan Carlson to a sporting goods store and had him buy a shotgun and some shells for him. Cobain took the gun and stashed it in a compartment behind one of his bedroom walls. He flew to Los Angeles and signed into Exodus Recovery Center, and three days later left undetected and flew back to Seattle. For five days, while Love, undergoing drug treatment herself in Los Angeles, sent friends and private detectives all over Seattle trying to find him, Cobain spent his last days on earth determinedly alone, preparing his successful suicide. Sometime during the night of April 7, he climbed into the upstairs of a caretaker's cottage on his property, injected himself with black-tar heroin, and shot himself in the head with the shotgun Carlson had purchased.

While it seemed that the whole city stopped dead in its tracks as the news spread on April 8, it also is true that Cobain's troubles were so well known that no one in Seattle was surprised by his death. For the previous year, at least, Nirvana observers had been on a death-watch. Almost from the time the band first became famous, Cobain's loved ones, friends, and fans had been watching him decline and expected him to die.

It would be another seven years, with the publication of Charles R. Cross's illuminating *Heavier than Heaven: A Biography of Kurt Cobain*, before the full story of Cobain's suicide and genetic predisposition to it became known. In the days following his death, the most moving excerpt released from Cobain's suicide letter cited the dead and empty feeling that overcame him when he walked onstage to the frenzied adulation of thousands. "For example," he wrote, heroin-addled, in his suicide letter, "when we're backstage and the lights go out and the manic roar of the crowd begins it doesn't affect me the way in which it did for Freddie Mercury who seemed to love, relish in the love and adoration from the crowd. Which is something I totally admire and envy. . . . Sometimes I feel as if I should have a punch in time clock before I walk out on stage." It struck me at the time as a classic Northwest reaction: an overwhelming distaste for fame, celebrity, attention. Having arrived at what he had taken for his Nirvana, Cobain was no better off than he had ever been, and now had nowhere else to go. He was still loathsome, still alone, still irredeemably miserable.

It also is hard not to consider Cobain's suicide as artistic composition, particularly when you recall the refrain from his "In Bloom," first performed in 1990, that describes a devoted, gun-obsessed fan who sings along when listening to Nirvana songs and is clueless about the meaning of it all. The refrain describes Dylan Carlson, whom Cobain befriended in 1986. An avid gun enthusiast, Carlson taught Cobain how to load and shoot firearms. Four years after "In Bloom," during the days when Cobain's suicidal intentions were on the minds of everyone who knew him, Carlson would purchase Cobain's suicide weapon at the singer's request, and later say to Cross, "If Kurt was suicidal, he sure hid it from me."

Of all the Seattle bands to hit it big during the heyday of grunge, Nirvana and Pearl Jam were by far the most popular, and Pearl Jam wasted little time in imploding—albeit less spectacularly than Nirvana—in the face of its outsized success. Lead singer Eddie Vedder was given more and more to growling sarcastically in public about his band's celebrity, and growing more surly and more drunk at performances, until finally the band picked a hopeless fight with TicketMaster (which controlled fans' and performers' access to nearly every concert venue in the United States) and dropped out of sight almost entirely after deciding not to tour at all in 1994. One day I called the band's manager, Kelly Curtis, to ask what had happened, and caught him in the mood for conversation. "You called me at a good time," he said. "I was just sitting here feeling bummed about it."

I walked over to the office of Curtis Management, which was located in a picturesquely seedy second-floor walkup above the Puppy Club at Fifth and Denny, near a fountain built around a bust of Chief Seattle. The headquarters looked like a private detective's office in an old B-movie. Its floors were slanted, its doors crooked, its walls grimy. It was furnished mostly with secondhand stuff—old desks, overstuffed chairs, a tattered couch—and was littered with magazines, piles of paper, discarded food containers, and a crowd of young hangers-on with assorted piercings, tattoos, and a tremendous amount of free time.

Curtis was sitting glumly alone in his office, smoking cigarette after cigarette, at a desk facing a wall on which was hung a guitar that Cobain had smashed at the end of a Nirvana show. He was thirty, but looked like he had been aged prematurely by chain-smoking and the stresses of his job.

Before I could sit down, he launched into his tale.

During its salad days, Pearl Jam's members resolved to keep their concert ticket prices low no matter how popular they became. Now, the most popular band in the world, they were in a position where they could more or less name their price. And prices were high: The Eagles, for example, sold out two performances in the Tacoma Dome, the Seattle area's most popular large concert venue, with ticket prices of $45, $60, and $85 that year. But Pearl Jam wanted its shows to be affordable to kids, and accordingly decided to set an $18 maximum ticket price. They first ran afoul of TicketMaster when they decided to stage some free Seattle-area performances over the 1992 Labor Day weekend. TicketMaster wanted to assess a $1 service charge for the free tickets, and the band balked, finally deciding to distribute its own tickets. For its 1993 tour, Pearl Jam charged $18 per ticket and forced souvenir and T-shirt vendors to lower their prices, absorbing a loss in income to the band that promoters estimated at $2 million.

In 1994, Pearl Jam went after TicketMaster, which had been charging between $4 and $8 in service charges for $18 Pearl Jam tickets. The band wanted TicketMaster to charge $1.80 or less, and when TicketMaster refused, Pearl Jam decided to tour without using the company for any of its concerts. After performing in New York and Detroit, the band discovered that it couldn't get into any more venues because TicketMaster had contracts with the venues stipulating that they never stage a show without using TicketMaster as their exclusive ticket distributor. If Pearl Jam wanted to stage concerts using a different distributor, it would have to do so in venues it somehow built itself. The band ended up canceling its 1994 tour. "It's possible to do a tour without TicketMaster," Curtis told me, "but it's an incredible pain in the ass." Pearl Jam decided to spend a year building a TicketMaster-free infrastructure in the form of outdoor venues that, Curtis said, "we'll build from the ground up."

The band also filed a complaint with the U.S. Justice Department, and two of its members found themselves testifying in 1994 before a Congressional committee. When Curtis and guitarists Stone Gossard and Jeff Ament flew to Washington to testify, they decided to spend their free time at the Holocaust Museum. Admission to the museum was free, but there was a $3 service charge for the tickets—distributed by TicketMaster. "That blew me away," said Curtis. "They had a service charge for a free ticket into the *Holocaust Museum*."

Pearl Jam had always been a little at odds with the other Seattle bands, partly because Vedder, a southern Californian, was a latecomer to the scene, hiring on with the band after Andrew Wood's death just as the Nirvana juggernaut was taking off. When world media started descending on Seattle in 1991, Vedder proved the most talkative, and he emerged in magazines and television broadcasts as the spokesman for and leading public figure in the Seattle "scene"—his relative lack of familiarity with it notwithstanding. Most other grunge musicians regarded Vedder's subsequent avowed discomfort with celebrity as a pose similar to his Californian's pose as a Seattleite—particularly since he displayed his angst so publicly. After the Screaming Trees' Van Conner unburdened himself to me about his woes, he begged me not to make too big a deal of his sorrows. "I don't want to come off sounding like Eddie Vedder crying about how 'It's *such hell* being a rock star,'" he said, mock-bleating.

After weeks of searching, I had tracked Conner down in 1996 in his home on Camano Island, an hour or so north of Seattle. The band had not released a record since 1992's *Sweet Oblivion*, and I mostly wanted to find out why they had vanished just when they seemed to have hit their stride as musicians.

Conner's home was about as far from civilization as you could get on the west side of the Cascades. It took me forever to get there—it was at the opposite end of Camano Island from the only bridge connecting it with the mainland, and had been built in some woods at the end of a series of almost unmappable twists and turns in the island's roads. Conner, with his wife and child, had been sitting out there for a couple of years— "working," as he put it, "on my problems." His house was surprisingly tidy, except for the room in which he did his songwriting. A small space with a small window looking out at some woods, it had a desk with an eight-track recorder on it, the rest of the room being strewn with tapes, discs, clothing, books, and discarded junk. In one corner, leaning against the wall, nearly buried in junk, sat the framed platinum record of the band's hit "Nearly Lost You," which was part of the soundtrack for the hit movie *Singles*. When I asked Conner about it, he just waved his hand dismissively.

A working band for more than ten years, Screaming Trees had had an unusually long and productive career. They started touring years before most of the other soon-to-be-famous Seattle bands had even been formed. Conner described those years now as an endless demanding lark. The rigors of touring the entire nation by van, playing every night for two-month stretches, was exhausting. Arrangements were haphazard: The band would play in one town, then send one of the members out into the crowd near the end of the performance looking for someone willing to put them up for the night. They would get up next morning, drive all day, play again. . . . "If I were going on tour like that now," Conner said, "I'd be about dead."

After five years—by 1988—alternative rock had grown into something economically viable for musicians. The scene consisted of a club network that took form largely to furnish venues to touring SST-label bands. The circuit sustained bands, like Screaming Trees, "whose music," Conner said, "was friendly enough that you could play it on college radio, but at the same time was too weird to be in the mainstream." Tour by tour through the late eighties, the Screaming Trees crowds grew larger, the record sales greater. By the time their last SST record, *Buzz Factory*, was issued in 1989, sales had climbed to over 30,000—pretty much as good as it got for an alternative label.

Although the band never made enough money to live on—generally, their record sales would barely earn back the advances given the group to make the record, and performance fees covered their expenses but little else while they were on the road—Screaming Trees found themselves playing in front of increasingly enthusiastic audiences. Twice they toured Europe, where they played to packed houses all over the continent.

Between tours, they would return to Ellensburg to work and save up money. Lead singer Mark Lanegan worked variously in pea fields, in a potato warehouse, as a fence-builder, in gas stations, in the Conner brothers' parents' video store, and so on. The jobs were easy to come by, Ellensburg being a refuge for underachievers. "It was the kind of town," Conner said, "where people gave you work that would free you up to follow your various pursuits—like watching television."

Sitting at his kitchen table now, Conner seemed to remember that time with tremendous fondness—as did Lanegan, who had met with me a few days before at Seattle's Elliott Bay Bookstore. "That was before being a musician just became a job," Lanegan had said. None of the band members expected to attain stardom or wealth, or to be performing and recording into their thirties. "We never really thought about music as a career or anything," Lanegan said. "We never dreamed we'd be doing it this long, or even looked down the road. It was just that we were having a lot of fun making records and goofing off, and for us it was just great to be able to get out of town and travel. We could make a little bit of a living when we were on the road. But then we'd come back and either have to get a job or quick make another record and get on the road again. We never really thought about the long-term possibilities."

Even so, as record sales grew and demand for Trees concerts grew along with it, the band eventually decided it needed a manager, as the rigors and obligations of nonstop touring grew into more than they could handle on their own. As nearly every high-profile Seattle band did in those days, they signed on with Susan Silver, who had a music-management company in partnership with Kelly Curtis until the two eventually formed separate companies. The first thing Silver told the band was that it needed to sign with a major record label. "We were like, 'What?'" Conner said. "Why would we want to do that? For us, music was just a lot of fun, more or less something we were having a good time doing. It beat sitting around Ellensburg working at those crappy jobs." They finally told Silver that, if she wanted, she could invite record-label representatives to attend one of their New York shows. Executives from Epic, who by 1990 decided that the alternative music scene had grown into something with commercial potential, showed up. Not long after, Epic signed the band, which began work on its first major-label record (eventually entitled *Uncle Anesthesia*), released early in 1991.

It should have been a thrill. After ten years of playing a grimy club circuit well out of the lucrative limelight, Screaming Trees was on the threshold of stardom and wealth, enjoying lavish support from the recording technology and marketing machinery of a huge record company. But no sooner did the state-of-the-art studio door close behind the band than they all wanted out. "We didn't even want to be in the same room with each other anymore, and it shows on that record," Lanegan said. Their sudden ascent into the commercial rock industry was utterly at odds with the definition the band members had always had of themselves. It was as if they had ascended into hell. "Everybody in the band was like, 'Big whoop,'" Conner said. "It was out of this weird thing of being on a major label all of a sudden. We just didn't have as much heart in it as our records before that."

The Trees reacted to their new major-label status by feuding constantly and "just going through the motions" of recording. When the record was issued, the band did a brief tour marred by onstage fistfights between band members. Even so, sales almost immediately hit 40,000. Given that the band felt *Uncle Anesthesia* was the worst work they had ever done—and indeed, it is the least interesting of the Screaming Trees' albums—the sales figures were shocking.

Still, the sales only made the musicians more depressed. Conner and drummer Mark Pickerel left the band, Lanegan went back to Sub Pop to record a solo album, and it looked as if Screaming Trees had hit the end of the road. But within a year, after having gone off to various forms of solitude to write songs, the band hired a new drummer—Barrett Martin—and started talking again about making music. "We decided," Conner said sardonically, "to make One Last Record, the best record we had ever made." They convened in New York late in 1991 to record, and "I don't know, it was really a lot of just feeling put into it or something that made it all really good. About halfway through, I remember listening to what we'd done and thinking, 'Wow, this is really going to be cool."

While the band was recording, Nirvana's *Nevermind* was released, and the grunge phenomenon was unleashed. For the first time, it was commercially permissible to play alternative music on mainstream radio. "Nearly Lost You," a song from the album Screaming Trees was recording—1992's *Sweet Oblivion*—started playing on radio stations all over the world. When the album was released, Conner recalled, "it just started selling, and we kept touring and touring and touring and touring, and it kept on selling." With album sales at 400,000 and rising, Screaming Trees had arrived.

Pleased as they were with the album itself—not only was it Screaming Trees' best work, but the best, with Nirvana's *Nevermind*, of all the grunge albums—the experience of hitting it commercially big was little more than *Uncle Anesthesia* writ large. Screaming Trees just couldn't seem to fit into the role of "rock star." Everything about the role, from the splendidly appointed tour buses to the large, luxurious performance venues to the endless series of interviews with fawning journalists, left the musicians feeling disaffected and alienated. It was as if they no longer knew why they were writing and performing songs. "When we were done touring," Conner said, "it was almost like all the smoke cleared and we were just standing in the middle of a field alone. It was like, 'What do I do now?'"

The band was surrounded by people who felt they knew the answer. "Everybody was telling us, 'You have to hurry up and put out another record! Right away! You've got to get out there while it's hot!' This time there was all this expectation, where in the past we would write songs because we liked them. So we tried writing again this time, and they just didn't come. The songs just did not come out, did not work. We wrote for like half a year or something, and I knew they weren't as good, but we thought that if we got in the studio, we could pull it off again somehow." By mid-1993, they met to record the new work. "And we went in there and there was no spark at all, there was just nothing. It was just really depressing. It was like trying to make something out of nothing, and it didn't work. So we kept writing, and we wrote more and more, and it seemed like every time we'd get something that we thought was good, it just like would fall apart." Eventually, they recorded an album's worth of songs, then refused to release any of them.

By now, virtually everyone among the big Seattle bands was in full retreat from center stage. The Screaming Trees members went their separate ways—Van's brother Gary Lee Conner to New York, Van to Camano Island, Martin and Lanegan to Seattle—to write in solitude. Lanegan recorded another solo album on Sub Pop, Gary Lee worked on a series of private music projects, Van wrote songs and built his new house, and Martin hooked up with bassist J. B. Saunders and two other disaffected grunge celebrities—Pearl Jam guitarist Mike McCready and Alice in Chains lead singer Layne Staley, who had been hiding in the mists of heroin addiction—to form the group Mad Season, which recorded and released a mournful album, *Above*, in 1995.

The nearly four years between the success of *Sweet Oblivion* and our conversation, Conner said, had been "hellish. For me, it's been really hard, and Mark's gone through hell too." Conner had spent the time writing songs with no particular purpose in mind, and going over again and again in his mind the reasons for having gotten into the music business in the first place. "It was really weird, going from 30,000 to 400,000. It's almost like we have been on this steady course for the last ten years, sticking kind of down the same road of being just a rock band, and everything just changed around us. We started out doing this and kept doing it and kept doing it, then all of a sudden we're in the mainstream now, and it's bizarre. It's like we went from being totally out in left field to being right in the middle."

He felt that all the Seattle bands who inadvertently hit it big had moved more or less along the same path. "We all just kind of like took our music seriously, I guess, but at the same time tried hard to not take it seriously. There's some kind of weird middle ground there, when you're playing your music or whatever, you're serious about it, but when it comes to thinking about it or making a living with it, it's more like, 'I really didn't have anything better to do.' We had absolutely no expectations of ever becoming actually successful as a band. There's some reason you keep going, although you don't know what it is. It's almost like we just walked into this blindly and ended up where we are today . . . The whole Seattle thing was just being totally balls-out and over the top, just having no respect for yourself, no restrictions when you're playing, you just kind of let loose." Insulated, isolated, he and his friends had thrived until the industry hunted them down and set them free from relative anonymity. "Now I feel like a guy who's been in prison for a long time, gets out, and doesn't know what to do."

Late in 1995, the musicians reconvened and began work on a new set of songs that would be released in 1996 as an album entitled *Dust*. It would be a swan song, of sorts—their last record—although they would tour one more time and do a few Seattle-area shows before breaking up in 2000. One song—"Dying Days"—stands as a requiem, with a little vision of Cobain, for the Seattle music community that fame destroyed. Describing what "used to be my city" as a "ghost town," the singer walks through the ruins of the Seattle that nurtured and sustained grunge, lamenting the misdirection success has forced all these musicians' lives to take. Near the end of the song, bereft, he moans, "Yes, it's too late, this life isn't mine," and he cries out to God for relief.

I'd quote more, as per the wishes of the song's writers, but the restrictive permissions policy of Sony/ATV, the corporation holding the copyright, prevented it.

Revelation

I was sitting in David Brewster's office one morning in 1995, during a *Weekly* editorial meeting, watching Brewster gnaw on his favorite bone: How to get at Seattle's identity. He had been exploring that issue in his paper for nearly twenty years now, and seemed no closer to an answer than when he first asked the question. He turned to his youngest staffer, Mike Romano, who had moved to Seattle from the East Coast immediately after finishing college, taken an internship at the *Weekly*, and parlayed it into a staff writing position. "Mike, why did you come to Seattle in the first place?" he asked.

"Because it's cool," Romano answered dismissively, as if the answer were obvious.

"That's so *fascinating*! I came here to save it!"

There *was* something shocking about hearing Seattle described as "cool," even after all that had happened by 1995. It made me wonder about my perception of the national perception of the city. I felt like I'd lived through Seattle's transition from Brewster's backwater to Romano's Rome without noticing it was taking place. All along, I had been regarding the rather stunning number of Seattle successes as aberrations—successes, like that of the grunge musicians, of Seattleites in spite of their Seattleness. Aside from the occasional lapse into pretension, the city—my version of it, at any rate—remained resolutely devoid of glamour, resistant to attention, disdainful of ambition, happily obscure, wise enough to understand that its happy condition, bestowed on it by Nature and a function of its remoteness from civilization, was far more valuable, sustaining, and satisfying than the shallow, showy, short-lived thrills afforded by ambition and celebrity.

Romano's statement, though, delivered with that unspoken "Duh!," made me wonder how a Seattle like that could be so attractive—so *cool*—in the eyes of a nation where nothing mattered so much as glamour, celebrity, hype, and promotion. Romano's very presence signaled that Seattle in 1995 projected an image opposite that of times past. Chronically anxious, constantly restless, disgruntled, always angling for ways to promote his byline, Romano was by far the most nakedly ambitious employee in the history of the *Weekly*. He pitched every story idea in every editorial meeting with the arm-waving earnestness of a kid convinced he'd found the shortcut to a Pulitzer. When not trying to sell his editors on grandiose ideas—exposing various Microsoft crimes, bringing what he insisted was grunge's racism to light, accusing a prominent family-values Republican congressperson of having had an illicit love affair—he was entering every journalism-award competition he could find and pitching stories to the *New Yorker* and the *New York Times*, often leaving copies of his query letters in the office printer or copier for his co-workers to find. His ceaseless pursuits made him the object of considerable mirth and derision at the *Weekly*, largely because they were so wackily out of scale, so silly in a Seattleite. As far as anyone at the *Weekly* knew, Romano was the only person in the city who came to Seattle to make his mark on the world; generally, people came here to avoid being scarred by it.

I used to watch him in meetings, pounding on the conference table and talking about "getting" Bill Gates, about "bringing that sucker down," about "going after" this or that public figure, and I'd find myself lost in a futile effort: trying to imagine a place for a kid like this in the Seattle I carried around in my head.

Deciding one day to try to quantify Seattle's cool, I wandered over to the Chamber of Commerce offices, which had a wall of file cabinets overflowing with newspaper and magazine clippings about Seattle from all over the nation. I discovered that the attention-surplus trouble started in 1989, when Seattle was listed as the nation's "most livable" city in five different publications. From then through 1995, the accolades accrued like barnacles. Seattle was cited variously as "the Number Two Best City for Raising Kids" (not, to judge from grunge, a designation the Seattle kids themselves would have bestowed), second-best city in which to locate a business, city with the best hotels in the United States, Number Ten on *Condé-Nast Traveler's* list of "world's top cities," *USA Today's* Number One City of the Future, the best American city for women, best city for business, best North American city for bicycling, sixth-best U.S. metropolitan area for working mothers, the "fifth hottest sports city" in the country, and—according to *Trailer Life*—one of the country's best destinations for "RVers." Even the Mariner-maligned Kingdome came in for an honor: "The Seattle Kingdome again remains the showpiece of the Seattle sky line, as it was intended 20 years ago," declared *Roofer Magazine*.

"Again remains"?

I slogged through reams of American newspaper and monthly magazine travel-section stories, all spinning fantasies about Seattle as a beautiful, exotic, nature-embraced city that provided an enchanting alternative to older, decrepit, frayed, and frantic urban centers. The Seattle described on these pages was alive with a vibrant culture, rustic charm, European ambience, a stunning natural setting, Inner Peace, and coffee, coffee, coffee. *Sunset* magazine, in an archetypal twelve-page feature replete with pictures of flower vendors, espresso stands, the Pike Place Market, Pioneer Square, "jolly and helpful" Seattle police, and various natural landmarks, described Seattle as "a relaxed city where life satisfaction is measured not in money but in quality of life." Not to be outdone, *Albuquerque Monthly* declared, "This is a city whose beauty and sophistication rival that of any in the country."

Perhaps, I thought, hyperambitious Mike Romano had set his sights on Seattle after coming across the issue of *Cosmopolitan* that dispensed this breathless advice: "Lady, you want a *lot*—and Seattle is the place to find it . . . Seattle is the place to go if you're competitive and want to throw yourself headlong into your career and make your mark. The quality of life is so high that the market attracts top talent, so expect to be up against the best and brightest . . ."

At the same time, *Mediaweek* was characterizing Seattle as "possibly the last bastion of counterculture." Was this a city that had something for everybody or what?

I finally decided it was not so much what all these publications were saying that was significant; the significance lay in the sheer number of them that were raving about the city. Seattle was your basic ravishing beauty, and the nation was like the adoring males around Marilyn Monroe in *The Misfits*. Driven to the brink of madness by the city's natural beauty, newspaper and magazine writers everywhere were trying to rationalize their reaction by finding proportionately extravagant depth beneath the extravagant surface. The details in their adoring declarations were more a function of their fantasies than of anything inherent in the object of their ardor.

Serious people in Seattle who studied cities, though, began believing that Seattle did indeed have as much to offer the mind as the eye—that its cultural environment was catching up to its natural environment. They believed that changes in the national economy, along with Seattle's public image, lured a new kind of citizen here whose presence drove the city toward ever-greater cultural improvement. Bill Beyers, a Seattle scholar who studied urban centers, told me that Seattle was locked in what Gates would call a positive-feedback loop: The natural splendor attracts a better cultural class of citizens, the newcomers increase the cultural splendor, which in turn attracts even better citizens. "One of the most rapidly growing areas of the economy here," he said, "employs people who sell information of one kind or another." People in this line of work can live wherever they want—they don't have to gravitate toward factories or other places dealing in tangible products or assets. "There's an undercurrent of very special businesses whose people have a degree of footlooseness that is unprecedented." These people become demanding consumers of cities, their decisions on where to live based more on what a city offers and less on employment opportunities, which no longer depend on physical location. Beyers believed that this new kind of citizen/worker was coming to Seattle because it had more natural gifts to offer; once here, the new residents raised the level of taste and sophistication, demanding more in the way of cultural gifts. This was more than likely the reason Seattle in the mid-1990s had more theaters per capita and a higher level of per-capita "book consumption" than any other city in the country. Seattle newcomers put a huge emphasis on what Beyers called the "quality-of-life industry," and the more they moved here, the bigger that industry grew.

Some days, though, it seemed that even among these cultured and career-successful migrants, the traditional image of Seattle as a haven for failure and haplessness remained its main attraction. It was a place to recover, seek redemption, start over—as it had been since the days of Doc Maynard and as it was being depicted now in movies (*Singles, Sleepless in Seattle*) and television (*Frasier*) in the 1990s. I met one newcomer, a twenty-seven-year-old computer professional named Ian Proffer, who moved to Seattle with no job prospects and in short order talked his way into a job at Microsoft. Proffer came to the city because he felt comfortably at home here in the wake of his divorce. "I saw the appropriate opportunity to end my marriage, quit my job, start a new life, all at once!" he said. Invoking *Frasier*, the television show about a newly divorced Boston psychiatrist who moves to Seattle in search of a new beginning and a new identity, and *Sleepless in Seattle*, in which a devastated young widower moves to Seattle for the same reason, Proffer encapsulated the reason he felt the city was made to order for him: "All the loser guys come here."

Long-time Seattleites, meanwhile, were beginning to fixate on the disadvantages of being the apple of the national eye. Sustainable Seattle, a civic group fearful that massive immigration was destroying the very charms drawing the migrant hordes, filed a report in 1995 packed with charts showing declining health in the city, including a lessening of civility and a loss of wetlands, biodiversity, salmon, and various other former hallmarks of Northwest living.

I was always oscillating between comfort and restlessness, complacency and rage, when I thought about these matters, and now I felt complacency taking hold as I read Sustainable Seattle's report. It struck me as the classic native Seattleite's reaction to change—panic over the downside, the conviction that every step closer to civilization is a stomping destructive step away from paradise. I decided to believe that all the forces trying to impel Seattle toward big-cityness would ultimately prove harmless, however infuriating they were in their beginnings, and that as vexing as were all the various gaudy displays of Seattle's emerging new wealth—particularly that galling future baseball stadium—eventually it would revert, as it always had in the past, to its Maynardtown essence. Change for the better here is always fleeting, I kept telling myself, and Seattle always goes back to being Seattle.

Already, you could see reassuring signs that the reversion was beginning. Clark Humphrey, noting with relief that the spotlight had passed over the Seattle music scene, wrote in *Loser* that Seattle would be better off for its return to obscurity:

> One of the biggest aspects about the Seattle Scene mania was its supposed authenticity. As the myth goes, this isn't something a couple of packagers in a penthouse office dreamed up. It's supposed to be a folk phenomenon, a community of ideas and styles that came up from the street. In fact, a lot of it *was* dreamed up by a couple of packagers in a penthouse office, but they exploited something that had been developing haphazardly for over a decade, digesting and rejecting assorted influences along the way. As

with anything real, its creators didn't give a damn about authenticity (much of the apparel and terminology was lifted from 1981 hard-core bands). . . . Nobody intended for the mania to happen the way it did, and just about everybody was glad to see it subside. . . . There is no singular "Seattle Sound," but there is a common Seattle attitude. We believe in making great music and art, not in the trappings of celebrity.

BBC documentarian Bernadette O'Brien, who came to Seattle to make a documentary about its charms, came face-to-face with that "common Seattle attitude" when potential subject after potential subject refused to be interviewed. She left the city baffled and furious. "There is this incredible *loser mentality* here," she said to me. "How could a company like Microsoft ever have come out of a place like this?"

It left me with the comforting sense that Seattle would emerge from its fifteen minutes of fame relatively unscathed. But then *New Republic* editor and *Crossfire* performer Michael Kinsley moved here. It was the most highly publicized move to Seattle in the city's history—a relocation viewed on the East Coast as proof positive either of an epochal shift or that Kinsley had gone mad. Pundits weighed in up and down the East Coast, interpreting the move, trying to decipher its meaning. *Newsweek* ran a cover story with Kinsley on the cover, posing the question "Is everyone moving to Seattle?"—the implication being that if he, the consummate East Coast wonk, could find happiness in Seattle, everyone could, and the rest of the country was about to be drained of the last of its brains.

One night shortly after Kinsley's move, Brewster called me and another *Weekly* staffer, Bruce Barcott, into his office and invited us to have dinner with him, Kinsley, and James Fallows, who was in Seattle promoting his new book, *Breaking the News*. The three Harvard-Yale alums were old college chums. The five of us sat down to dinner in a new, high-end restaurant with such a bewildering array of cutlery at each place that I would have spent the entire meal trying to figure out when and how to use all of it had I not been so busy being starstruck. Barcott and I, Northwest natives, sat through the proceeding drinking like maniacs and staring at each other in disbelief, guffawing like a couple of backwoodsmen astounded at the famous city-slickers they ended up sitting with, nudging and pinching each other like people trying to figure out whether they're asleep and dreaming or awake and living a fantasy. The fiasco ended with the three Ivy Leaguers engaging in a ritual east-coastern "Tut-tut, old fellow" Zemblan wrestling hold struggle over the check— "No, no, my good man, I insist!"—while I tried desperately to get another bottle of wine ordered before they settled the argument.

We walked through Pioneer Square afterward to Fallows's reading at Elliott Bay Books, after which Kinsley decided to go home rather than go out for drinks. "This," he said of his move to Seattle, "is the great adventure of my life." By now, it was nearly midnight and he was afraid to walk back to his car alone—a fear-habit, I decided, left over from his days of living in Washington, D.C., one of the most dangerous cities in the world. I offered to walk him back to his car, wondering, with my Seattle native's condescension toward newcomers, how long it would take him to realize how *different* Seattle was, and how there was no longer any need for those survival skills that had gotten him through his crummy life back east.

We walked back through Pioneer Square, the buildings empty, the streets deserted, Kinsley looking around nervously and asking me constantly if it was "safe" to be walking around downtown this late at night. There was something almost quaint about his inability to relax—his scars from a lifetime spent in East Coast cities clearly would never heal. "You'll learn," I kept insisting, "that life here is legitimately different—we don't have the kinds of problems you lived with back there."

I got him to his car and watched him drive safely away, then walked back through Pioneer Square to the ferry terminal, feeling alternately like a yokel and a sophisticate. Then the next morning I read that a man had been stabbed to death by two derelicts in Pioneer Square.

This is when I first started noticing that outsiders were looking more and more at Seattle as a wrecked paradise. An acquaintance from New York, Rachel Schnoll, visited and delivered herself of this postmortem when she was back in New York: "Portland's more my image of Seattle than Seattle was. Seattle seemed kind of industrial and sprawling. It wasn't even *raining*. It wasn't as hip when I got there as its reputation. And there's no more grunge—that's just sort of evolved into alternative, which is really mainstream now."

There is no question that she was right about grunge. The only band still producing good music was Screaming Trees, and after the 1996 release of its *Dust* album—which would be its last—the band vanished again, with lead singer Mark Lanegan lapsing into drug addiction. The rest of the movement had been killed off by celebrity, money, heroin, and *Vogue* magazine, which had published a grunge fashion spread with supermodels draped in $2,000 designer-labeled, artfully torn flannel jackets and wool sweaters.

I had to admit too that everything linked in the national public mind with Seattle now looked monstrous, predacious, power-obsessed, infinitely greedy. The most-livable-city stories started giving way to stories of Seattle-based corporate evil. Boeing, after driving all its other American competitors out of business, was buying up its sole remaining U.S. rival, McDonnell-Douglas. Microsoft, once a computing-power-to-the-people revolutionary, now was under renewed siege by the U.S. Justice Department and perceived around the world as a monopolistic monster, with revelation after revelation highlighting its drive to crush the life out of its competitors. And on a visit to Minneapolis, I was driven past a new Starbucks outlet while my escort berated me for being from Seattle. "We *hate* Starbucks here," she said.

I was stunned. "Why?"

She pointed across the street to a locally owned, locally beloved coffeehouse. "Because they keep moving in next store to our Caribou Coffees, and charging really low prices until the Caribou place goes out of business. Then they jack up their prices. They're just trying to kill everybody off."

The business pages back home, meanwhile, were displaying new Seattle-sellout stories every day. Starbucks signed a distribution deal with Pepsi, Redhook with Budweiser, Microsoft with the creators of Barney. And then *Billboard* announced one day that Sub Pop was bought by Time Warner for $20 million.

That last deal was a telling shocker. I called Jonathan Poneman—who only a year before had told the *Weekly* "I did not get into this business to discuss deals"—to ask if it was true. It was, he said, then added excitedly, "Bruce and I are really psyched about this deal."

By 1995, technology money—all of it either directly or indirectly generated by Microsoft—was flooding through Seattle, dramatically changing its urban and suburban landscape and the expectations and values of its citizenry. Suddenly, money and the young people who held massive amounts of it were showing up everywhere—highly visible, powerful, *worshipped*. Kathryn Robinson reported in the *Weekly* that $570 million in vested Microsoft stock options (excluding the wealth of Bill Gates and Paul Allen) now sat fat in the local economy, and the most visible effect of that infusion was the dramatic change in size, scale, and design of the new houses cropping up everywhere along the eastern shores of Lake Washington.

Local fundraisers from medicine, politics, the arts, and philanthropic organizations saw a sea change taking place: Old-money Seattle was giving way to Brand-new money Seattle. They were adapting as quickly as they could, developing new habits and new pitches. "I had to learn," one veteran fund-raiser told me, "to take off my tie before driving across the lake to have lunch."

The imprimatur bestowed on an enterprise either by Microsoft money or by someone holding it was seen as an unquestioned sign of the undertaking's legitimacy. Microsoft retiree Scott Oki became the first techno-millionaire to take a seat on the board of the University of Washington, amid great expectations that he would shake things up and make the university modern, more efficient, more agile. (Oki, still in his thirties, cut something of a hilarious figure at UW board meetings. Sitting in an ornate, echoing, Gothic room at a massive table among doddering graybeards, a laptop perched in front of him, he looked wackily out of place as the proceedings droned on around him like the parody of a British legal proceeding.) Another retiree, Ida Cole, took over the landmark Paramount Theater and began a massive rehabilitation project there, her $40 million fortune seen as the landmark's salvation. Retiree Tina Podlodowski won election to the Seattle City Council on the theory that she would bring high-tech efficiency to chronically inefficient government. Allen built a splendid new library on the University of Washington campus, with Gates building a new hall nearby. Millionaires, most of them still in their thirties, were starting new companies and moving into philanthropy or political action all over town. "No other company," Russ Prince, president of a Pennsylvania research and consulting firm specializing in the philanthropic activities of the affluent, told Robinson, "has the power that Microsoft has."

The prevailing belief in Seattle held that the secrets to Microsoft's success—drive, focus, high intelligence, endless energy—would be transferred via these retirees to the rest of the region. Schools—where many young Microsoft retirees devoted their attention—would become wired, efficient, more effective; government, notorious for stifling process, would become a juggernaut, delivering unprecedented return on the taxpayer's investment; new businesses would bloom in Seattle, many of them recreating the outsized success of Microsoft (the phrase "the next Microsoft," in fact, was heard everywhere) as the Pacific Northwest moved entirely into a "new economy" of high-tech businesses run by founders with a new kind of intelligence so powerful as to be virtually mistake-proof.

Microsoft alums stood out by virtue of an affected manner characterized by rapid speech, frequent interruptions of others, and demands that meetings stay "focused" or "on track" and lead quickly to a set of "takeaways" leading in turn to resolution or success. The anointed tended toward impatience with mere mortals, who were by definition less intelligent than those "forged in the crucible" of the company, as one young retiree put it in a conversation with Robinson. Longtime philanthropists and board members of charitable organizations were appalled at the arrogance of these newcomers, who seemed to believe that their presence and brainpower alone were worth far more to society than their money. "One could argue," wrote Robinson, "that overconfident overachievers have been Microsoft's most significant contribution to the world thus far."

Lured by the prospect of putting in a few years' hard work and long hours in exchange for retirement by age forty, people began leaving mainstream businesses for jobs at startups with no products, customers, or apparent means of ever making money. Writers and editors I knew started drifting out of journalism to work for Medio, a Microsoft-alum-founded company publishing a "magazine" on CD-ROM. Others went to work for an array of electronic publishers creating everything from multimedia educational products on CD-ROM to electronic reference works to CD-ROMs that taught you how to play the guitar. Companies siphoning marketing and engineering talent away from the Boeings of the world included Virtual Vision, which manufactured a head-mounted television set slightly larger than a pair of eyeglasses; Virtual i/O, manufacturer of a head-mounted video display for movies, games, and television; startups making video displays for exercise equipment that would make it possible to run on a treadmill through video-rendered landscapes or to play tennis against the digital video image of a pro tennis star; and on and on and on and on.

By far the most prolific father of new companies, buildings, yachts, jets, and other visible assets bought with Microsoft money was Paul Allen, who proved more than profligate in the 1990s. His purchases of a Boeing 757, another jet, two massive yachts, a 387-acre camp on Lopez Island in the storied San Juans, an entire San Juan island, a Montana ranch, and various other land parcels, companies, buildings, technologies, and toys kept him almost constantly in the news.

While Gates was buried in the work of growing Microsoft and fending off armies of federal regulators, the retired Allen was constantly turning up as a conspicuous consumer of companies and celebrity. He bought and sold TicketMaster and a large share of America Online, and was investing heavily in wireless communication, TV cable companies, Hollywood studios, and Internet enterprises, apparently intent on becoming a new-media mogul. His media enterprises included a company he founded, Starwave, that was to help pioneer the movement of print and electronic media onto the Internet. Starwave, which entered into various deals, including one with ABC News to create abcnews.com, started madly hiring editors and contracting with writers to establish an online publishing empire.

A typical Allen story—this one in the *Seattle Times*—included this characterizing item: "Last month, Allen hosted a lavish bash in Venice, Italy, for 200 friends, family and Hollywood stars, including Robin Williams, Geena Davis and Sting. He flew them in from California, then shuttled them by gondola to a medieval masquerade ball where they were entertained by jazz saxophonist Tom Scott, guitarist Carlos Santana and Allen himself, who also played the guitar."

Allen bought or funded a tremendous number of companies in the 1990s, began building what would eventually be called the Experience Music Project—a high-tech rock-and-roll museum and entertainment venue—and announced, in 1995, his intention to buy the languishing Seattle Seahawks, whose current owner, California real-estate baron Ken Behring, was trying to move the team to Anaheim.

The Seahawks purchase, though, came with a condition attached: Allen would "save" the franchise, as local fans were clamoring for him to do, only if taxpayers entered into a "partnership" with him by replacing the Kingdome with a new state-of-the-art, taxpayer-financed, $425 million football stadium. Given his net worth of $13 billion, paying for the stadium himself would have been equivalent to something like a $15 investment from me, but Allen nonetheless insisted that he could not save the Seahawks unless local citizens joined him as partners in the salvation effort.

Immediately, King County politicians reacted in horror, having just been through their battle with Nintendo and the Seattle Mariners. "Allen's purchase doesn't remove the financial pressures on us in any way," said Ron Sims. Added fellow councilmember Maggie Fimia, who had voted against the baseball stadium funding package, "We've signaled with our arrangement with the Mariners that we have no bottom line. We talk tough, but when we get pressure from the business community and the fans, we give in."

The battle over building another stadium would rage into 1997, with local resistance to another round of stadium taxes strong enough to result in the state legislature putting a voter referendum on the ballot, asking citizens statewide to approve a $425 million stadium tax package. The referendum would be held in a special election in June 1997, with Allen—in an historic move—underwriting the $4.2 million cost of the vote.

The billionaire put another $500,000 into selling the package to voters, declaring in a television ad that "I can't do it without you." *Seattle Times* sports columnist Blaine Newnham insisted that the deal was a good investment for taxpayers because Allen was a proven winner. "My guess is that within five years Paul Allen's Seahawks will be in the Super Bowl," he wrote, "and have at least as great a hold on the community as the Mariners do now." Then he floated the fear forever lurking in the background whenever Seattle was afforded the opportunity to rid itself of a professional sports franchise: that the team would move elsewhere and immediately win the championship that could have been Seattle's. "But then someone in Quebec probably said that of its long-struggling hockey team, the Nordiques, who left anyway for Colorado, where, of course, they would win a Stanley Cup and break more than a few French-Canadian hearts."

The weirdest and most telling thing about the debate was the assumption by proponents and opponents alike that Allen was a successful man. The mere fact that he had $13 billion in Microsoft-minted money conferred on him the status of a can't-miss genius. Yet his wealth had been made not by him but by Gates, who built Microsoft into the money machine it became after Allen left the company in 1983. And Allen's record as an entrepreneur was terrible: None of the more than twenty companies he started had been even mildly successful, and his most successful investments—in TicketMaster and America Online—had been in already-established companies that he bought and sold at the right times. *Wired* magazine, in a 1994 feature, called Allen the "accidental zillionaire," and seemed thoroughly puzzled by his image as a brilliant success. "Allen's own companies," wrote the magazine's Paulina Borsook, "suggest that if he hadn't hooked up with the Jay Gould of our era when they were both teenagers, he might have ended up no more than, say, an engineer at Boeing or an employee at a software company."

There always seemed to be complications with Allen's enterprises. What he first called the Jimi Hendrix Museum project became mired in a lawsuit with the musician's father over the rights to Hendrix's music, with the result that the museum's name was changed to The Experience Music Project. The first company Allen founded, Asymetrix, was known in Seattle as "the reorg of the month club," and had not produced a market success in its ten-year history. Virtual Vision parlayed a hefty investment from Allen into laughter (one of its ads showed a golfer standing on the links, club in hand, while watching television on his Virtual Vision headset, blinded to the course around him) and bankruptcy. An employee from Vulcan Ventures, one of Allen's investment companies, told me that his term for any Allen-owned company was "black hole." Yet, declared the *Seattle Times* in instructing its readers to vote for the stadium referendum, "Allen is the reason to vote yes, his willingness to buy the team, to pay a portion of construction costs, to cover cost over-runs and, most of all, to provide the best product money can buy."

The campaign would prove to be ferocious, the almost-daily polling as election day neared showing the yes votes drawing inexorably closer in number to the nay-sayers. Even in 1995, when outraged opposition to the subsidy was almost unanimous, it was clear that the script would play out the way it always did in Seattle and elsewhere, and the billionaire would get his stadium. Yet nothing about either stadium deal made sense, economic or otherwise. When the dust would clear in June 1997 and a narrow majority approved the gift to Allen, a perplexed Art Thiel would write in the *Seattle Post-Intelligencer,* "We just agreed to build a stadium with a roof for playing baseball in summer, and a stadium without a roof for playing football in winter. Think about it."

In 1996, the *Weekly*'s connection to the Internet consisted of a single computer in the editorial department with a modem and an America Online account. Writers would use it only occasionally, to research the particular odd topic that had information about it residing somewhere on the Web, or to send an e-mail message. The machine was painfully slow, and few people—myself included—had much use for it.

I came into the office one afternoon, though, and found a group of writers gathered around it. They were looking at a new Web site for a Seattle company called Amazon.com, and I could hear them reacting with a mix of confusion and admiration: "Look at that! Look at that!" "How do they do this?" "I can't figure it out. . . ." Then, above the tumult, came the voice of Mike Romano: "I think it's, like, a scam to get people to give them their e-mail addresses."

After they dispersed, I sat down to study the site in detail. It claimed to offer electronic access to one million book titles, along with the ability to purchase them online and have them delivered to your door. A million titles! The largest bookstore in Seattle, located in the lavishly updated University Village shopping center, was a Barnes & Noble reputed to be the second-largest Barnes & Noble in the country, and it held only 150,000 titles. Amazon.com appeared to make available every American English-language book currently in print. I started randomly typing in authors and titles, and for each one I got back a screen with a picture of the book, its price, and the number of days it would take for the book to show up at my house.

The site seemed at once ingenious and obvious. It looked like a giant step toward what Bill Gates had called, in his recently released *The Road Ahead*, "low-friction, low-overhead capitalism" that created "efficient electronic markets that provide nearly complete instantaneous information about worldwide supply, demand, and prices." You could see at a glance what the Web site presaged: direct connection between buyer and seller, over the Internet. No more retailers! Pretty soon there'd be no more wholesalers! Even Amazon would eventually be obsolete! Everything was going to be cheaper! And the first company to demonstrate how well it could work was right here in Seattle!

Wowed, I explored the site, found a telephone number, called it up, and arranged to interview Jeff Bezos, the company founder. I walked down to Amazon's offices, which were in a crumbling light-industrial zone south of the Kingdome, directly across from the mammoth old Sears Roebuck store—an old-economy landmark that had been closed, sold, and converted into Starbucks's corporate headquarters.

It was not easy to find Amazon, which was on the second floor above a store selling tile. The door opening onto the staircase leading to Amazon was crooked, warped, and adorned with the company name in stick-on letters. The staircase was narrow, the stairs themselves worn nearly all the way through. Making my way up, I felt like a junkie calling on a dealer.

Amazon occupied a warren of small offices that looked across at the Sears/Starbucks building. The furniture was secondhand—the only new touches in the place were a few desktop personal computers and a cluster of programmers and Sun Microsystem servers off in one corner. Bezos emerged from a tiny office and greeted me with tremendous enthusiasm. He was a small, unprepossessing man, only thirty-one years old, with the happiest facial expression I've ever seen, and he had a disconcerting habit of punctuating his stories with a booming laugh that left me feeling uneasy at first, then increasingly nervous—I kept steeling myself for the next explosion, and found it harder and harder to concentrate on my questions.

"It was clear a couple of years ago that interactive retailing was coming," Bezos said. "I mean, people have been predicting that for ten or twelve years. But only now, and only for some types of products, are there enough people online for interactive retailing to make some business sense. And even at that, looking at it now, I decided that books was the only feasible product to sell this way. You look at the demographics of people online, and the demographics of people who buy books, and the demographics line up very nicely."

After getting his computer science degree from Princeton, Bezos had gone to work first for Bankers Trust, then D. E. Shaw & Co., building and maintaining computer networks for investors. In 1993, "always interested in the juxtaposition of computers and anything," he spent a few months researching the Internet, put together a business plan, rounded up investors, moved to Seattle, and set up his business in the summer of 1994, officially opening online in July 1995. Bezos built his store by acquiring connections with the electronic inventories of the nation's seven largest book wholesalers, all the formats of which are incompatible with all the others. He then wrote translation software that made all the databases readable by his computer system, and wrote more software to make the resulting "inventory" accessible by his customers.

The business was at once ingenious and simple: A customer found the book he or she wanted on Amazon's site and ordered it. Amazon in turn ordered it from the wholesaler who had it in stock, having it shipped overnight to the company's Seattle address, where it would be unpacked, combined with other books from other wholesalers in the same customer's order, repackaged, and shipped that day to wherever the customer wanted.

"Why Seattle?" I asked Bezos. With all the technology money washing through the city streets, and with all the startups taking form, I still couldn't think of Seattle as a place where people came to make it big. "Because it is only one shipping day away from the country's three largest book wholesalers," Bezos answered, "and because there is a readily available supply of talented software engineers here. A great programmer can differ from a good programmer by a factor of a hundred."

After a mere six months in business, Amazon was "growing ahead of our projections" and had already outgrown its space. Bezos and his programmers worked in their little suite while down in the basement of the building, in series of low-ceilinged rooms I had to stoop in order to walk through, legions of employees were frantically filling orders. Bezos already was looking for bigger quarters.

Early Amazon customers loved the site. Coming back to the office, I spent some time navigating through it again, and came upon a page entitled "What our customers are saying about us." All the messages there were from exuberant, enthusiastic customers astounded at their unbelievable luck. One comment in particular stood out, largely for its conciseness. "You guys," it said, "are going to make a billion dollars."

You just knew the correspondent was right. You could feel the massive good fortune in the offing as soon as you stepped into Amazon's offices. And it just seemed so *weird*. A Microsoft, you would think, judging from history, might come along once in the life of a city—and then only if some massive technological shift is under way, like the deployment of electricity or telecommunications or the internal combustion engine, and if by fluke the person born to exploit it first happens to be living there. Now it looked like Seattle, not even a century and a half old, was going to have two of them in ten years. The world was full of thousand-year-old cities that had never been through anything like this. Where would it end? How big could it possibly get? What was going to happen? Seattle had been through booms before, but this one was homegrown, and it was going to be immeasurable by any normal Seattle scale. I sat there staring at the Amazon interface on the screen, getting what felt like a privileged glimpse into the future. It was a religious experience—I felt at once awestruck and fearstruck, the recipient of Revelation, unable to tell whether the grandeur confronting me was marvelous or horrifying.

I wrote an enthusiastic story about Amazon and its prospects, ending with that billion-dollar quote from that ecstatic customer, and went on with my primitive life at the *Weekly*. But I found myself returning again and again to that Internet-connected machine and going directly to Amazon's site. I would sit there clicking directionlessly around on it for what seemed like hours at a time, reading the little descriptions of books, quotes from reviewers, reviews sent in by customers, reading again and again the little introductory essay about "Earth's biggest bookstore" on Amazon's home page, and brooding more and more obsessively about my prospects in my flat little world in relation to Amazon's prospects in its burgeoning, booming world of endless, eternal, instantly acquired prosperity. It was as if Microsoft had set off a chain reaction of nuclear proportions, and everybody that ventured into technology in Seattle now was going to be swept up in a firestorm of wealth.

One day, I saw at the bottom of the Amazon page a link I'd never noticed before: "Jobs at Amazon.com." I clicked on it and looked dully at the long list that came up of positions for programmers and financial wizards—jobs demanding skills as foreign to me as the skills brain surgeons have. I felt like a logger forced to move from his denuded wilderness into a city, where he finds himself obsolete, unemployable, helpless, adrift, useless, ignored, scorned.

Then, at the bottom of the list, I saw a listing for "editor." It took me forever to believe it was really there, and when I clicked on it and read the description—they wanted someone to read and write about books, supervise a staff of like-minded and-hearted people, good literature-loving souls every one, and collect a technology-industry salary and stock-options package into the bargain—I fell into a depressing trance. The newsroom noises around me faded to near-inaudibility, the ringing phones, clacking keyboards, conversations, whine of printers, rustle of papers all dissolving into a noisome indistinguishable background sludge while I pictured myself in an office alive with purpose, novelty, a sense of real mission, real possibility. The kind of experience the ad listed matched my own so perfectly that I felt called by it.

I sat and thought, sat and fantasized, sat and pictured myself in a new setting with new responsibilities and new dreams. In the near distance, I saw the day when I was no longer scrambling for money all the time. Then, as if awakening suddenly from deep dreamy sleep, I stood up and went off to talk to my boss.

Reincarnation

After growing up in eastern Washington and graduating from the University of Washington in 1974, Katherine Koberg had gone to New York, taken a job at *Newsweek* magazine, put in her time back east as per Seattle tradition, then come back—as per Seattle tradition—in 1983. She went to work for the *Weekly*, where she proved to have tremendous editorial gifts and a vision for alternative journalism—particularly when it came to arts coverage—that rivaled Brewster's in both energy and clarity. She also had an aptitude for management—writing budgets, firing underperformers, demanding ever-greater effort from writers, giving direction, setting vision—that is rare in the world of writing, where artistic temperaments and willfully impractical minds predominate. In short order, she became arts editor, then, in 1986, the paper's managing editor. In the years since, she discovered and developed the *Weekly*'s best writers and established the paper as the preeminent voice in Seattle arts coverage and criticism. Anyone writing a story of significant length or complexity wanted her as an editor—everything she touched, she made better.

By 1996, the *Weekly* was best known for rigorously crafted cover stories and great arts-and-entertainment coverage—the areas of the paper falling under Koberg's aegis. I had arranged—largely through screaming and begging—to have her edit both my books. I still keep among my most treasured possessions manuscript pages decorated with her handwritten comments, my favorite among these being "What could this possibly *mean?*"

Koberg was the boss I approached in the wake of reading the Amazon.com ad, and during my short walk from the *Weekly*'s Internet lifeline to her office, I underwent a rigorous and pointless self-examination. I thought about the rare opportunity I had been granted to escape the *Weekly* just as it was falling too far behind the technology boom ever to return to relevance. Seattle was about to be transformed into something the *Weekly* would never understand, and I had a chance to experience the transformation firsthand. I was convinced that Bezos and I had hit it off and that he must have been so pleased with what I had written about Amazon that the job was mine for the taking. (Out of a sense of obligation, I wallowed for a while in self-recrimination over the ethical lapse signaled by that fantasy.) And mostly I thought about the opportunity I'd missed at Microsoft; here I was now, being handed a second chance, a chance at hitting it rich for life after a few years' work, if only I had the guts to leap onto the passing freight train bound for glory before it picked up too much speed.

Everything in the office around me looked shabby. Amazon's offices, in a far more decrepit building than the *Weekly*'s trendy refurbished digs, looked somehow more splendid, more alive. Amazon was the future—success, power, prosperity, glamour—and the *Weekly* was the failed past: complacency lapsing into bewildered nostalgia.

No one would understand this more than Koberg. A year or so before, she had hit the wall I was hitting now. She had made tremendous personal sacrifices for the sake of a paper that now was fading from glory and losing connection with the city it was supposed to chronicle and civilize, and she spent increasing amounts of time alone in her office, with her door closed, sunk in a gloom she could neither understand nor control. My attempts at consoling her faltered largely because I felt the same gloom coming over me. My work was decreasing in quality and giving me decreasing satisfaction. I had failed to notice and appreciate the *Weekly*'s grungy young buildingmates before they became famous "alternative" musicians—a lapse I was beginning to regard as the defining failure of my self-styled "alternative" paper. It was harder to get excited about story assignments, partly because I felt less connected to the *Weekly* readership. Something was wrong with the paper—the creative energy in the air was gone, as was the sense that we were doing something of use to the city. I could feel myself following Koberg into a depressing cul-de-sac, having carved out a career in a tiny niche occupied by a single publication. Where does an aging alternative journalist go? Not to the daily papers; not to an adult job with adult responsibilities and adult schedules, where you are expected to behave like an adult and have an adult's resume; and certainly not into a Seattle job market where the only employers are software companies hiring engineers half your age.

So the Amazon ad was a gift from God—a chance not only to survive Seattle's latest boom (which, I realized, I had unconsciously been setting as the outer limit of my life's dream) but to actually cash in on it like everyone else.

I walked into Koberg's office and closed her door behind me. While my head was trying to figure out what to say to her, my mouth opened and began making the sounds of speech. And I heard the words:

"Katherine, I might have found the perfect job for you."

She whirled and looked at me with more energy than I'd seen from her in years. Her eyes lit up like a happily surprised child's. I brought her out and showed her the Amazon ad, and she withdrew immediately to her office to write an application letter.

I went back to my desk, where my head immediately began haranguing my heart, demanding to know why, why, why?

My heart had no articulable answers.

I told myself the usual lies—that companies like Amazon took you away from your family, that to go to work for money and the potential for a quick payoff was a sellout, that it would be a crime to abandon my calling—but none of that really rang true. The truth was that I always recoiled, instinctively and irrationally, from good fortune. And I can only attribute that to some dark impulse lurking deep in the soul of certain Seattleites. Striking it rich is for others—if it were for people like me, we never would have settled for living in Seattle in the first place. We would have gone off back in the 1980s to wherever it was that people were supposed to go to seek their fortune. Now, Seattle had turned into that place, ambitious people were pouring in here, and you felt driven into a kind of internal exile where you hoped to hide until the boom was over and things returned to normal.

In 1996 I began trying to strike an uneasy compromise between my vanity and my avowed urge to hide from the boom and its effects. Fascination with the personal computer had given way in the human imagination to far more fervid fascination with the Internet, which everyone began pegging as the next revolutionary development in computing, communications, and entertainment. The Internet was going to grow into ubiquity, this thinking went, the only question being how it would sustain itself economically once everyone was hooked up to it. How would the people building it find a way to make money off their investment? How would the new medium generate income, and for whom?

As my luck would have it, the first guess was what the guessers called "content." They believed that the Internet would be populated with "publications" or "shows" that would be free for the viewing or reading. Users would be drawn to a given site by the quality of its content, and advertisers would pay escalating rates, in proportion to the number of a given site's visitors, to be seen along with the content drawing users there. This "business model," as these fantasies were called, was identical to the *Weekly*'s—a free paper supported entirely by advertising, with ads arrayed around its stories.

The word "content" was everywhere in Internet strategyland. Even Amazon.com's investors insisted that the site needed content, in the form of book reviews and annotations, in order to draw users and get them to purchase books. Bill Gates entered into a partnership with NBC to launch MSNBC on both the Internet and television, Paul Allen's Starwave launched an abcnews.com Web site in partnership with that network, Microsoft launched Kinsley's *Slate*, and media companies around the world suddenly were in a panic to get on the new communications medium. Everywhere the conviction was the same: Only sites with compelling content would survive the coming shakeout on the Internet.

I began getting calls, many of them desperate, from Web site editors faced with the pressing need to fill their vast, empty sites with . . . well, they really weren't quite sure what to fill them with. All they knew was that whatever it was they wanted, it was worth a lot of money. Sites were willing to pay three or four times the going print rate to "content providers"—their highly entertaining word for "writers"—in return for pieces that took three or four times less work than printed pieces took. For a writer-cum-content-provider like myself, their pleas amounted to hilarious fantasy: "Could you please give me a piece of opinion writing quickly, on any subject you like, for this extravagant amount of money? And one more thing—could you make the story you write really, really short?" The only thing any of these new cyberpublishers believed they knew for sure was that people reading prose online would have extremely short attention spans. Therefore, stories published on the Web would have to be short enough to keep readers from clicking off to some new site before they finished reading.

So, the less I wrote, the more I got paid. If this was what "New Economy" meant, I was all for it. I resolved never to say no to any of these people, and accordingly published on a wealth of sites that had extremely short lives. It proved laughably easy to supplement my *Weekly* salary with these freelance pieces, many of which took less than an hour to write. Before long, my monthly income had increased by more than 50 percent, I was dashing off my "thoughts" for sites that would leap into and out of existence in a matter of months, sometimes weeks, thus sparing me the embarrassment of keeping these things in "print," and was writing a weekly opinion column for abcnews.com, whose offices were just across Lake Washington, in Bellevue. Judging from what ABC/Starwave was paying me—around $200 an hour, by my reckoning—that site didn't figure to be in business for long, either.

All over Seattle, freelance writers and cartoonists who had been starving for years were awash in cash. I would run into these people and ask how they were doing, and they would just burst out laughing. The cartoonist Michael Dougan, also feasting off abcnews.com—mostly by doing caricatures of me—found himself making an adult income for the first time in his life. We felt like con artists whenever we met, both of us taking advantage of the epic stupidity of the nouveau riche kid trying to spend his way to glamour and acceptance across the lake, and our refrain was always the same:

"How you doin', Mike?"

"I'm livin' the dream, baby! And so are you!"

At the *Weekly*, meanwhile, I was directed to write more or less exclusively on the technology industry and its effect on Seattle. High-tech had become the only story in town. That mandate and the crying needs of Web publications had me thoroughly—if only vicariously—immersed in the Seattle technology boom. Between the sheer number of pieces I was writing and the youth and energy of the people I was writing about, 1996 through 1998 went by in a blur allowing me no time to luxuriate in doubt, depression, disapproval, self-loathing—the hallmark emotions of the Seattle-souled. I found myself instead getting swept up in the new Seattle Zeitgeist—the chase for the Next Big Thing, the invention or idea or new application that would catch on worldwide and make its local progenitors billionaires. Everyone seemed to believe that the Microsoft story was endlessly rewritable, that Gates's success was the prototype for a new norm in business. Just as Microsoft had supplanted IBM, so now would some new Seattle entrepreneur supplant Microsoft—a company that was seen increasingly by Seattle's techno-revolutionaries as representative of the staid computing establishment, the old way of doing things, the past, the obsolete.

I would almost immediately have grown appalled at the greed-to-brilliance ratio in this demimonde, where talk devolved exclusively to the A, B, C, D . . . rich storyline, all stock options and IPOs, and at the lack of passion for improving the world that I had found in the heart of Bill Gates, had I not chanced one day to visit the Human Interface Technology Laboratory at the University of Washington. The HIT Lab, as it was called, was founded by an electrical engineer named Thomas Furness III, a technical evangelist with a tremendous idealistic zeal for bringing the power of computer technology to bear on the world's most pressing problems.

Furness had stumbled into his life's work when he graduated from Duke University in 1966 and landed, because of an ROTC assignment, in an Air Force laboratory in Dayton, Ohio. There, charged with designing cockpits that would make fighter-jet piloting more efficient and less dangerous, Furness was overcome with sympathy for pilots under siege from technological advances. The modern pilot, he noticed, was sealed in a tiny compartment, so cut off from the outside world that he could see virtually nothing through his helmet visor and the tiny canopy overhead. Contact with reality was furnished through interface with an instrument panel that had proliferated around all sides of the cockpit, surrounding the pilot of the F-15A fighter jet, Furness said, "with 75 different displays, 300 switches, 11 switches on the control stick, and 9 switches on the throttle. And those switches change their function depending upon what system you happen to be in at the time."

Disconnected from the surrounding environment, forced to interact with reality through the complicated interface furnished by his instrument panel, the besieged pilot had to contend with a set of information sources so complex that learning how to read and interpret them was harder than the act of flying itself. He also had to perform this task while traveling faster than the speed of sound, while the jet was pulling Gs and taking him constantly to the brink of unconsciousness, and while someone was trying to shoot him down. The worse conditions grew for processing information, the more complex became the information he had to process. "Anytime you go to coded information," Furness told me once, referring to the instrument panel displays, "you get into a situation where the more coding you do, the more you have to learn how to do the decoding." As a result, pilots devoted more brainpower to deciphering information than reacting to the information itself. "So—especially when there's a lot of workload—you're really busy, your brains sort of ooze out of your fingertips."

Furness was tremendously moved one day early in his career when a pilot gave him a drawing of what he called "the pilot of the future"—a man with six arms. Everything the lab was doing, Furness realized then, was backward: Instead of tailoring jet interfaces to the needs and abilities of humans, it was trying to tailor humans to accommodate these infernal machines.

From 1968 through 1982, Furness worked on a system that would accomplish the opposite: make jets interface with the human on human terms. He wanted to replace the conventional instrument panel with computer-generated images and sounds that represented the real environment around the aircraft and brought back a modern version of the old days of open-cockpit flying, when a pilot could look down and see how far above the ground he was, or tell by the feel of the wind in his face how fast he was flying. (This being the 1970s, it took a roomful of VAX computers hooked up to a flight simulator to deliver Furness's dream.) Being in Furness's experimental cockpit was like being inside a video game—the pilot was surrounded by an artificial environment, rendered by computers reading the reality around the aircraft, that sent information about speed, altitude, presence of friends and enemies, fuel levels, and so on to various senses rather then displaying an array of abstract numbers and letters that had to be constantly read and interpreted before the pilot could react. The idea was to make it possible for the pilot to react instinctively, just as humans and animals do in the wild, rather than read and translate a bewildering array of abstract symbols representing reality. Furness called this system the "Visually Coupled Airborne Systems Simulator." It proved tremendously effective—both trained pilots and novices, including schoolchildren, learned how to fly on it far faster than on conventional simulators, and the VCASS launched countless pivotal studies on human perception and performance in computing environments. It was the precursor both of the graphical user interface in personal computing and the term "virtual reality," which was coined twenty years after Furness began this work by Jaron Lanier after he saw VCASS technology at NASA in 1989. It also was the precursor, by nearly thirty years, of a kind of fighter only now beginning to take off: pilotless aircraft, controlled by a pilot sitting at a computer on the ground.

Furness, then, was a legitimate pioneer—one of a handful of scientists who set the computing revolution in motion by directing researchers' efforts toward making computer interfaces intuitive—making, as Furness himself liked to say, "machines more humanlike rather than humans more machinelike."

This essentially humanitarian entrepreneurial drive—Furness wanted to make the world better, whether or not doing so made him rich—made him stand out starkly from everyone else in the Seattle technology landscape of the late nineties. He had left the Air Force in 1987 and resolved not to enrich himself but to find a way to turn his discoveries into a powerful weapon of moral and social change for the better. He wandered the country looking for an academic laboratory that would further his vision rather than a corporation or startup that would fatten his wallet.

That Furness found hospitality to his dream in Seattle I took as a sign that the city was still somehow "Seattle," its outsized boom notwithstanding. From his new lab, he began launching countless research projects into the development and use of VR hardware and software, with particular emphasis on "human factors"—the ways in which people assimilate and disseminate information through computer interfaces.

There was a quixotic element to Furness's endeavor. His laboratory was chronically short of money—partly because of an innate dreaminess that prevented him from managing his affairs in anything resembling a practical way, and partly because he was looking into computing areas far beyond the horizon of investors' imaginations. His technological visions were decades ahead of the state of the art in hardware and software. He was dreaming up applications for devices—head-mounted displays—that did not yet exist in any useable form, and few people believed they would ever have any practical use no matter how well-engineered they were. While Microsoft was selling the world on the breakthrough advances of Windows 95, Furness was talking about putting on head-mounted displays and motion-tracking hardware, inhabiting three-dimensional, computer-rendered "information environments," and "walking along an insect's eye" or "wandering around on the nucleus of an atom." He was trying to get software and hardware companies to underwrite work in his lab that was at best years away from having any practical or profitable application during a time when companies were under intense pressure from shareholders to turn research into bottom-line results almost immediately. And he was trying to interest investors and researchers in hardware and software projects that might bring about social good but were unlikely ever to make anyone particularly rich.

Furness was a deeply religious man, a convert to Mormonism, and religious fervor was his most characterizing trait. He treated his work as a vocation in the religious sense—a calling to redeem fallen humankind. "It was really clear to me that there was a revolution taking place in computing," he told me of his departure from the Air Force, "and that the capacity of computers was going to continue to grow, that there was no limit. But no one was working on interfaces! We were still sitting at screens, ploinking on a keyboard! And we had all this computing capacity on one end, we had this incredible human on the other side, and we had this barrier in between." What had started out as a means of bringing relief to fighter pilots had turned into a cause that burned in his heart. He saw the lab as a kind of seminary: "I decided that I wanted to train missionaries, I wanted to train these disciples, as it were, who understood where we could go with this interface."

He particularly wanted to develop interfaces and devices that eased the burden of handicapped people. I was to hear him talk repeatedly, in public addresses and in private, of building "electronic prostheses" for the paralyzed, allowing them to "inhabit virtual bodies" that can travel through "virtual shopping malls," and to build headsets that "allow the blind to 'hear' a room" or even "allow the blind to see." "I want to give humans the ability to learn experientially, to enhance their creative abilities so that their creative juices might find easier and better expression. I want them to be able to communicate with each other, especially across vast distances. I want them to *be there*, literally reaching out and touching someone across 9,000 miles. And I want to recapture lost world citizens, the ones who are lost because of physical disabilities or cognitive disabilities." He felt that all humans were tremendous spiritual and intellectual creatures trapped in physical bodies that kept them from realizing their full potential. Furness dreamed of setting everyone free by "creating symbiosis between the human and the machine" and "building a transportation system for the senses" that will "unlock human intelligence" and "transcend human limitations."

I first met Furness when I visited the HIT lab to see a demonstration of a prototype headset that relieved the suffering of people afflicted with Parkinson's disease, a neurological condition causing debilitating tremors that make ordinary tasks impossible. Working with a veterinarian, Dr. Tom Riess, who was in the advanced stages of Parkinson's, lab researchers devised a see-through headset that displayed a row of vertically scrolling dots, superimposed on reality, as the wearer walked along. This was a high-tech version of a trick Parkinson's patients use to overcome the disease's breakdown of the brain's "visual cueing" mechanism—the breakdown that triggers their tremors. Often, Parkinson's sufferers lay out rows of playing cards on the floors of their homes because such evenly spaced visual aids eliminate their tremors and disorientation, and Riess wanted to build a portable system that would work that magic wherever he went by making it look as if the floor or sidewalk before him was decorated with the evenly spaced dots superimposed there by his head-mounted display.

When the display was turned on, it immediately eliminated the tremors and twitches caused by Riess's disease. I watched him at the beginning of the demonstration, twitching and flailing so violently that he could scarcely maintain his balance, get himself fitted with the headset and belt-pack-mounted computer that rendered the scrolling dots. Then, once the display was in place and turned on, his symptoms vanished, instantly, miraculously, and Reiss started walking around the lab, even breaking into a run at times. It was one of the most powerful, affecting spectacles I'd ever seen: a man who one moment was flailing and trembling spasmodically, then the next was walking and running gracefully, exuberantly, up and down the hallways of the laboratory.

I spent a lot of time mystified by Furness's charisma. He was spellbinding—both as a public speaker and in private conversation. A great deal of his success was due to his personal charm, and a great deal of that could be attributed to his rural North Carolina roots. Disarmingly down-home, he seemed by turns to have stepped right out of either *The Adventures of Huckleberry Finn* or one of Faulkner's Snopes family sagas. (I asked his mother once what she remembered of his early childhood, and she said, "Whut was it he made that first rocket out of? Snuff cans, I think it wuz.") He had a rich, rolling accent and an arresting manner that was at once courtly and folksy. Along with his spectacles and graying hair and beard, his accent gave him the avuncular air of a Colonel Sanders. He was formal in a way not commonly seen in modern America, opening doors for women, shaking hands every time he greeted a friend, and pulling chairs out from tables for his guests. His speech, marked by a musical drawl, was determinedly homey, packed with odd, strangled sounds as if consonants kept getting swallowed in mid-expression by his sinus cavity. "Isn't" he rendered as "idn't," "ninety" was "niney," "want" was "won't," "presented" was "bresented," "student" was "stunent," "my" was "muh," and so on.

Furness also had an approach to his work—or, at any rate, to the promotion of his work—that was epically romantic, in the Sir-Walter-Scott-by-way-of-the-American-South sense. This could cause a tremendous amount of head-scratching among the no-nonsense engineers in the HIT Lab. They were particularly bewildered when Furness wrote a call to arms in one of his lab-anniversary messages. "I have long held the belief that humans have unlimited potential," it began, and went on to declare Furness's intent to attack

> hunger in the world, and wars and crime and places where our children are not safe. . . . I believe that we can solve these problems. That we can go where no man or woman has gone before. That we can soar by spreading wings we don't know we have. And that we can do this by creating new tools which tap that incredible resource of our minds, allowing us to amplify our intelligence, much as the pulley or level amplifies torque, giving us a new strength and empowerment to address contemporary issues and the frontiers of our existence. . . . In the end, perhaps we are not too different from our early ancestors, when the invention of the wheel provided a new kind of mobility. We, too, are dedicated to a new kind of mobility—mind moving—but with the end goal of making our lives, and those of future generations, more complete and fulfilling. For as we move here, a candle flickers in Tibet.

"Good God," said Rich Johnston, one of the lab's electrical engineers, by way of a typical reaction among the lab's scientists. "My job is *not* to solve world hunger. My job is to solve specific engineering problems!"

Furness's students differed from him considerably in other ways as well. Many of them viewed the lab as a stepping-stone to wealth—particularly those intent on leveraging their HIT research into a discovery that could attract funding for a startup. The Diaspora of HIT lab alums that Furness envisioned going off to universities and established corporate laboratories to further his visions were instead going off to startups hoping to strike it rich. Lab discoveries that Furness envisioned being licensed to corporations with the finances and infrastructure to invest for years in commercializing new research were instead being licensed to startups more interested in winning an immediate gamble on the stock market than in putting in the years and millions it would take to turn research into world-changing industrial products. Furness's most important scientific achievement—an invention he called the "virtual retinal display," which scanned images directly onto the retina rather than the back of a screen and that showed long-term promise in fields ranging from relief of certain forms of blindness to development of featherweight, screenless head-mounted displays—had been licensed to businessmen from a company called Microvision who felt none of Furness's love for the invention or its potential. Furness came to believe that they saw it simply as a financial opportunity. They seemed to him to be intent on capitalizing on the high-tech hype that was sending more and more money after less and less plausible ideas; they were hoping to hype his invention's potential, cash in on the stock market, and abandon his work instead of carefully building a viable business around it and remaining committed to its success over the long haul. As evidence, Furness cited numerous instances in which the company either tried to evade its quarterly license fees to the lab or complained without justification that Furness was channeling that fee money—which was supposed to be devoted to VRD research—into other, unfunded lab projects. In the years since Furness licensed his invention to Microvision, he had grown increasingly disenchanted, referring to company management more and more often as "clowns," "clueless," and "freeloaders."

Furness also grew increasingly bitter about what he viewed as a broken promise to grant him founder's equity in the company equal to that of the members of the founding group. "It was a handshake deal," he told me. When the stock never materialized—particularly after the company went public and the shares would have made Furness a millionaire—he was convinced he had been robbed. The more he pondered the slight, the more valuable the shares grew in his mind and the more outraged he felt. "So here I am," he said one day, "after all this time, and I'm going to come out with *zero shares*. And I see all these clowns that are on the board of directors—where do all these guys come from? I mean, I see another one of my babies going to the dogs."

Furness's feelings about the stock were complicated. On the one hand, his religiosity drove him to be indifferent to material wealth—and, in truth, he cared little for it, his mind taken up almost entirely by hopes and dreams. On the other hand, he had put more into Microvision than had all sorts of investors who were granted substantial shares of stock for their financial contribution but who had put no work into the invention or the company. He felt on principle that he should be rewarded for his ingenuity, his labors, his faith, and his generosity. It was as if someone had sneaked into his head and stolen his life's work, and with each passing day the situation seemed to eat away at him even more.

For a long time, I couldn't figure out why I was so thoroughly enchanted by Furness. I parlayed his charm and importance in the technology world into another book contract and followed him around for months, recording his every word, writing down his every move. I watched as countless brilliant students came to the HIT lab from around the world to study under him. I watched representatives of the leading American and Japanese software and hardware companies come regularly to the lab to see what was happening there. I watched him struggle to establish a new settlement on the fringe of the computing world, his struggle as much against his own dreaminess and idealism as against the hardships imposed on him by the frontier. And as students lured by his dream came to his lab, then went on to build their own personal fortunes out of what they found there while he remained locked in his struggle with exterior and interior demons, I watched him give in alternately to joy over what was taking form around him, in the hands of his followers, and dismay over how little he was profiting from it personally.

I finally decoded his enchantment—of me, at any rate—when I followed him to the Boeing Museum of Flight one day to watch him pitch a typically ambitious project proposal. The museum, a lavish institution on the Boeing grounds, underwritten in large part by Boeing family members, had been talking with the HIT lab for months about building a relatively simple kiosk about space flight. Typically, Furness turned the idea into a multimillion-dollar extravaganza, stretching the limits of computer technology. He proposed that the museum build a "Starfleet Academy," in which visitors wearing VR headsets would sit at flight controls in a mockup of the flight deck of the starship *Enterprise* and navigate through a virtual outer space. Visitors would have this experience in groups, all of them networked on a system that would render the surrounding universe in "real time" while allowing the crew members to communicate with one another and with a "ground control" back on virtual Earth.

Furness spent most of his time at the HIT lab trying to raise money, and he was an uncommonly practiced pitchman, deftly mixing in homespun humor and folksy informality with rational-sounding technological explanation. Now, in the Boeing boardroom, he set up two large-screen displays, one connected to a VCR and the other connected to his laptop, miked himself, and strolled into his presentation with a studiedly nonchalant allusion to his Air Force career—"black airplanes and fighter cockpits and things like that"—before moving on to the presentation proper. "What we want to build here," he said, "is a six-degrees-of-freedom museum."

On the oversized video screen off to one side was playing an animation showing an astronaut on a spacewalk making repairs to his spacecraft. On the screen behind Furness, a series of slides stored on his laptop were on display: a rocket, an Air Force VR helmet, a picture from deep space taken by the Hubble Telescope.

Furness began going through a long story about the boyhood he spent dreaming of flight and space travel, building homemade rockets—"I came up with this fuel mix that burns real fast . . . matter of fact, it burns so fast it sort of *explodes*"—leading his listeners through a story of various high school science fair awards, a week he spent with the Navy for winning first prize in a state competition, a meeting as a kid with the Mercury astronauts, his acceptance out of high school into the Air Force Academy, which was the realization of his boyhood dream . . . and how he was turned away at the Academy door because of poor eyesight.

"And lemme tell ya," he said, "I was *heartbroken*."

Next he began telling a story from late in his career as a scientist with the Air Force—the career he settled for after being denied a career as a pilot—when he traveled down to NASA in Texas to help implement a display to be used for landing the space shuttle. While there, he revisited another of his creations—a VR system with a stereographic helmet-mounted display that was being used to train astronauts for future repair missions in outer space. It was called the Manned Maneuvering Unit. Trainees would don a spacesuit and the helmet with its virtual display, then navigate through a virtual outer space, repairing a virtual spacecraft.

This was the system being displayed on his video monitor, and Furness, pointing now at the space-suited figure floating on the screen, called his own experience in the Manned Maneuvering Unit the belated realization of his boyhood dream. He made it sound as if his entire Air Force career had been a long, circuitous way of inventing a form of virtual flight to compensate him for the crushing disappointment delivered him by Nature. "They let me put this on, do a walk in virtual space," he said, pointing at the figure in the video. "It was just a joy to finally get a chance to fly."

There wasn't a dry eye in the house.

Furness paused for a second, giving his listeners a chance to compose themselves, then launched into his description of his plans for the museum project. "We want to build a Starship Center," he said energetically, "a virtual learning environment for future leaders and explorers of the universe." Kids taking part in the project would sign on through the Internet to a project Web site, do preparatory lessons on science and spaceflight, then subsequently come to the museum. There, they would undergo a brief orientation, go on a mission into deep space, and upon their return would be "debriefed"—report on what they had learned. The lessons would continue indefinitely, again over the Internet, as the students continued their studies and their relationship with the museum through the World Wide Web.

This was 1997—years before the widespread deployment of broadband Internet access—so even that minor dimension of Furness's project, to an informed and practical mind, sounded almost impossible to implement.

Furness's presentation went on to cover a description of the project, its costs, how it would be built, and how it would work; an argument for using an immersive VR approach in education; an enumeration of the ways such a project would benefit the museum; and a presentation of some of the visuals the starship visitors might see through their headsets. His laptop was displaying an accompanying array of slides up on the screen: now some charts showing the components, time lines, and costs of building the starship; now a breathtaking, full-color picture of a star being born; now a view of Earth from outer space; now a schematic diagram of the school's Internet connection, or "virtual schoolhouse," the flight deck of the starship *Enterprise*, the debriefing room, and the post-flight, Internet-mediated revisitations to the starship; now the landscape of Mars, now a field of stars; now figures showing that television viewership among children had declined in the video-game age. "Studies show kids prefer interactive entertainment . . . Kids are getting bored with traditional ways of education."

Although Furness, who never raises his voice, eschews the shouts and dramatic exclamations of garden-variety techno-orators and evangelists, he nevertheless communicates powerful passion and conviction when he speaks. His language is rich, and the range of his intonations wide and deep. He has the odd ability to project his voice across a packed room in a way that makes it sound as if he is standing next to you, talking quietly and persuasively to you alone. His presentations always have woven into them an ardent argument for the virtual-world interface. "Computers are still *outside in* . . . You can't *go to a place* . . . Building a virtual world leads to building a much more robust mental model. We want to present a circumambience of visual information, we want to build a high-bandwidth interface with the mind."

Now the presentation was building to something of a crescendo, with the understated rhetorical flourishes and images on the screen coming thicker and faster, richer and more colorful. Furness was offering the museum an opportunity to *change the world*, to *shift the paradigm* of education, to "open the portal between information and the mind." With the system he envisioned, "if you want to, you can crank it up to a hundred Gs and juggle on Jupiter." Even after more than thirty years of work on this interface, he still was reduced to an awestruck kid whenever he thought about its potential: "Y'know, I was thinking to myself, '*Gosh. . . .*'"

The museum not only had a chance to join him in unlocking the human mind and changing the face of education, it also could set humans free from the prison the PC age was slowly building around them. "Computers are basically symbol processors," Furness said. "And to use them, we've had to act like computers. The only innovation in interface in the last twenty years is the mouse—that's about it."

Moreover, the museum could do this at relatively low cost—could, in fact, work the spatial equivalent of the miracle of the loaves and fishes: "The beauty of this is that your real estate is *unlimited*. The cost per square foot of virtual real estate is *infinitesimal*—because you can *roam the universe*. The only limit on where you can go is your imagination."

By now, Furness's listeners looked liked kids in Disneyland. They sat stock-still, their eyes riveted on him, their mouths agape, as he segued from the dream portion of his speech to the practicalities of realizing the dream in the museum. Furness detailed the "scalable, modular system" he wanted to build—one that would allow the museum to plug in or remove computer modules as software and hardware advanced, so that the system, one that "might be a real precedent in the world," could be kept constantly state-of-the-art. He could get started, he said, with "an R-O-M—Rough Order of Magnitude—of $1.4 million," which would get the starship and its support system "through construction." He would like to get started as soon as possible, he added, "because we have several projects that are ramping down."

In truth, he needed to get funded as soon as possible because he was on the verge of having to close the lab's doors.

I sat through the presentation alternately swept up in the soft whirlwind of Furness's speech and mindful of the intimidating technical obstacles standing between the museum and its virtual Jupiter—obstacles that approached those of a spaceflight to the real Jupiter. I started thinking of the enormous difficulties of getting a network of computers to render the real-time, rich, collaborative environments that Furness was describing. I wondered how he would maintain and repair the headsets he wanted to use without the support of the manufacturer, which had gone out of business. I wondered how the system would stand up to the punishment sure to be inflicted on it by kids with no experience using VR equipment, and by museum employees who could be taught to deal with its interface but who would lack the expertise to tweak broken or misbehaving hardware and software. And I realized that Furness was promising to deliver something no one had ever managed to deliver anywhere.

And most amazing of all—Furness actually believed he could pull this off. He had an amazing ability to keep seeing the desired as the actual, the vision as the reality, no matter how many times his dreams fell short of being realized. He never seemed to know how to get from the imperfect here to the perfect there, but he knew in his heart that someone somehow would get there someday. If it was good and useful and something humankind desperately needed—and Furness was convinced that his virtual-world interface was all those things and more—then it was as if he had already found the way there and had only to pull the less imaginative up into his paradise.

The presentation was a resounding success—at the end, the audience came up and surrounded Furness. "Great presentation!" someone shouted. "Outstanding!" said the museum board chairman. "My goodness!" said the museum PR director. "I didn't realize you were going to come down here with bells and whistles and dancing girls!"

And then, as happened again and again with Furness, the museum board backed out of the project when it came time to write the check a few weeks later. Once his spell wore off, the board members came to their senses.

The night Furness told me that, sitting in early evening in his office with the darkness settling in around him, wearing his disappointment like an old familiar favorite sweater, I recognized him at last—and found the source of his hold over my imagination. It was just a matter of waiting for the room to grow dim enough for his real features to emerge.

He was Doc Maynard reincarnate, "dreaming the right dreams too soon," in Murray Morgan's words, who had come out to Seattle from Ohio, just as the first Maynard had, full of amazing visions and the unequalled ability to see them come to fruition in one way or another. But he was also destined, as Maynard had been the first time around, to see his grandiose dreams fulfilled not by himself but by others—less imaginative, less daring, and ultimately far more rich.

Money for Nothing

While Furness was struggling for money inside the HIT lab, the gold rush was raging outside it. In February 1997, Coopers Lybrand reported that sixty-one Washington companies had closed venture-capital deals in 1996, bringing $295.5 million into the state—a significant chunk of the $10.1 billion invested nationwide in such deals, particularly given the size and remoteness of Washington. "It probably doesn't get any better than it is right now," the Puget Sound Venture Club's Gary Rittner told the *Seattle Times*. "These angel investors are feeling pretty good. If you're the right guy with a good idea, you can probably get the money."

Weirdly enough, it was going to get a lot better than it was right then, and you didn't even have to have a good idea. In retrospect, the years 1996 to 1999 can be seen as a classic mania of the sort that overtakes financial markets in times when money, being in oversupply, sends people into a paradoxical panic to make a lot more of it. At the time, most Seattleites viewed the boom as evidence that economic rules and models were changing and that Seattle was helping lead the world into a new economy, the workings of which were inexplicable to minds trained to think in old-economy terms. In time, the believers insisted, the new rules would become clear, the behaviors and results rational and reasonably predictable.

Cooler heads tried to prevail. Even as early as 1997, people in Seattle and elsewhere were floating comparisons between the dotcom boom, as it was beginning to be called, and the seventeenth-century Tulipmania disaster. Excited as Seattle was by the surge in wealth, growth, and energy, there also was the profound sense among many here that something was tremendously wrong about the city's headlong rush into unreasonable prosperity—particularly given the obvious fact that many of the local companies reaping millions in the stock market or from private investors would never, under any circumstances, turn a profit.

Examples abounded of nonsensical investments. Virtual i/O raised first-round cash of $20 million, most of it from the cable television company TCI, to build head-mounted displays, on the theory that millions of consumers would eventually want to wear their televisions. FreeShop.com, a Web site that compiled free offers for consumers, had a market capitalization of $203 million at the close of the day it went public. Amazon.com, emerging as Seattle's biggest startup story, having lost $5.8 million in 1996 and on its way to losing $1.75 billion through mid-2000, filed for an initial public offering in 1997, generating infinitely more excitement than old-fashioned, profit-making, outmoded Microsoft had when it went public in 1986.

By the end of 1997, there was very little talk in Seattle of where technology was headed or what technological bets would play out well in the long term. Talk had devolved exclusively to what idea would catch on fabulously enough to take a company public, cash in, and make its promoters millionaires. After that, who cared what happened? Money, which a few years before had been the means by which a technical vision could be fulfilled, now was the end in itself, the vision or hallucination being funded a mere means to instant riches. Instead of betting on a company's prospects for turning into a solid business, investors were betting on companies they thought would generate enough hype to lure in huge numbers of subsequent investors immediately. It was like watching people bet on racehorses that would be taken out and shot as soon as they crossed the finish line—even if and especially when they won.

I tried, both in the *Weekly* and on abcnews.com, to sound various alarms about moral decline, long-term costs, the dangers of turning America into a nation of shareholders, and boom-delivered damage to the soul of the city, but my heart wasn't in it—partly because I was growing tired of my own determined-Seattle-loser shtick, and partly because casting aspersions on everybody clever enough to cash in on the boom was coming across more and more as either sour grapes or idiocy.

And really, what was the point of turning away free money? What was to be gained? I fell prey to the conviction that I was missing out on the inevitable, the wonderful, out of some misguided set of values that felt more and more like crankiness or pretension. Almost everyone was having a great time and getting paid lavishly for it, and they all were supremely confident about where they were headed. They were wiring the world! Building the future! They were young and rich and happy, and I was old and irascible and getting poorer by the minute relative to everyone else.

The explosion in salaries and net worths in Seattle and the tremendous influx of young, moneyed new residents set prices and real estate taxes on a steep upward curve that made supporting a family on a writer's income increasingly difficult. I started to fear that I was starving my children to feed my ego. Seattle's cachet—or at least my high dudgeon about it—was costly to people like me, and I would sit at our dinner table in the evening imagining I was leading my family to financial ruin by refusing to buy into the boom. If only I'd pursued those opportunities with Microsoft and Amazon! (By now, I imagined they had been outright job offers I'd turned down.) My kids would be better fed, more secure, happier! We could be sitting here over dinner trying to figure out how to diversify the family stock portfolio!

Instead, we sat through dinners night after night in deepening silence, and I kept hearing the same conversation in my head:

"What's for dinner tonight, Daddy?"

"Moral indignation."

"Not *again*!"

It didn't help that the boom took shape largely as a generation-gap dispute, with the beneficiaries and righteous promoters of the new Seattle way of living large being kids, and the confused, disapproving, and nostalgic being their elders. To watch young people getting richer at age thirty than I would ever be, and staying excited all the time about what they were doing, only deepened my sense that the *Weekly* and I were out of touch with the city and the times. We had missed the significance of grunge; a rival paper, the *Stranger*, had come on the market in 1991 and by now had thoroughly captured the young moneyed market the *Weekly* couldn't seem to understand; and all the themes and preoccupations we thought made our paper great were passé now, boring and backward.

This young-dotcomboomer-vs.-old-babyboomer divide in Seattle played out in particularly stark fashion at the *Weekly*, which lapsed headlong into a cataclysmic identity crisis in 1997, when the paper was sold by its founders to Hartz Mountain Pet Foods. The founding investors in the

Weekly were retiring from active investment, turning their portfolios over to their children, and the children wanted to take their money out of publishing and put it where it could earn a far higher return. Katherine Koberg, who had been only half-heartedly pursuing that job at Amazon, took one look at the new owners and bolted for the bookseller. The pet-food people—New York corporate types in tasseled loafers—had big plans for using the *Weekly* to gain entrée into the newly cash-rich Seattle market. They never uttered the word "Seattle," in fact, unless it was attached to the word "market." The first thing they wanted to do was retarget the paper toward all those new-moneyed youngsters who were reading the *Stranger*. "They're going to want to make some significant changes here," a shamefaced David Brewster, who was to retire as a condition of the sale, told me. "Advertisers want to reach readers in the eighteen-to-twenty-eight age bracket, because they're more impressionable."

Moneycentric kids were taking over the city, then, along with all its institutions—including the one that had most affected disdain for money, status, ambition, material progress. The *Weekly* was to be transformed from gadfly to booster, from iconoclast to corporate cog. Hartz Mountain bought the *Weekly* for $8.5 million, which seemed a staggering sum for something I had always regarded as resolutely anticommercial. It was also a depressing sum, proof positive that the *Weekly* was turning into yet another Seattle sellout story, going the way of all Seattle craft movements: grunge had gone to mainstream record labels, Sub Pop to Time Warner, Redhook to Budweiser, Starbucks to Pepsi, Microsoft to monopolist, and now the *Weekly* to Hartz Mountain Pet Foods. The new owners would soon be forcing us to add two new sections—Technology and Rock Music—at the expense of the fine-arts-coverage franchise Koberg had worked so hard with Brewster to build. We would all be working on ad-revenue-driven trend, lifestyle and pop-culture pieces that would be as boring to write as to read—but then, if I read the signals properly, the paper was no longer to be targeted at people who read.

Watching Koberg leave in the face of that certainty was the most painful experience I'd ever been through at the *Weekly*—and not only because of the immeasurable loss to the paper. By the time she completed her months of negotiation with Amazon, Koberg had gotten so steeped in Seattle's emerging new boom-culture that already her interests, passions—even her speech—had changed dramatically. When she first began serious talks with the Amazon people, she would come back from her meetings there laughing at their peculiarities. "They asked me what my

SAT scores were," she said one day. "I just had to *laugh*." She had taken the SATs twenty-six years before, and like the rest of us back then had barely bothered to notice what she had scored, let alone bothered to remember it. A meaningless, momentarily entertaining number then, an SAT score now was apparently a credential—something, Koberg noticed, that people at Amazon would always contrive to work into introductory conversations about themselves.

A woman who had never deigned even to feign interest in technology or popular trends, focusing instead on arts and culture, Koberg was talking by the end of her negotiations with Amazon like a brainwashed convert to technoboomism. "The Web isn't going to be about content," she said, with a surprisingly straight face, during one of our last conversations before she left. "It's going to be about transaction." I felt like the last terrified, uninvaded human at the end of *Invasion of the Body Snatchers*.

The Seattle glass artist Dale Chihuly had spent the previous ten years turning himself from an artist into an industry. By the mid-1990s, he had left his bowls and baskets and seaforms behind and was doing huge hanging "chandeliers" that looked like massive Medusa-esque tangles of glass, and mounting gigantic indoor and outdoor installations all over the world, all these efforts faithfully chronicled in lavishly produced books and videotapes. His crews cranked out "Chihuly" pieces virtually around the clock in two factory-like facilities—one on Lake Union, the other in Ballard—in numbers that took on assembly-line proportions.

In 1989, Chihuly Inc. began producing glass pieces decorated with "putti"—plump little glass nude boys perched in various playful poses, connoting inextinguishable mischief and joy. By the late 1990s, he was practically mass-producing them. Regarding them one day, I was struck by how much a departure they were for Chihuly, and I was wondering if they signaled a dramatic new direction in his art when I looked up from my desk in Tom Furness's HIT lab to discover that two of the putti had put on clothes and come prancing into my life. Named Michael "Squish" Almquist and William J. "Joey" King, they were among Furness's most promising protégés, and by far the most perversely interesting creatures ever to come through his lab.

From time to time over the previous several months, I had heard about "Squish and Joey" and their adventures inside and outside the lab. They were variously believed to be either delusional or enlightened, their dreams of starting companies that would produce entirely new, highly

advanced computer and communications interfaces being tremendously—and, many believed, impossibly—ambitious.

The two wanted to build not so much a single company with a single
product as an entire industry manufacturing an entirely new set of
devices that would be part of what King called "a tightly coupled system"—a computer system wired so thoroughly to the user that it could
react to wishes and mood changes without the user having to bother issuing a command. King wanted to realize the vision of the scientist J.C.R.
Licklider, who wrote in a famous 1960 paper, "The hope is that, in not too
many years, human brains and computing machines will be coupled
together very tightly and that the resulting partnership will think as no
human brain has ever thought and process data in a way not approached
by the information-handling machines we know today." To that end,
King wanted to develop computer interfaces that were "dyadic" or "sym-
biotic," in that they could be designed to accept, as he put it in a 1994
paper, "facial nonverbal behavior (i.e., facial expressions, eye movement
or gaze, and pupil size) . . . as a novel input channel to computer systems."
King believed that a computer could be made to have an "active or proac-
tive" interface that could interpret human behavior and facial expressions
so quickly and accurately that it could, in effect, answer questions before
they were asked. King liked to call these dream machines "imagination
amplifiers." "One of the things that I do when I want to modulate my own
behavior is play different music," he told me the first time we met. "And
I'm often annoyed because I'll be doing something and the music won't be
right, and I'll have to change it. And there's no reason why I should have
to do that. I don't think it would be very hard to have a machine do that
for me."

Where King's expertise was in human-computer interaction,
Almquist's was in networking, virtual reality, and interactive content, and
he dreamed of producing Internet systems that would move data at hitherto undreamed-of speeds, allowing people to connect and communicate
in rich, immersive, three-dimensional multimedia environments. The two
first met in 1992, and within a few weeks were spending hours upon hours
together fantasizing about future ideal interfaces and applications making
use of King's tightly coupled systems and Almquist's high-speed-
network-mediated virtual environments.

Their dreams ultimately took form as a communications system in
which as many as eight different people in eight different locations could
put on a little head-mounted display connected to a small box that was in

turn connected to the Internet, and "meet" face to face in a digitally rendered "environment," in which they could manipulate and collaborate on any kind of digitally stored file. The system would allow all forms of collaboration and competition, from simple face-to-face conversation to working together on three-dimensional models or playing complex computer games.

The dream in itself would have sounded bizarre and impossible had not the HIT lab already built an experimental version of it. Working with a team of researchers at Japan's Fujitsu Research Institute, Furness and his assistants had built a system in which a team at the HIT lab appeared to be sitting in the same virtual environment with a Fujitsu team on the other side of the Pacific. The environment was crude, and there was tremendous latency in the communication of data. When a person moved or spoke, several seconds went by before the others in the environment saw the action or heard the speech, moving images were displayed in slow, jerky, frequently interrupted motion, and speech and mouth movement were poorly synchronized. But the experiment proved that the concept could be workable with future technology.

The tenuous technological feasibility of their dream aside, there was the more difficult matter of the credibility of the dreamers. Almquist and King struck the sane as unlikely builders of a digital communications empire. Cherubic, mischievous, chronically boyish, poorly groomed, and given to long, energetic, free-form disquisitions on any subject anyone brought up, the two were like a high-tech Tweedledum/Tweedledee tag team, tormenting whoever came near them with rapid, insistent, almost frantic speech that could be hard to track—particularly when, as was often the case, they finished each other's sentences. King had a tendency toward sarcasm and impatience with the rest of the world, which he and Almquist both deemed irredeemably slow. A Texan, he talked in a high-pitched drawl that made him sound like Slim Pickens played at too fast a speed. Almquist, for his part, could never wipe the murderously mischievous look off his face. He didn't so much walk into rooms as come bursting into them, spewing wisecracks one after the other, the one-liners related to one another by tenuous puns or connections no one else could see. He described himself to people he met as a formerly "dyslexic and autistic" child, and accompanied this confession with the hissing, spitting, head-shaking fit of someone trying to force a million ideas at once out of his brain through an interface that can only accommodate one statement at a time. He also liked to describe himself as a latter-day Godzilla—

"I am *vast!*" he would thunder, "I romp and stomp and devour small planetoids!"—a presentation that could be off-putting, if not frightening, to people he had just met.

I first met Almquist when he dropped by the lab to visit Furness, who brought him by my desk for an introduction. As he shook my hand, Almquist fixed me with a piercing stare. "There's a lot of craters out there," he said, "and I don't intend to be one of them."

King, while less intense, was no less odd. He rigged up a computer with a hidden camera that could photograph faces of users without their knowledge, then wrote software that made the computer respond incorrectly to common commands. He conducted months of experiments in which he secretly photographed users' faces as they stared in confusion at the rogue machine.

While King was pursuing a combined psychology–computer science Ph.D. on human-computer interaction and trying to convince someone, somewhere that his "facial expression work" was worth doing, Almquist left the lab in 1994 amid considerable controversy and started a virtual-reality company, called Ambiente, that failed within a year. He then sunk into a long depression before emerging in early 1996 to start another company, F5 Labs, with a young venture capitalist named Jeff Hussey. King went to work part-time for F5 as its "chief scientist," charged with designing its interface. Almquist, the "chief technical officer," led a four-person team of programmers, and Hussey—the "CEO"—busied himself raising more money (the two had easily raised $1 million to get started) and hectoring Almquist and his fellow programmers to work faster, faster, faster.

From 1996 into 1998, when not slogging through the emotional morass at the *Weekly*, I followed Almquist and King around downtown Seattle, gathering material for my HIT lab–centered book, as they fought for their dream against various demons. F5 was building what Almquist called "a load-balancing switch," which was software, installed where a Web site connected with the Internet, that monitored the array of PC boxes or servers comprising the Web site and distributed information requests—the data packets that came in over the Internet—to the least busy among them. The device would allow a site owner to replace extremely expensive server boxes with extremely cheap personal computers and dramatically increase the speed of a Web site, thereby allowing both for simultaneous communication with more users and the display of richer multimedia content.

The switch, which Almquist named BIG/ip, was to be the first in a series of devices he envisioned for the Internet of the future. Only when all these products were deployed would the Net be able to deliver full-featured multimedia and virtual-reality experiences like the ultimate communications system Almquist and King envisioned.

What fascinated me about King and Almquist was their mix of insanity and immaturity with technical brilliance and apparently solid strategic thinking. When talking about BIG/ip's technical features and role in the development of the Internet, they sounded extremely credible, sober, rational. But watching them in action—watching, for example, as they worked through a complex conference call with a customer while Almquist knelt on his chair making infantile faces at the speakerphone, or referred to a potential business partner as a "poopyhead," or tried to run a simple meeting without cracking jokes incessantly, or even just tried to order lunch—they seemed willfully helpless and helplessly childish.

They lived together in a house on Queen Anne hill that was packed with gadgets, junk food, wine, technical magazines, the works of George Orwell, books of Nostradamus's prophesies, comic books, and video games. They were obsessed with MTV's *Real World*, taping all episodes and watching them repeatedly, particularly the Miami episodes in which the group tries futilely to launch a business. They were inseparable and often indistinguishable—so much so that one of my colleagues at the *Weekly* told me once, "I thought Squish and Joey were the same person."

Sitting at lunch with them one day—they had ordered deep-fried ham sandwiches, genuinely horrifying fare—I started telling them about my dinner the night before. "My wife," I said, "made a normal macaroni and cheese casserole, but then did something really cool—for the topping, she crumbled up Tim's Cascade Style potato chips and sprinkled them over the whole thing." Tim's is the Seattle craft potato-chip equivalent of Starbucks and Redhook.

Simultaneously, their jaws dropped and their eyes started glistening.

"That's a *great* idea!" exclaimed Joey.

"That woman's a keeper!" said Squish.

Squish in particular often came across not so much as an entrepreneur or software engineer but as a performance artist, his role of the moment being that of the founder of a high-tech startup. He had an odd kind of frenetic energy—if you looked closely enough, you could see little lightning bolts constantly crackling from him. He referred to any event, however traumatic, disastrous, strange, unexpected, or distressing, as "the usual madness," and he could not keep himself from incessant play, no matter what purportedly serious task might be occupying him at the moment. E-mail detailing what needed fixing in BIG/ip was always a mix of technical arcana with maddening asides. "Root need to start em off with either: bash, tcsh, or 'STTY TERM PC3'! Otherwise blood will shoot out of my eyes and fingertips!" he wrote after inspecting the first test version of BIG/ip to be installed at a customer's site. "This merits some documentation and perhaps an 'install script'?! Something—blah blah blah! . . . ALL of this PLUS the following are 'ACTION ITEMS' that Sally and I are negotiating. When we've come to an agreement we'll DEFINITELY LET YOU GUYS KNOW! The pressure is BIG and so are the payoffs! ACK ICK OOK OCK!"

I watched him end one argument over programming strategy by looking at his interlocutor and saying, "Is that your face or did your neck throw up?" And one day when Hussey—a crisp, impeccably coifed young man who showed up every day in F5's grimy little office suite in a suit, tie, starched shirt, and scowl—was screaming at him for having missed a deadline, Squish looked coolly at him and said, "When I said we could make that date, I was smoking crack."

Every day I would faithfully chronicle the signs of failure I could see all around me at F5. There was the utter disorganization of Squish's mind; the repeated failure of successive builds of BIG/ip to work consistently; Hussey's apoplexy; and the growing tension and distrust among Squish and the other programmers, growing to the point where Squish would sit at his computer with headphones on and his CD player turned off so that the people around him, thinking he was listening to music, would talk freely about him, not knowing that he was listening to their every word. Hussey would rail at me in private about how he was teaching himself programming in order to get rid of Squish and take over the faltering programming effort. F5 had hired a receptionist, a sales vice president, and various other people who appeared to have little or nothing to do, and they would sit in the F5 offices all day long either trying to look busy or playing solitaire on their computers. Hussey had a stock ticker installed in his office, clandestinely hooked up to the stock feed at his old employer, A.H. Capital, which was also an investor in F5, and would spend his day trading stocks instead of running his company or raising more money for it. F5 had a version of BIG/ip installed at the Tower Records Web site in northern California, and spent hours every day anxiously monitoring and maintaining it from Seattle, always coming within seconds of having it crash. Squish and his minions consistently treated the exercise more like a game than a business: "Arrrggghhh, the ol' rust-bucket [BIG/ip], she be takin' on water . . . she's goin' down fer sure," I heard Squish say during one typical BIG/ip flameout. (He liked to pretend he was a pirate.) And always in the background, like a loudly ticking clock on a time bomb, was the countdown to when they would run out of money.

Through it all, when you would have expected everyone involved to be focused and panicked over trying to make BIG/ip stable and successful, they instead spent increasing amounts of time brooding about what they perceived as unfair allocation of employee stock. Avi Bar-Zeev, a programmer and erstwhile friend of Squish's, quit when Squish wouldn't grant him options on more stock. Squish was convinced that Hussey was being awarded stock far out of proportion to his contribution to the F5 effort, Hussey insisted more and more vociferously that Squish should lose some or all of his stock for his consistent failures to meet company milestones, and I watched all this, amazed that people were devoting so much energy to fighting so strenuously over something that was likely never to be worth anything.

The more the pressure built at F5, the more Squish/Joey and Hussey maneuvered against one another, each hoping to persuade their investors that the other was to blame for the failure they all feared was coming. Squish and Joey would sneak into F5 in the middle of the night and go through Hussey's e-mail and papers, looking for evidence that he was stealing money for himself. Hussey would rail at me about the shortcomings of Squish and Joey, calling Squish an "unredeemed fuckup" and Joey an "arrogant little shit." To Squish, Hussey was "a wee little man! A wee little man!"—a term he invoked almost constantly whenever Hussey came up in conversation.

One day, I walked across downtown Seattle with Squish to a suite in the Westin Hotel that had been converted to a home for Web servers. F5 had a test site there that was serving pornography for free, Squish having decided that that would be the best way to test BIG/ip under constant, exceptionally heavy demand. (He was right about the level of demand— the site handled thousands of requests per minute, around the clock, many of the requests coming from Hussey's computer.) Since he routinely dealt with the fulminations of Hussey and the constant series of disappointments and disasters at F5 with a series of exclamations ("Incredibly humorous!" "Highly amusing!" "Quite hilarious!"), manic facial expressions, pirate-speak, and long stretches of what he called "coding like the wind," I had not noticed how frantic, depressed, and exhausted he had become. But we no sooner settled down in the room at the Westin than he started tinkering with his machinery and screaming out his frustration and anger. "The whole situation has become so incredibly ludicrous that it's difficult for me to get really upset about it," he began. "Yesterday I was incredibly *pissed*, incredibly mad, which is weird, because that now makes the tenth time in my life I've ever been really mad. There are so many people milling around, fighting, screaming, backbiting, and milling about because they don't have a clear vision or clear focus. So I went home really pissed, really burned out, and this morning I woke up and said, 'It's obvious! Fire everybody!' This is not, like, 'Things are broken.' This is my last recourse. This is, like, a moment of *absolute calm*. A moment of absolute clarity."

He saw the end coming for F5 before it could start selling BIG/ip and making money. Not only was his company running out of funding, but Cisco Systems, a multibillion-dollar Internet company, was one of many established companies also at work on load-balancing solutions. If it was going to survive, F5 would have to get to market before the others with a better load balancer. "Now, is this a crater in the making?" Squish asked rhetorically. "We've got, like, two or three more months. Two or three more months from now, we'll find out. But we can't continue on the course we're continuing."

He had failed before, both at the HIT lab and with Ambiente, but this potential failure loomed as monumental by comparison because the potential payoff was so much larger. Squish had carefully researched the state of technology and the state and direction of the Internet marketplace, realized that it was too early in the development of the Internet to think about full-blown virtual-reality applications, and come up with a can't-miss motherlode of an intermediate, Net-building idea at exactly the right time. Now it looked as if all he was going to take away from his F5 adventure was yet another lesson: The greater the potential success, the more devastating the failure. "*I nailed BIG/ip and the BIG line squarely on the head.* People are begging for this. Now sometimes we talk about the half-full kind of thing. You know, we've got a prototype, it works, got a proof of concept, we've got a market, we still have half of our money, we still have some time . . . But my gut tells me that if we can't get BIG/ip done, fixed, and out there in the field within six months, we're toast."

He felt trapped in a loop, endlessly repeating the same mistakes, enduring the same swirling cycle toward failure every time. "You know, I keep thinking, 'Wow! I've learned *so much* doing this! Wow! You know, I'm going to make like an *incredibly great* person! I'm incredibly experienced, incredibly *wise*, I've condensed the learning of like a lifetime, or job experience, which may be like five years of being at a job, into like *two weeks!*" He saw the impending failure of F5 as yet another manifestation of the recurring theme in his life: "You know, it's kind of been like my life, like at the HIT lab, at Ambiente, you know . . . it's just like how *I've always been*."

For every portent of doom, though, there always seemed to be an equal and opposite portent of success—or just enough of one to keep Squish (and me) hanging on to the F5 story. For one, you could see more and more investor money chasing after less and less promising Internet businesses, and F5, with an actual product meeting a demonstrable need, showed much more promise as a business proposition than nearly every company raising venture capital or mounting a successful IPO. And things that should not have worked out in F5's favor always seemed to find a way to do so.

My favorite example of the latter was a request from *PC Magazine* to review BIG/ip as part of a cover story the magazine was writing on Internet products. It was a tremendous coup for F5 even to attract the notice of a magazine of that stature, and a review of BIG/ip, if it were at all favorable, would virtually guarantee F5's success.

Unfortunately, Squish and Hussey were no sooner arranging for the magazine to run tests on BIG/ip than they discovered a flaw that would take months to diagnose and fix. BIG/ip could run at full strength for only a few hours, then its memory would overload and it would crash unless an operator were online to empty its memory and make various other adjustments. If Squish were to take a BIG/ip down to the magazine only to have its testers uncover the flaw—a high likelihood—the company would be ruined. Not to be part of the story at all, however, would be almost as bad: More visible, established competitors would be showcased, the world of Web site owners and operators wouldn't even know F5 existed, and service providers all over the world would be making their one and only load-balancing investment in someone else's product, effectively freezing F5 out of the market before BIG/ip was finished.

Hussey and Squish agonized for weeks over which would be worse: to be slammed in a review or ignored. Hussey kept begging Squish to find a way to survive the magazine's test protocol, and Squish kept saying he didn't think it could be done.

Finally, though, Squish realized that they really had no choice but to try, so he took two other employees with him and flew to California with a BIG/ip box. Once there, he was relieved to see that his interrogators and testers were relatively unfamiliar with Internet issues, and he performed what he called his "Full Godzilla," staging an elaborate, entertaining, and energetic presentation for which he pulled out all the stops on his considerable and eccentric charm. He regaled his audience with his vision of the Internet's future, the infrastructure weaknesses contributing to its present problems in handling traffic, and his invention of a real-time load-balancing switch that dramatically upped the power of a Web site.

Finally it came time to set up for the test, and Squish, with excruciating care, managed to get his BIG/ip configured and running without letting the testers see how tenuous an operation the launch was. Then the magazine writers asked him and his companions to wait outside while they hooked up sixty computers to BIG/ip, all of them sending it constant connection requests. Once the test was running, they all went off to have lunch together while the program put BIG/ip through its paces.

When they returned two hours later, a visibly upset tester came out and said to Squish, "Um . . . can you come in here for a second?"

His heartbeat on hold, Squish followed him into the room and looked at the bank of monitors hooked up to his machine. Each was supposed to be displaying either a large "R," for "Running," or a large "D," for "done." Instead, every screen in the room was displaying a large "X."

"What happened?" Squish asked.

"For some reason, our test program stopped functioning."

BIG/ip, though, was humming happily along. Squish looked at its log and saw that it had overloaded almost immediately and put all sixty test machines on indefinite hold until the test program, hopelessly confused, crashed. Squish looked around the room and saw that the testers were going over the source code in *their* program, looking there instead of in BIG/ip for the error that caused the crash. Suddenly he saw an opportunity for salvation. Hurriedly offering regrets, he told his hosts that he and his companions had a plane to catch, and he packed up his BIG/ip and ran out the door.

Back in Seattle, he explained to a transfixed Hussey what had happened, and offered him a ray of hope. "Now if they're smart guys," he said, "they'll be able to figure it out. But they were only going to spend a day on each box they tested—they were up against a deadline. I think that *incredibly* smart guys would be able to figure it out. *Regular* smart guys would need more than one day to figure it out. *Really stupid idiots* are going to need like a few weeks or something to figure it out. So they're spending one day on each product, and actually today they're writing the article. Today they're supposed to have all the testing done, of all four products, and they're going to write the article."

They had to wait a month to find out what happened. "True to its name, the BIG/ip, from F5 Labs, is up there with the other big boys in our load-balancing roundup," the review began. Then, after describing BIG/ip and comparing it favorably with its more expensive competition, the review went on to note that BIG/ip "was in beta at the time of testing, but it should be shipping by the time you read this."

It wasn't, but it didn't matter—F5 had finally caught a break.

The difference between the meltdown at F5 and the meltdown at the *Weekly* lay in the persistent faint hope of success, transcendence, at F5. The trauma at the startup stemmed from frustrated ambition rather than the slow death of complacency and illusion that overwhelmed me at the *Weekly*. Instead of making Squish and Joey despair, F5's travails only seemed to make them grow more feverishly hopeful. They were energized by defeat rather than rendered comatose by it, as I was at the *Weekly*. I saw in Squish and Joey this perplexingly admirable mix of altruism and greed—a determination to change the world for the better and cash in extravagantly on their kindness along the way—that you see only in American optimists. By comparison, I felt like my mission at the *Weekly* was to keep an outdated and pretentious cultural franchise alive so I wouldn't have to do real work for a living. Squish and Joey were kids with the city's—the world's!—future in their hands; I was a faltering, doddering adult losing his grip on the past.

I could feel myself willingly giving in to the glamour Squish and Joey represented. More and more of my abcnews.com articles now were about startups with weird and fantastical business models that I began seeing in a favorable light. I sat through employee meetings at Zombie, a virtual-reality game company, where company founders explained to their employee/shareholders that they were only one game title away from an IPO or acquisition by a deep-pocketed company. At Go2Net, a company creating Web sites where players could meet to play chess, poker, hearts, and other competitive games online for free while the company decorated the margins of their screens with paid advertising, I asked, "Are you profitable?" and was told, with a laugh, "It's in the business plan for next quarter!" (Although they never made it to profitability, they did make it to millionairehood.) At a tiny startup in a Pioneer Square loft, I listened to two young company founders explain how they would make millions selling hardware over the Internet and licensing content from home-improvement magazine and book publishers. "People log on and describe the project they want to do—like remodel their bathroom—and our site shows them how to do it, listing all the supplies they will need, and they'll buy those supplies from us, and they'll be on their doorstep the next day. . . . It's all about content! Content is our differentiator from the other sites selling hardware!" Everywhere you looked, someone had a Great Idea—and everywhere you looked, those Great Ideas were getting money either from venture capitalists or the stock market.

How could all these young people making all that money possibly be wrong?

Months passed. BIG/ip, while still incomplete—although the term "incomplete" came more and more to define "lacking a new feature a potential new customer asked for"—grew gradually more stable. Tower Records grew more and more thrilled with its Web site's BIG/ip-enhanced performance. Market conditions grew even friendlier to start-ups launching IPOs. F5 rounded up some second-round investors, prepared to hire more people and move to larger headquarters, and in 1998 began preparing for a mid-1999 IPO.

The more real the impending IPO became, the more the pressure inside F5 mounted, and the more bitter grew the battle between Hussey and his Squish-Joey nemesis. Gradually, then more and more often, and with increasing vehemence, Hussey threatened to fire Squish and take back all his stock.

By this time, I had finished work on my book and tried to get on with my life. In the past, I had talked my way into people's lives; put up a "duck blind," as Squish termed it; watched, listened, recorded everything I heard, saw, and read; then had written my report and moved on. But Squish and Joey wouldn't let me move on—they had come to regard me as a permanent fixture in their lives, their personal historian—and they turned up wherever I went, like the two tormentors of Joseph K in Kafka's *The Trial*. I would come back from a meeting at the *Weekly* to find them sitting in my office, one of them going through my desk drawers while the other was fooling around with my computer. They would take me away, usually for lunch, to regale me with stories about Hussey and F5, about the HIT lab, or about their personal lives, which consisted largely of admiring girls from afar and trying without success to figure out how to strike up a conversation with them. They would pepper me with endless questions about everyone they saw in the *Weekly* offices, connecting faces with bylines. And they would mock me constantly about the moribund nature of the place, its depressing atmosphere, and what a loser I was for working there. "The place is *dying*," Joey would say. "Shit, it's already *dead*. You're working for a dinosaur, for God's sake! The *Stranger's* way cooler—the *Weekly's* just a fucking *lame-o* rag now . . ."

They would sit in my office going through that week's issue of the *Weekly* and reading quotes from it, laughing. And when they weren't denigrating the paper, they were talking of the day when they would hit it rich from F5's IPO, use the resulting wealth to launch their dream companies, and make me come work for them. "We gotta get you out of this place . . . you're dying in here . . . you need to get with the real world, the future . . . you need to come and work with a *real company* for *real money* [they were particularly amused by my salary]. Look how depressed everybody is around here . . . this place is *killing your soul*."

Squish and Joey had a lot of time on their hands at the end of 1998 because they had finally been thrown out of F5 by Hussey. Some months before, after showing up at my office and dragging me off to lunch, they told me that Hussey had told Squish that now he really was going to fire him and confiscate all his stock—nearly half the stock in the company. Incredibly, Squish—depressed, ill, burned out—had more or less concluded that there was nothing he could do about it. I gave him the name of an attorney—Jon Kroman, a friend of mine—and insisted he hire him. He did, Kroman served papers on Hussey and F5, and in the ensuing discovery found that Squish had signed away the rights to anything he ever invented, for the rest of his life, to Hussey, and had indeed given him the right to fire Squish at will and take back all of his F5 stock.

Now that he had an attorney, though, Squish had tremendous leverage. The last thing F5 needed on the eve of an IPO was the company cofounder and sole inventor of its technology suing F5. And Squish made sure Hussey and his board knew he would do it, as he said to me, "just to see the look on Jeff's face." So he was able to negotiate an exit allowing him to keep nearly all of his stock—well over a million shares—and winning back ownership of his future intellectual property.

This battle went on for months, with Squish and Joey disappearing for days at a time, then surfacing in my office to regale me with the latest stories. One day they called and told me to meet them down on the street outside the *Weekly* because "we're going to take you somewhere."

"Where?"

"You'll see! You'll see!"

I went downstairs and in a few moments they arrived, in Joey's decrepit Chevrolet station wagon. They were both dressed in oversized shorts and baggy, threadbare T-shirts. They drove me up to the Columbia

Tower, home to some of the poshest offices in Seattle, parked in its underground garage, and led me to the elevators and up to an office somewhere above the fiftieth floor. We walked into the offices of Cairncross and Hempleman, F5's—and Hussey's—law firm. It turned out that the negotiations over Squish's severance from F5 had broken down over $3,000 in credit-card bills Squish had rung up on his personal credit card, and he was refusing to sign the deal, which F5 now desperately needed, unless the debt was paid off by the company. F5 finally had agreed, on the condition that Squish show up in the Cairncross offices immediately to collect his check and sign the deal.

Of course the two found this hilarious, and they were particularly entertained by the alarmed looks they kept getting from the business-dressed people in the Columbia Tower. And at the Cairncross offices, which were done up to look like a British gentlemen's club, with overstuffed leather chairs, leatherbound books lining the walls, a tremendous number of pricey Chihuly seaform sculptures, and massive, ornate, Cairncross-logo metal coasters on all the tables, they walked in snorting derisively at the reek of money and failed attempt at gentility. When a suited Cairncross partner came out, scowling, to get Squish, he followed the attorney off to a distant office, looking over his shoulder at Joey and me, laughing and making faces.

The deal signed, we left the place as fast as we could, got back down to the parking garage and into Joey's car, and made our way out of the garage. At which point Squish pulled from some hidden place in his clothing one of the Cairncross coasters. Brandishing it, he was shouting now, laughing: "Who cares what else happens? I got a fucking coaster! I win!"

When not following Squish and Joey around, I was back at the *Weekly* trying with decreasing zest and utter lack of success to cope with the crippling malaise that came over the place in the wake of its sale to Hartz Mountain Pet Foods. Brewster's and Koberg's departures left a vision void that the paper's old-timers were too disoriented and the paper's youngsters too narrowly oriented to fill. The oldsters wanted the paper to remain what it always had been, covering politics and arts and culture for people advertisers no longer had any interest in reaching, and the youngsters wanted to devote coverage exclusively to technology companies and the club scene. The oldsters wanted to pretend their corporate owners didn't exist and that the *Weekly* could forever refuse to run itself like a business;

and the youngsters looked eagerly to their new corporate masters to rid the paper forever of the oldsters and their outdated vision of the city.

Never the best of friends, the two factions started waging all-out war against one another in a microcosmic, high-voltage version of what was happening to the city as a whole. Editorial meetings turned into exercises where an older staffer would bring up a story idea and the youngsters would sigh and roll their eyes in exasperation, radiating the rage of a grounded teenager at a tweedy dad. And when the kids would suggest a story or an angle, the adults would stare at them in bewilderment and horror, afraid to say anything out loud. One youngster—the rock-music critic the *Weekly* hired in its attempt to appeal to new young rich mindless Seattle—suggested "Extreme Gardening" as the title of our annual Home and Gardening Supplement issue, and "Rehab Chic" for the annual Fashion issue. As idea after idea of his was rejected—often because his managers couldn't tell whether or not he was serious—he finally stopped coming to meetings entirely.

The *Weekly* devolved into a dysfunctional family as two successive managing editors attempting to fill Koberg's shoes quit in frustration, forcing the company finally to settle for me. Late in 1998, I moved into the office next to the editor, Skip Berger, and together we watched in dismay while our "children"—as we took to calling the young writers—came whining and wheedling and complaining to us constantly, insisting on massive raises and holding out the threat that they would bolt for the technology sector and its monstrous salaries if they didn't get them.

Between the behavior of the children and the pressures from New York to make the paper unreasonably profitable, Berger sank into a massive depression. It got to the point where he almost never left his office, avoiding conversations as much as humanly possible. He would sit either at his desk with his head in his hands or at his computer, surfing the Web and staring into his monitor in search of relief. In our "family," Berger was the Dad, withdrawn and detached. I was the Mom, constantly trying to find a way to placate the children, and to get Dad to notice how miserable they were and how desperate we all were for something to be done. More and more days ended with me hunkered down with Dad in his den, wailing with him about the behavior of the children, who were coming to me constantly during the day to whine about Dad's neglect of them.

At one time or another, before giving up on talking to him entirely, the staffers had been coming to Berger one by one demanding raises. After only a year or two at the paper, they were insisting on salaries it had taken writers of Berger's and my generation nearly twenty years to earn.

Berger would just sigh and shake his head in disbelief when talking about these matters with me. "What's wrong with this generation?" he kept asking over and over again. "They just feel *entitled* to things we always felt we had to work so hard for!"

He was right about their behavior, which could be stunning. Each one of these exchanges was more demoralizing than the one before. Squeezed by the paper's paymasters, Berger had no money to offer anyone, as everyone well knew. He would try, as gently as he could, to explain this to people demanding more money, but they were unmoved. I was sitting in my office working late one night when I heard a staffer shout at him, "But the budget *is not my problem!*"

The problem was not, as Berger thought, that there was some fundamental moral difference between our generation and the children's. Rather, it was that salaries and financial expectations were being thrown thoroughly out of whack by the technology industry's massive, inexplicable abundance of money. The kids in our employ all were either getting huge freelance paychecks for small tech-industry side projects, had friends working for some Internet startup making three or four times what the *Weekly* paid, or had friends who were made instant millionaires by stock after their company went public. David Brewster had always found a way to pay writers a living wage—an anomaly in alternative journalism—but the boom had redefined "living wage" as "chump change."

Although I was more aware than Berger of the depth of this problem, I took some comfort in the idea that the nature of the work at the *Weekly*—thinking and writing about matters of the mind, things that mattered, doing work that made your life meaningful—would make up for the lack of material pay. (I managed not to notice that these consolations had long since ceased to work for me.) The way I did the moral math, being paid 100 times as much to do work that was a million times less satisfying would always strike good writers as a losing proposition.

I was wrong. Koberg, for example, by all accounts was thrilled with her new job, and when I would run into her from time to time she would be almost unrecognizably different, speaking in that rapid, clipped speech that characterized inhabitants of the technology sector about how "focused" everyone at Amazon was, how "brilliant" Jeff Bezos was, about "strategies" and "emerging new sectors," and how she never had time to think about anything but Amazon, Amazon, Amazon. And after months of strenuous efforts to get Berger and me to raise her pay, Claire Dederer, a talented and—formerly, at least—enthusiastic film critic, walked into my office one morning and quit. "I went home last night," she sniffed, "and there were two checks in my mailbox. A freelance check from Amazon, and my *Weekly* paycheck." Amazon's check, for a few hours' work writing reviews of children's toys, was bigger than the *Weekly*'s check for two weeks of full-time work. She stood there holding her hands out, palms upward, one up high, the other down low, as if one was hefting something lightweight, the other something infinitely heavier. Then she shrugged as if to declare that the answer to the equation was inescapably obvious, and turned and left.

I realized that I was fighting a losing battle. Looking for new writers, I could find only people who were unemployably eccentric or chronically depressed. Any writer who was even marginally functional was distracted to the point of resentful preoccupation, at best, with the explosion of wealth in the city. For the young at the *Weekly*, being underpaid became more than a simple matter of money. It was a sign that they were uncool, out of place, out of time, out of luck. Soyon Im, a talented writer on culture, film, books, behavior, and cool, turned in an essay one day in 1999 entitled "How do you cope with watching all your friends get rich?" While her coevals were paying cash for new condos and new sports cars, she was scraping by in a crummy apartment with an unreliable car and no prospects for upward mobility. "Although I love being a writer," Im wrote, "I would be lying if I said that I don't feel doubts now and then about my career decisions. Lately, the money issue has been rearing its ugly head: Not part of the high-tech clique that made this city famous, I find myself suddenly feeling poor, unskilled, and surrounded by rich people my own age."

The boom had, either directly or indirectly, cost her a relationship with a boyfriend who worked at Amazon.com. "A year ago last spring . . . my boyfriend, who had been working as a customer service representative since the company's early days, cashed in his shares. The very next day, he went out and bought a condo on Capitol Hill. A few months later, he 'retired.' He is 31 years old."

Im viewed the condo as a meretricious, high-concept place built for someone with no taste. "In short," she wrote, after describing what was in essence a stylized studio apartment, "it's a glorified bachelor's pad with a glorifying price tag."

The place triggered a crisis of envy mixed with contempt; now she saw her boyfriend in an entirely different light. "I didn't admit it to myself then, but the reason I didn't like the place wasn't its self-consciously modern design; it was that I knew there was no way I could afford something like that on my own. He is only a year older than I am, but we were living and buying as if we were a generation apart."

The sudden change in her boyfriend's status left Im depressed. "He didn't get the best deal on the condo, but he didn't need to. It may have been overpriced, but he was rich and could afford it; he wasn't being compromised. Not in the way that people like myself—who earn an annual income lower than one year's college tuition—are compromised every time we write our rent checks, buy furniture, or purchase plane tickets to go home for the holidays."

Inevitably, they broke up. "It wasn't about money, but the disparity of our buying powers didn't help. He is still retired, spending his days pursuing personal projects—which consist largely of drawing comic strips, going to the gym, and smoking pot."

I knew—maybe even more than Im did—what she was feeling, because I felt it myself: an unpalatable, unendurable mix of horror, envy, disgust, and prurience.

Circling the Drain

By 1999, it was no longer possible to imagine the *Weekly*—or, for that matter, Seattle—recovering its equilibrium. And, with each passing day, it was increasingly difficult for me to tell whether I wanted it to. The city was spinning glamourward, and while there had been times (a year ago, a few months ago, last week, yesterday, a minute ago, a few minutes hence) when I regarded such a trend as the death of everything I treasured, now I found myself more often than not excited by it, convinced that the Squishes and Joeys of the world were Promethean purveyors of the technological fire that would make gods of us all. I decided that the flow of wealth toward them for business models that made no apparent sense was proof that they knew something profound about the future that the rest of us could only dimly sense was there, and I came to believe, happily, that my destiny, and the city's, lay in the direction they were taking it.

I became quite insufferable on the subject, dismissing my erstwhile coevals' alarm over the opening of upscale retail outlet after upscale retail outlet—Pottery Barn, Restoration Hardware, Tiffany's—as Chicken-Little thinking, the panicked focus on risible side effects when Seattle's ascent into glory was the real story. We are not, I would insist, being transformed into Bellevue, Sausalito, LA; what is really happening is that Seattle is coming of age, leading the world into the twenty-first-century

Technological Era, and being well compensated for it in the bargain. We were changing from backwater to bellwether. The dramatic transformations all around me—the quickening of the pace of life, crowding on the freeways, the frenetic rush everywhere all the time, the heightened sense of urgency and excitement in the streets—all testified to Seattle's arrival at the cutting edge, and the mushrooming population here testified to the world's endorsement of The Seattle Way. We were arriving at a point relative to the rest of the world that back in 1990—during the hype and heyday of the Goodwill Games—had been mere pretension. Rushing headlong into the New Technology and the New Economy, following the Squish-and-Joey generation, we were realizing that long-held vision of the Greater Seattleites of yore: Seattle had finally arrived among the trend-setting cities of the world. New-York-Pretty-Soon had grown into More-Than-New-York-Right-Now.

Yet I fell prey at the same time to an unacknowledged unease. I lapsed into a careful, steady schedule of drinking through the workday, editing and writing *Weekly* stories in an anesthetized haze, downing pints of sanity-pickling local microbrews at lunch and dinner, and employing massive doses of coffee to get me through the mornings. I couldn't see that I was in mourning. While my dismayed family watched me grow fat, glum, and comatose, Squish and Joey chose to be enormously entertained by this regimen, and came down to my office nearly every day to take me to lunch and watch me drink while they sat there regaling me with insults, tales of their travails and battles with the Wee Little Man, and visions of the world after F5 went public and made them multimillionaires.

They insisted constantly that I didn't really work for a living, and that my enterprise—the *Weekly*—was an outmoded, no longer useful artifact from a bygone age. Hence my depression. When they hit it rich, they were going to give me a real job with a real salary. I was going to be half employee, half biographer, writing business plans and product documentation for them while gathering material for a new masterpiece—about them. "Squish and I aren't gettin enough lovin'!" Joey would complain. "You gotta get started on another book!" Until I did, I was essentially useless. Joey's greeting whenever he popped up in my office was always the same: "You're not workin'! You're slackin'! Let's go to lunch!" With each of them at an elbow like guards escorting a condemned man to the Chamber, we would head off to a nearby tavern, Joey calling me "slacker," "bum," "derelict, "loser," and other endearments along the way, pointing out the occasional drunk slumped against a wall or lying on the sidewalk, saying, "That's you in five years," while Squish would be acting out what he saw as my life's quest: the search for the "Magic Beer." Growling, twisting off an imaginary bottle cap, pantomiming a drunken draining and tossing away of a bottle, repeating the cycle again and again, he would mutter, "Where's the Magic Beer? Where's the Magic Beer? Are you the Magic Beer?" Then suddenly he would be brought up short when a "beer" bleated, "Don't drink me! Don't drink me! I'm the Magic Beer! I have the secret to eternal wealth! Eternal happiness! All you have to do is not drink me, and you will be happy forever!" Pause. Baffled look. Sudden guzzle. Growl: "I don't care! I can't help it! It's worth it!"

Safely in the bar, pint in my fist, I would listen to their tales of impending glory. F5 would go public, their stock would make them insanely rich, and they would then build what they were calling their "Empire": a two-company communications conglomerate that would realize their worldwide system of networked human-computer dyads. One company would be an "Internet backbone" company, deploying a worldwide fiber-optic network with Squish-designed hardware throughout. Built with state-of-the-art telecommunications equipment, and enhanced by Squish's "magic boxes," the network would be by far the world's fastest, allowing for true, real-time, multimedia communication in immersive environments. The other company would be an "applications" company that would market the conferencing product allowing up to eight people to meet in a "virtual environment" for face-to-face conversation and collaboration. The evolution of the Internet, the rise in consumer expectation, the wiring of the world, and the development of Squish and Joey's products all were converging at exactly the right time for their long-held dream to be realized.

And I was going to be there with them! They were going to take over the world, and I'd be there to tell the story—from the inside! No more editing lame fashion supplements! No more writing stupid lifestyle stories for a dying alternative newspaper! No more books about that boring Bill Gates! "Think of it!" Joey would say. "The day we're on the cover of *Business Week*, your book about us will be in every bookstore in the country! You'll finally write a book that *sells*!"

There were days when they made me feel like Jesus in the desert with Satan whispering in his ear, sweeping his arm out over the expanse before them, insisting, "Someday this can all be yours . . . just turn these stones to bread . . . work a pointless miracle."

Get thee behind me, Squish and Joey! (Drunkenness and apostasy had me mixing my Bible stories.)

The better I got to know them, the harder it was to believe that any of their dreams were realizable. Sometimes, in the dim tavern light, hunched over their massive meals, eating and talking at speeds ordinary humans can only imagine, spraying food and words all over the bar, Joey looked like Bill Murray in *Caddyshack* and Squish looked like the gopher. How could creatures like this possibly mastermind the birth and sustained performance of a multimillion-dollar corporation?

I also doubted that F5's IPO would ever come off. Without Squish, and with the mercurial Wee Little Man at the helm, it didn't seem possible to me that the company could get itself into IPO-marketable shape. How could they possibly be making progress on BIG/ip if its inventor had been thrown overboard? I knew that the company had a new VP of sales and marketing, and that the board had taken enough control of F5 to consign the Wee Little Man to the sidelines, but even so it was hard to believe they could pull off an IPO without a fatal hitch.

Yet less promising enterprises were going public for hundreds of millions of dollars almost every day. Sitting alone in my office, surrounded by the escalating horror at the *Weekly*, it was impossible to imagine a world in which F5 failed to go public and give Squish and Joey the means to rescue me. But whenever I found myself in their company, it was just as impossible to imagine them as multimillionaire captains of industry.

I wasn't the only one struggling with this question. The *Weekly* by late 1998 had turned into a vale of tears. Men and women alike would come into my office just to cry, with the crier who most touched my heart being a young woman named Sumi Hahn. Raised in Ohio, educated at Harvard, she had moved to Seattle for the usual reasons, talked her way into a job at the *Weekly*, and had scarcely established herself there as one of the editorial leaders when the paper was sold and went into its tailspin. With both the paper and the city that had drawn her here changing into something foreign and unpalatable, Hahn grew so desperate and depressed that Squish with all of his peculiarities emerged in my beery imagination as an actual solution. I introduced them, on the theory that I could rescue two people simultaneously from their private hells: Squish from his involuntary (and possibly lifelong) celibacy, and Sumi from the kind of psychological collapse that had nearly overcome Katherine Koberg.

Almost immediately, Sumi and Squish started spending all their free time together—a development that gave me some relief from Squish and Joey's constant attentions, since now they were as likely to settle in Sumi's office as mine when the invaded the *Weekly*. But then just when it looked as if things were getting legitimately serious between Sumi and Squish, Sumi took a job with the *New Orleans Times-Picayune* and fled town.

In our frequent telephone conversations between here and there, she spoke of New Orleans as if it had everything Seattle had promised and withdrawn from her. It was a culture of words and food—she had moved there to be the paper's lead restaurant critic—steeped in a pre-technological tradition that New Orleans was committed to preserving rather than destroying. The computers in the newsroom were just writing machines—they weren't hooked up to the Internet. To get e-mail, you had to go to a machine in a separate room and log on. Men showed up for work in a shirt and tie, books mattered more than bucks, people were allowed to walk the streets with drinks in hand—"You'd love it here, Fred! You'd love it here!"—and "no one here *ever* talks about Microsoft . . . no one seems to have even *heard* of Microsoft. Down here, it's like none of that exists!"

I felt a tremendous and telling surge of envy—not because she was in New Orleans instead of Seattle, but because she seemed to be in a city more like "Seattle" than Seattle was now.

When I talked with her about Squish, or about Squish and Joey, she would turn furious, ranting scornfully at me about how their dreams of empire and even of simple impending wealth were "pipe dreams," how they were "just dreamers who would never amount to anything," and how F5's impending IPO was a "fantasy." "They're just talk!" she said again and again, whenever I tried to bring her up to date on their efforts and hopes.

Whether because of Sumi or because of what Squish would call "the usual madness," Squish and Joey's pretensions seemed less and less plausible to me as the date for the IPO—now scheduled for late spring or early summer 1999, the date constantly moving back—drew closer. Joey learned that Hussey had just finalized a divorce, and his estranged wife was unaware of the coming F5 IPO and his attendant massive wealth. He drove across Lake Washington one day and mailed an anonymous postcard to Hussey's ex-wife, telling her that an upcoming "liquidity event" was going to make her Wee Little Ex-Husband a multimillionaire. Hussey's divorce was re-opened and in the ensuing discovery proceedings, Joey fed various company documents to the erstwhile Ms. Hussey's attorney. At one point, intending to return the documents to Joey, the attorney mailed them to Hussey instead. (In the context of Squish-and-Joey stories, this did not seem a particularly odd or surprising development.) No sooner did Hussey learn that Joey was the source of his trouble than he and F5 sued Joey for breach of company confidentiality. Squish, possibly trying to evade getting swept up in the lawsuit, took off in pursuit of

Sumi, Sumi kept calling me trying to get me to dissuade Squish from visiting, and Joey came down with Bell's Palsy—a paralysis of one side of his face that was caused, his physician assured him, by massive stress.

Not exactly a series of developments presaging riches and fame.

Things percolated along in this fashion for some months. I stopped thinking about the IPO, having decided that it would never come off. Even Squish and Joey stopped talking about it, Squish's talk being mostly about Sumi's disappearing act and his heartbreak, and Joey's talk being mostly about his and Squish's declining health. On those infrequent occasions when they brought up the IPO, I tended to tune them out the way you do to people who can't let go of a fantasy that's over, over, over.

Then one day F5 dropped its lawsuit against Joey, and a few weeks later—June 3, 1999, to be exact—Squish called to say that the next day F5 would be going public. When I got to work that morning, I logged on to NASDAQ and saw that F5 was indeed trading. It would close the day at $14.87 per share—a price that set Squish's worth at nearly $20 million.

Then Squish and Sumi were reconciled and Sumi was on her way to getting bejeweled, married, and pregnant before the year was out. And a few weeks after the IPO, shortly after a visit by Squish to New Orleans, a cartoon by Walt Handelsman appeared in the *New Orleans Times-Picayune*. It depicted two chubby little boys, ten years old or so, wearing T-shirts and shorts, standing outdoors with an MCI Worldcom executive. They were holding bananas to their ears as if they were telephones, and talking to one another. "I gotta go, Joey," one was saying. "I was just offered a million six for my banana!"

There was this weird way in which Squish and Joey's sudden wealth was an abstraction. They still hung around my office and hectored me about my worthlessness, just as they always had. They still talked in vague ways about my future with them. They still bought lunches and beer for me— although now we went to fancier establishments. They still dressed and acted like aggressively crude slacker adolescents. And although much of their talk now was about brokers and financial advisers and Goldman Sachs people and this whole new world they had been vaulted into nearly overnight, they didn't seem materially changed—it was as if the money they had now was symbolic, or virtual, or in some way not entirely legal tender. And it grew more abstract in my imagination with each passing day as the stock price shot into the stratosphere.

Perhaps it had to do with the unreal way they went about spending.

Squish went out one day and bought a mansion—a huge, turreted, classic old home on Queen Anne Hill, looking down at the Space Needle. It had four stories and more rooms than I could count. He moved his three pieces of furniture into it and rattled around like a ball bearing in a boxcar, e-mailing photos of it to Sumi as part of his campaign of persuasion to get her to marry him ("Look at the house I bought us!") and calling me at home in the evening, offering me endless beer if I would just come over and keep him company. He would lie there alone at night wide awake and frightened by one noise after another, like a little kid alone in a haunted house.

Another day, he and Joey drove across Lake Washington and bought three new Mercedeses (two Kompressors, Joey's being silver and Squish's the color of a pumpkin, and a larger, black four-door E320—the bigger car, Squish e-mailed Sumi, being their eventual "family car"), and came racing back across the lake in the Kompressors. A few days later, Joey drove his over the mountains to eastern Washington, where the highways are straight, and floored the accelerator. He was traveling at 160 miles per hour when the radiator hose burst. Night after night, Squish would come back to his mansion in his Kompressor after dark and crash into the pillar on one side of his garage door, the turn being too tight for him to make in the dark. Within weeks, he managed to make a $60,000 car look like a splendidly appointed piece of junk.

Squish also decided to "spread the love," as he put it, by doling out extravagant gifts. He started giving away F5 stock—he gave 100 shares each to everyone in my family, among many others—and told me he would buy me whatever I wanted for my next birthday. The first thing that popped into my mind was a private Screaming Trees show at the Showbox—a legendary music venue in Seattle—and Squish told me he would write the check for it as soon as I made the arrangements. (Ultimately, relative sanity and sobriety prevailing, I opted instead for a family trip to Korea.)

Watching the vertical climb of F5's stock price, it occurred to me that the unreality of Squish and Joey's wealth might have something to do with the fact that no matter how fast and furiously they spent their money, the stock price was rising so much faster and more furiously that they could never catch up. Instead of depleting their stockpile, it was as if spending made it grow. One month after going public at $14.87, the stock was selling at $50.75; six months after F5 went public, the stock hit $160.00, and Joey had a net worth of $6.6 million, Squish a mind-numbing $200 million.

$200 million is not a number that can be made to make sense. Obsessively, I would check the share price every day and multiply it by 1.3 million, give or take a few thousand shares, trying to find a way to describe Squish's wealth and its metastatic growth in terms that could make it "real" for me. The raw number might as well have been in a foreign language—I couldn't picture what it was, really. I could not look at Squish and find a way to see him as someone with $200 million in the bank, nor could I find a way to look at the two years or so of F5 work he'd done and make it seem worth $200 million.

In fact, I couldn't think of *anything* that was worth $200 million.

Squish, though, grew less and less aware of the roles of luck and market mania in his enrichment, and more and more convinced that he had earned his $200 million the old-fashioned way. He noticed that whenever he was out in his Kompressor, people would shout insults at him and flip him off—an indication that not everyone was thrilled with the Seattle technoboom and its overnight millionaires. "I feel like screaming, 'Fuck you! I worked hard for this!'" he told me, as if his millions were an appropriate reflection of the quality and quantity of his work at F5. And while Joey, with his relatively modest $6.6 million, began selling his F5 stock off in pre-planned, scheduled installments, Squish decided the stock would rise to at least $300 per share, so he sold as little as possible, keeping his eye on the bigger prize.

I suppose the height of the mystery came the afternoon Squish was in my office directing me to bigcharts.com. He guided me to its "market capitalization" entry for F5, pointed to the figure there, and said, giggling, "Hee-hee . . . look at me! I started a $3 billion company!"

The last time I had been in the F5 offices, the place was a mess, Hussey was jumping up and down on his desk screaming "Mother of God!" over and over, waving his arms, and the programmers were safely behind a door they had duct-taped shut, with a sign on it telling everyone else to stay away unless they were willing to sacrifice a goat to gain entrance. Safely behind the barricade, they were playing networked Duke Nukem. Now American investors had decreed that F5 was worth $3 billion, and Squish expected it to be worth nearly $6 billion before the run was over.

I walked out of my office a few hours later, with that "Hee-hee . . . look at me!" still ringing in my ears, and looked around at a wasteland. I had just spent the afternoon editing down Mike Romano's unreadable 7,000-word piece on the New Pornography to an unmemorable 2,000-word piece entitled "Not Your Daddy's Porn." That was my job now—

turning the unreadable into the unmemorable. The walls looming up behind the cubicles in the *Weekly* looked like they were crumbling; the computers were covered with grime. Only a few dispirited souls were still there, trudging around as if trying to cultivate that precious updated Dickensian look. I hadn't had a beer for four hours and was a walk, ferry ride, and bicycle trek away from my next one. Soon the *Weekly* would hit the newsstands with a dull thud, a few days later the leftover copies would be retrieved, a new *Weekly* would thud standward, the owners in New York would call to complain about each issue the day after it was released, and the bad copy would come pouring through my computer from writer to reader, just keep coming and coming and coming like that relentless hair would, years hence, through that unbearably depressing barber shop in the Coen brothers' *The Man Who Wasn't There*. Every word I edited and sent on to typesetting was an unnecessary stain on silence and nothingness.

How much was the despair I felt about the *Weekly* at that moment, in those days, in the ensuing months, a function of Squish's astounding, inexplicable wealth? I would look at him and think he could see where the world was headed while I—helpless, old, outdated, Seattlebound, Maynard-blinded—had no idea what was happening around me. I saw my life at the *Weekly* as a pointless exercise in fighting a losing battle to keep a failing paper from abandoning a tradition not worth preserving. And all the while, Squish and Joey were ridiculing me for feeling hesitant about leaving the *Weekly* and going to work for them.

They found my doubts about their next enterprise to be tremendously amusing. "Why the hell are you hesitating over this?" Joey asked me one day. "It's like a book contract with a salary—you won't have to live on those disgusting publisher's advances anymore, you won't have to edit all those lame-o articles anymore."

"What if the economy starts turning down?" I asked one day.

Joey looked at me as if I'd gone mad. "Why would the economy go down?" he asked. "And even if it did, the technology sector wouldn't!"

They were certainly betting heavily that it wouldn't. They contracted with Seattle's Sabey Construction to build a Network Operations Center south of Seattle, in Tukwila. They formed a property-management company, called Limpopo Properties, which bought leases on land in the Fremont District, northwest of downtown, and began construction of three buildings—one for Indaba, their applications company, which would take up half of the building, the other half being leased out to technology tenants; and the other two to be leased to more technology tenants, the income from their renters covering the costs of their construction loans and ownership and half-occupancy of one of the buildings, while delivering them extra cash in the bargain. They spent their days now either hectoring me, laughing about how easy it was to get richer once you were rich, or meeting with architects, financiers, prospective employees for their two new companies, and countless other crisp business types of the sort who inhabit the world of multimillionaires.

They loved taking me out to lavish "business dinners" where we would eat and drink and talk about their empire-building. They would run through the rapid-fire math of their property management "scam," as they loved to call it. They would sketch out timelines to their next IPO, with Squish, who had officially become a millionaire just after his thirty-first birthday, crowing out his life's plan: "A millionaire by thirty, a billionaire by forty!" Joey would talk not about *if* I came to work for them, but when—as if the decision, while yet unmade, was too obvious to deny.

I met them after work one night at El Gaucho, a high-concept steak-and-martini place in Belltown, to spin fantasies while eating and drinking to excess. Everyone in this place, except for me and the courtly old men who were our waiters, was young. I sat down, picked up a glass of million-dollar wine, sipped it and was stunned at its marvelous taste, set down my glass, and looked across at Joey, who was wearing an enormous Stetson and grinning from ear to ear. "You're gonna live high on the hog now!" he bellowed, lapsing heavily into his native accent.

A few days later, I had lunch with Katherine Koberg. She was like the Katherine of old, only incredibly happier. Amazon's stock had soared so high since she signed on that ordinary human-built computing machines could no longer calculate its value. The famed (and now notorious) analyst Henry Blodgett had predicted it would hit $400 per share, and now, factoring in splits, it was nearly there. "I can't believe how my life has changed," she said. "I have *four* financial advisers now." She said this as if it were the most unlikely thing that ever could have happened to someone like her. "I just can't believe . . . I tell people all the time, you know, the story about how you found this job for me. It's my favorite story—I just . . . Fred . . . thanks. Thank you."

I walked back from that lunch in the usual energetic stupor—lingering effects of hangover complicated by massive doses of caffeine further complicated by lunch's microbrewed anesthetic—called Squish, arranged for the date I would begin working for him and Joey, and gave notice at the *Weekly*. A few days later, I gathered my beleaguered editorial minions and gave them the news. One of them asked me what I was doing next, and I said, "Going to work for a startup."

"Yes!" he shouted, punching his fist in the air. "Every journalist I know is going to work for a high-tech startup! All right!"

And a few weeks after that, I found myself wading through the WTO riots to my new life.

The Return of Little Shat

Squish and Joey learned from their F5 experience that starting a company was a practically effortless exercise in getting rich quick. Not for them the slow building from scratch of a Microsoft or Aldus. The New American Way was to come up with an idea, sketch out a big-picture view of its product line, get started, raise money, and go public. A, B, C, D . . . rich.

If two years of blood, sweat, and insanity at F5 could make them millionaires, they reasoned, they could be *billionaires* if they started not one company, but *three* simultaneously. The three would complement one another, providing a seamless, synergistic suite of services and technologies that would transform the world of digital telecommunications.

Accordingly, they launched Zama Networks, Indaba Communications, and Ahaza Systems in 1999. Zama would be a Pacific Rim company connecting the western United States, Japan, Hong Kong, Singapore, Malaysia, Korea, and other nations with a high-bandwidth, fiber-optic network. Ahaza was to produce a line of products that boosted the network's performance, passing data packets at dizzying speeds, thereby enabling immersive three-dimensional communication. And Indaba would make the communications interface: the software for the boxes and peripherals people would use to inhabit virtual environments and communicate "face to face."

For Squish, the core endeavor was building the best imaginable high-speed digital communications network. In his mind, the guy who moves data packets fastest wins. For Joey, the core endeavor was human-computer symbiosis—making people better and happier through fusion with digital machinery. His theories of communication and interface were informed largely by research he'd done in Japan, where he had worked in laboratories on virtual communications environments that people "inhabited" by donning a virtual-reality headset connected to a box connected in turn to a network of these devices. The devices tracked the details of facial expression—pupil size, mouth and eye movement, etc.—and used that data to animate a three-dimensional model of the user (similar motion-tracking and animating technology is used in such video games as *Tomb Raider*). Instead of e-mailing or talking blindly on a telephone, Joey believed, an Indaba user would see these expressive models of his or her interlocutors and have as rich a communications experience as if they all were physically face to face.

I could never figure out whether this was the most ingenious or the most insane thing I'd ever heard of. But Joey had a videotape of these communications sessions from the Advanced Telecommunications Research lab in Japan, and it was fascinating. There was very little difference in look between a person using one of these devices and the model representing him or her. "And remember," Joey would say excitedly, "that was 1990s technology! It's just going to get better and better!"

The Indaba/Ahaza/Zama product line was a fusion of the Internet, computer, video-game machine, television, telephone, and VR devices—the ultimate example of digital convergence. Squish and Joey's empire would change the world, make them and all of their friends—including me, of all people—rich, and make everyone forget Bill Gates, Paul Allen, Andrew Grove, Alexander Graham Bell, Thomas Edison, Edward Gibbon . . . Squish and Joey were winners—until now, a rare commodity in Seattle—and all I had to do was go along with them for a couple of years, win with them, cash out, and retire to concentrate on my life's work, free at last of financial anxiety.

I had my moments of unease about this bargain, but tried to think of it less as the sale of my soul than a high-interest loan of it. (Not being much of a business thinker, I could never work into the metaphor any kind of reasonable motivation on the part of the borrower.) Looking back from a safe emotional distance now, reassessing (or reinventing) my state of mind, I believe that I derived some comfort from the subconscious conviction that I was signing on with a doomed proposition. For indeed I was: Eighteen months to the day after I left the *Weekly* for Indaba, the company died. And the other two republics in Squish and Joey's empire were out of business six months after that.

The decline and fall was a typically tedious soap opera of the sort chronicled in countless dotcom-failure books. As sources of money for startups finally dried up—a long-overdue, and entirely natural, market correction that began the day I left the *Weekly* for the empire—Squish and Sumi lapsed headlong into a terrible paranoia about their fortune, and turned first on Joey, then on nearly everyone else involved in their effort. They threatened to sue, sued, or were sued by various would-be business partners, investors, vendors, and contractors. They fired employee after employee, including various experienced CEOs and other executives, most of them retired US West managers whom Squish and Joey had hired to run their companies. Squish and Sumi blamed each of them in turn for the Empire's failure to raise investment capital. Countless others—myself included—blamed Squish and Sumi for destroying, with their paranoia, the empire's chances at success.

The whole group exercise was a misguided search for a scapegoat to blame for a natural and inevitable economic trend: the slow burst of the speculative boom-bubble that was already under way when the empire was launched. Trying to blame someone for that was like trying to blame someone for a tornado.

Largely for the sake of my own sanity, I have distilled my memories of Indaba's eighteen-month death spiral down to a series of snapshots— evocative little pictures behind each of which lurks a series of events the size of an iceberg.

The first is of Squish on the first day I met with him after leaving the *Weekly*. We were having lunch. His brand-new cell phone was ringing almost constantly, and each time he would pull it from his pocket, look to see who was calling, and wearily put the phone back without answering it. All the exuberance of his pre-IPO days was gone. He had the dead eyes of someone under constant siege—in his case, from people wanting access of one kind or another to his money. I realized that the joy he derived from being alive—the joy that characterized him, made him vast, grandiose, *Squish*—stemmed from the struggle to succeed against insuperable odds, with little or no money. Now, having made his fortune, he found himself constantly on the defensive instead of on the attack. He had been robbed of his youth, deprived of the struggle to build something substantial for his old age. He was a rich man beset on all sides by people after his fortune who looked more like scoundrels every day. At thirty-one years old, he was living the endlife of J. Howard Marshall II. How long, I wondered, could he survive like this? And how long before I looked to him like one of the scoundrels?

The next snapshot is of Squish standing in an AT&T Wireless store in downtown Bellevue. He had decided he wanted all his new employees to have cell phones so he could reach them whenever he needed to, wherever they were. There were only three employees besides him and Joey, so it was a relatively small matter. He drove me across the lake to Bellevue, bought me a state-of-the-art cell phone—my first—set me up with the priciest plan AT&T Wireless offered, and loaded me up with the most expensive options possible. "You'll want the quicker battery recharger . . . you might as well get the vibrating battery." Then we went to lunch.

I look back now on these as the halcyon days—the days after I was gone from the *Weekly* and before Sumi returned from New Orleans for good. (This may be because, upon moving back to Seattle, she immediately began reining in Squish's wildest impulses, among them those directed at me.) Squish was footloose, as he had always been, and impulsive, and mindlessly generous. This day, he waxed dreamy about what he was going to do with his second round of wealth, after making billions from the empire. "I want to build a big theater just for musicals!" he said. "Live performances, every night . . . *Little Orphan Annie*, *The Sound of Music*, *Don Quixote* . . . you know, all those 'Dream the Impossible Dream!' musicals. It'll be great! Great! *Great!*"

Next I see Squish handing me a check for $10,000 for our family trip to Korea. It had been nine months or so since he promised me whatever I wanted for my next birthday, and I had grown increasingly loath to remind him of his promise because I felt that his and Sumi's attitude toward their money was changing dramatically. Sumi was growing more and more vocal about Squish's naiveté and how nearly everyone they dealt with was "robbing him blind," and Squish seemed increasingly prone to looking at the world through her eyes.

But one day he e-mailed me a rebuke for failing to pick up the check from him when we met the day before. "You goof!" he wrote. "You forgot to remind me! I'm coming to get you this afternoon." He picked me up in his Kompressor and whisked me off to his empty mansion—Sumi wasn't home—where he briskly wrote out a check and handed it to me. "Just don't tell the wife," he said, winking.

It seemed like a matter of only a few days later that we were on our way to the airport to fly to Korea. We had signed on with a Seattle couple, Tim and Kim Holm, who volunteer their time each year to take groups of adoptive families back to Korea. (He is a Korean/Caucasian adoptee and she a Korean who emigrated here after marrying him in 1988.) The Holms arrange meetings with the social-service agency in Korea that handled your child's adoption, visits to the clinic or hospital where he or she was born, and an examination of the agency's files on your child. Sometimes these explorations can unearth surprises—the existence, for example, of birth siblings, an extended birth family that is searching for the child it lost, a dramatic birth-family story, or the discovery of a genetic predisposition to a particular disease. So we took off on this trip with a heart-rattling combination of high excitement and jangled nerves.

Although we were preoccupied with our own private quest, we couldn't help but notice cultural marvels everywhere we went in Korea. Seoul in particular amazed us. It is like a cleaner, more optimistic Manhattan, adorned with a far cooler alphabet. It is positively packed with people—half of South Korea's forty-three million citizens live in Seoul and its surrounding area—and the flow of people through the streets and subways is overwhelming. Yet we hardly ever heard a car horn go off, no matter how clogged with cars the streets were. It was a level of driver quietude that made Seattle's vaunted civility look unimpressive, and I couldn't help but wonder if it was the Asian influence on Seattle rather than the oft-cited Scandinavian influence that made it so laid back in comparison with the rest of our country.

The trip turned into a series of massive emotional rushes. We were walking through an open-air market one afternoon when a woman in a shoe stall looked up at our family, then turned to Anne and asked, pointing at Jocelyn, "Daughter?" When Anne nodded, the woman ran over to Joceyln, hugged her, and said in English, "Welcome back!" A few days later, in Taegu, where Jocelyn was born, we were taken to a tiny temple with a little metal gate, midway down a narrow alley off one of Taegu's busiest districts. Here, our guide said, is the site of what had been a small obstetrics/gynecology clinic in 1986. It was here that Jocelyn had been brought into the world and temporarily dubbed Huh Ok-Kyung. Overcome, I turned and looked at her: She was blushing deeply and sporting a massive, hilariously outsized grin. It is the look she gets only when she is tremendously moved, a smile so much bigger than her face that it looks like something she's trying to hide behind.

Back in Seoul for the last few days of our journey, we set off for the agency offices. We looked through Jocelyn's files, which contained nothing we hadn't already known, and gave the agency an album of pictures of Jocelyn and a letter for her birth mother, in the hopes that someday she might be reassured at finding what a happy and healthy girl her daughter had grown up to be.

Then came the time to meet the foster mother, Shin Hae Soon, who had raised Jocelyn from birth until she was three months old. She turned out to be a tiny, shy woman who was clearly excited and moved at the prospect of seeing our Jocelyn. We noticed that she came in carrying baby pictures we had sent to Korea eleven years before, and that she had kept them in pristine condition, like treasured relics. She came in and sat down, hugged Jocelyn, and began babbling in Korean, stroking and studying her hand as if it were the most amazing thing she had ever seen. Jocelyn weighed only five pounds at birth, and now towered over her foster mother.

As she sat there fondling Jocelyn's hand and wiping away tears, we were told that only 2 percent of Korean adoptees ever return to Korea, and only 1 percent of them while still children. Hae Soon told us, through an interpreter, that Jocelyn was only the second to return among the scores of babies she had nurtured over seventeen years. And when we gave her a photo album of Jocelyn's life, she hugged it as if it were Jocelyn herself.

We were to spend the afternoon with Hae Soon, first at the agency offices, then during lunch at a nearby restaurant, then visiting her and her family in her home. Jocelyn and Hae Soon kept looking at one another and smiling fondly as if they'd spent the better part of Jocelyn's life pining away for one another. The afternoon felt like the emotional climax not only of our trip but of the journey we all had commenced the day Jocelyn was delivered to our home.

I didn't see Squish again until two weeks or so after we returned. I was still brought to the brink of tears whenever I thought about the trip, and when I ran into Squish in the hallway at Indaba, I was choking them back as I blurted out a clumsy and florid thanks. "Squish," I said at the end of my little speech, "you did a really, really good thing."

"Shuckins!" he shouted, more embarrassed than I'd ever seen him. "*You're* the one who took her there!"

Now I see Squish in profile, driving his car as we make our way out to the construction site of Zama's Network Operations Center. Squish put $17 million into funding the construction of what has turned into the most robust such center in the world. Everything in it, down to the two diesel generators that automatically kick on when the power fails, is state-of-the-art. It is a massive building, a colossus—the best that an unlimited budget can build. And Squish is freaked out about it. He lost faith in the CEO he hired for Zama almost as soon as he hired him, and the building had gone tremendously over its original budget even as Zama's attempts at securing second-round investors was being constantly frustrated. Pulling into the parking lot, Squish says of the CEO he had been ecstatic about six months before, "He's turning into a befuddled old man before my eyes." It is a pattern I was to see again and again through the high-speed wax and wane of the empire. Squish would hire technical experts or experienced managers away from other companies, rave about their abilities—"He kicks ass!" "He's a genius!"—then invariably spin toward blaming them for missed deadlines or failed attempts at securing venture financing a few months later. "Everybody's a genius when Squish hires them," Joey would tell me near the end. "Then they turn into 'fuckin' morons.'"

Now I see Squish in his Indaba office, packing up his equipment to move down to Zama. He has decided to focus his attention on Zama and feels he needs to be there every day. Seven months after F5 stock hit its high of $160 per share, it is trading at $42 and still dropping. It would close on the last trading day in 2000 at $9.20. Joey had sold nearly all of his stock, but Squish is still hanging on to his. At first he had been convinced, against all evidence to the contrary, that it would rebound and climb far beyond $160. Now the magnitude of his mistake is beginning to sink in. He is trapped: To sell now is to sell at an unbearable loss—a psychological impossibility—but to hang on is to head for unbelievable losses. He finds himself hoping for a rebound he knows will never come. He has been through the seven emotional stages (denial, bargaining, etc.) Elizabeth Kübler-Ross details in her classic *On Death and Dying*, arriving now at a grim, exuberant fatalism. "I'm riding this sucker all the way to the bottom!" he shouts. "Yahoooo! Yee-haw!"

Later, I run into a dismayed Joey in the hallway. Squish, he says, is in full retreat, wanting to shut down two of their companies and concentrate on Zama—the least interesting, in Joey's view, and the least promising of the three enterprises. "Shit," he says, "Squish is letting his money own him. All he can think about now is how much he's losing." Joey, who comes from the boom-and-bust culture of Texas, grew up on stories of his family making and losing countless fortunes over countless generations—a legacy that accounts for his careful stewardship of his F5 winnings. He had sold his stock off according to a prearranged schedule, at an average price of $110, and put his winnings in tax-free municipal bonds, content to live on the income they generated. Squish, he tells me, recently sent him an e-mail explaining that he couldn't put much more money into the empire because he and Sumi decided they needed to set aside $60 million to "live on." In less than two years, Squish had gone from living on virtually nothing to feeling he couldn't survive without $60 million in the bank. And the way the F5 stock price was dropping, his fortune might dwindle to less than that even if he stopped spending money entirely. Watching Squish lose his grip on both his money and his sanity, Joey feels helpless. "It was just greed," he says, shaking his head. "It was just greed that made him hang on to that stock too long."

Now I am looking at James L. Acord's sculpture, *Monstrance for a Grey Horse*. I am standing in a triangular, tumbleweed-strewn lot at the point where state Highway 240 enters Richland, in eastern Washington near the Hanford Nuclear Reservation. *Monstrance* is standing there covered with dust and bird droppings outside a three-walled shed that Acord had been living and working in until he abandoned it in despair back in 1998.

I am there photographing the sculpture because Joey, during a conversation a few months before, suddenly asked me, for no particular reason, "If you could have any work of art in the world, what would it be?" Before I realized what I was saying, I blurted out an answer: "*Monstrance for a Grey Horse*." Joey stared at me, flummoxed. "What the hell is that?"

I told him the whole Acord-and-*Monstrance* saga. It all came pouring out of me—the ten-year effort, the move to Vermont and back, the canister of live nuclear material . . . I also told Joey about what Acord had gone on to do next: He moved to Richland in 1991 as part of his quest to get someone to let him use a nuclear reactor. He wanted to transmute technetium—nuclear waste—into ruthenium, a member of the platinum family, and use the transmuted material in a sculpture.

Joey was enthralled. Watching the look of absolute wonderment unfold on his face, I realized that I had found in him the perfect audience for my Acord story. As someone who lived in the technology startup world, he could appreciate the kind of obsessive visionary who spent ten years and moved across the continent for the sake of building the best sculpture possible; as a computer scientist, he could appreciate the science in Acord's art; and as a Texan, he had an almost fatal love for grandiosity. "Shit," he said when he recovered his powers of speech. "Find out if it's still for sale and I'll buy it for you—as long as you agree to have your ashes interred in it when you die."

Getting Joey to buy the thing was the easy part; far harder was getting Acord to sell it. I tracked him down—it turned out that he had no home, and was just drifting among friends' homes between sojourns in downtown homeless shelters—and that his life had been more or less on the skids since he spent seven years working nights in a frozen-french-fry warehouse and working days at trying and failing to get the Hanford Nuclear Reservation to collaborate on one of his live-nuclear-material art projects. I did manage to reach him by phone one day, at the Fremont Fine Arts Foundry, and I got him to name a price for the sculpture— $25,000. But getting him to collect the check was another story. Meeting after meeting fell through because he didn't show up. Months passed. Friends of his, insisting that he owed them tremendous amounts of money, tried to get him to double the price of the sculpture so he could pay them back. I found out that he had been offered upward of $200,000 from galleries but had never accepted an offer because he had an aversion for galleries and financial transactions in general.

Finally, he showed up as prearranged one day, at Elliott Bay Books, and we chatted for a while. "I know this is my masterwork," he said. "I'll never do anything this good again." He still seemed to be debating with himself whether he could sell what amounted to his life's work. At last he decided he could, and I handed over the check, which he hurriedly pocketed without looking at it. "You know," he said, "it meant a lot to me that you remembered *Monstrance for a Grey Horse* [he always referred to it by its full name] for so long—that you never forgot it. I feel now like it has a good home. I feel good about that. I've had galleries offer to sell it for me, but I never wanted to do that. I don't know . . . my business affairs. I've just never been able to handle the practical matters of life very well. I actually was supposed to live on a different planet, but somebody screwed up." Then he abruptly got up, shook my hand—one of his fingers was permanently curved against his palm, another was missing entirely—and vanished.

An hour later, Joey's cell phone rang. It was a local branch of his bank. "There's someone here trying to cash a check you wrote, for $25,000," a voice said. Acord, it turned out, didn't have a bank account.

The check safely cashed, Acord disappeared. Weeks passed. Months passed. Occasionally Joey would call me or pop into my office and bellow, "Where the hell's my sculpture?" I would call the one Acord friend I knew who had a phone, hoping to find out what happened, and he would say, "I gave up a long time ago apologizing for James." Acord would call once in a while, obsessively describe the detailed plan he had to drive with a friend over the mountains to Richland, pick up the sculpture, bring it to Fremont to clean it up and get it ready for "the installation," and deliver it to my home, where he and a crew of his friends would install it in my yard "as part of the price you paid for *Monstrance for a Grey Horse*." But the plan, somehow, would never come off—the more detailed Acord's plans were, I soon learned, the less likely they were to reach fruition.

Then, improbably, everything came together. Acord brought the sculpture to Fremont, came over to my house to pick a spot for it, did some final work on it, and one Saturday morning came over on the ferry with a crew of six to do the installation. I had rented a forklift and dug a large hole by way of preparation, and stood by with video camera in hand as Acord and his crew drove up.

After a few hours of hard work, with Acord operating the fork lift, the sculpture was properly installed, and all of us—Acord and his crew, Joey and I—stood there regarding it in a state of happy shock. We consumed celebratory beers. We laughed in disbelief. We declared that the spot Acord had picked was the most beautiful spot on earth for his sculpture. And indeed, it looked splendid beyond belief. We all stood around for an hour or so, listening to Acord tell hilarious stories about his life and troubles with the *Monstrance*. Then everyone but Joey and I left.

"Damn," Joey said. "This thing's gonna outlast human civilization!" Then he left too, and I was alone again with the masterpiece, astounded at my unbelievable luck.

Now I see Squish talking with his attorneys about the empire's complex arrangements. Nearly all the seed money for all three companies is Squish's, but he is fully in control of only one: Ahaza. For the other two, he has hired experienced CEOs, one of whom he's since fired, and he and

Joey share relatively equal power on the Zama board. And Squish has divorced himself entirely from Indaba, in which he invested $500,000. He feels cheated; he is telling the empire's attorneys that Joey's intellectual contribution to the effort is minimal when measured against his. "It's like if we were making a VCR," he says. "I'd build the whole thing, then Joey would come in at the last minute and say whether the buttons should be square or round." It makes me think of what Gates told me about his industry's beginnings. "Everybody should be pretty modest," he said, "because it took a lot of pieces." There is the most telling difference, I realize, between Gates and the pretenders who came after him: Gates is both the most accomplished and the most humble of all of them.

Now I'm looking at a ravaged Maynardtown near the end of the 2001 Mardi Gras riots. Mardi Gras in Pioneer Square is a traditional bacchanal in which drunks roam the streets beating one another up and groping women, with the police looking on tolerantly, ready to step in when some-one crosses an essentially undefined line. The New Orleans Mardi Gras is a family-values festival by comparison. This year, the police are over-matched—much as they had been during the 1999 WTO riots—and they cordon off the square, implicitly designating it a riot zone. One man is beaten to death, another is critically injured, and seventy-one others are injured seriously enough to be hospitalized. Two of the injured have gun-shot wounds. A large number of cars are destroyed and storefronts smashed. The catastrophe devolves into a race riot—the assailants in the death and injuries are black, the victims white, with the assailants emerg-ing over time as lifelong victims of benign racist neglect—and it gives the lie to Seattle's self-styled racial enlightenment. I see the riots as irrefut-able evidence that old Seattle is dangerously defined by its complacency—just as I had thought in my youth. The riots prove that the city's treasured vision of itself as an exemplar of racial tolerance is a delusion. Voters seize on the tragedy as one more reason to send Mayor Paul Schell packing. I seize on the tragedy as justification for my flight to the boom. It's not about money, about greed—it's about *values*. I'm fleeing the same city I fled in the 1970s—self-satisfied, antiprogressive, locked in a form of denial that keeps it from realizing any of the visions it has of itself.

Now I'm looking at Squish, walking away from my office at Indaba. All the lights save one over my desk are out, it being late at night. I have been working on Draft 25 of the Indaba business plan—a document I've been revising or revisiting in one way or another for more than a year. I am working alone, everyone else having gone, when Squish emerges from the Ahaza offices downstairs and comes strutting into mine. When I greet him, he says, "I'm just looking around at all the stuff I'm going to be taking over soon."

I was to have only two more conversations with him after that, both of them being about Joey, on whom Squish had grown increasingly fixated as a villain. He often referred to him as "another Jeff Hussey." He came to be convinced that Joey was stealing from him, writing Limpopo checks to himself without Squish's permission and, by mismanaging Indaba, effectively stealing Squish's investment in that company as well. Near the end, when I ask if he has any actual evidence that Joey is stealing from him, he reluctantly says, "No," then cites a series of meaningless incidents as "data points" proving Joey's evil. "Well, you should at least find out whether your fears are justified before you freak out completely," I say. It turns out to be the last time we speak to each other.

The view now is through a window in my home, looking out at the *Monstrance*. I am struck by how still it stands, utterly stolid, in the tumult of the earthquake tumbling and spinning around it. The house is creaking and rocking and jangling, the earth roiling, and the sculpture stands there as if it is the pivot around which everything else is drunkenly orbiting.

In the days following the February 2001 earthquake—the most violent in Seattle's recorded history—I walk through Maynardtown, which seems to be where all the serious damage was confined. The OK Hotel, where Nirvana first performed "Smells Like Teen Spirit," is damaged beyond repair, never to be reopened. In a last spasm of optimism, of hope for the boom's future, my future, I decide to believe that the earthquake is a great symbolic act: By confining the damage to Seattle's past, to the storehouse of its most storied loser's legacy, the cosmos is endorsing Seattle's headlong rush into cyberspace, the future, the New Economy, the brave new world where everyone is a winner.

Now I see Joey sitting forlornly in my office at the end of another day. He and Squish have been growing gradually more estranged from the day Squish and Sumi married, and now are speaking only through lawyers.

Their long-standing friendship is in ruins, and soon their companies will be as well. "I'm the ex-wife, Fred," Joey is saying. "I'm the ex-wife."

On May 1, 2001, we were told that Indaba would be going out of business in thirty days. Since Joey had already told me a week before that the company was dead, and since I had been watching over the previous year as technology stocks collapsed and tech companies shut down all over town, the news came as no surprise.

Yet I reacted as if it were a tremendously surprising shock—the last thing in the world I would have expected. It was the ending I had always known was coming but had never been able to imagine. And when it arrived more or less on schedule, I came apart like I'd been blindsided.

Shock almost immediately gave way to recrimination. I couldn't understand how I could have known as much as I knew about the uncertainties, risks, and fundamental insanity of the technology market and still jumped wholeheartedly into it. I must have been determined to manage my life in such a way as to steer myself to the worst possible ending: out of a job in my fifties, with a family to support, and no prospects for survival in sight.

On the other hand, it was drearily predictable—at last I was the loser I'd always pretended to be.

For that last month, I came into the Indaba World Headquarters every day, walked through a roomful of empty cubicles to my well-appointed little office with its view of the ship canal in Fremont, and sat there at my desk either staring out the window or reading newspapers on the Web. I would drink the usual for lunch. On my sole active day that month, I worked up just enough energy in the morning to fill out résumés online at monster.com and hotjobs.com, but the exercise of summarizing my professional life in résumé form—I hadn't written one since finishing college—only served to deepen my hopelessness. I was fifty-one years old, had never had a respectable job with real responsibilities, could never take corporate culture or effort seriously, hated daily journalism, hated what alternative journalism had become, and demanded a high salary for my inexperience, old age, lack of ambition, and reflexive disloyalty. My résumé read like an official Certificate of Unemployability.

Hoping to deepen my hopelessness, I took constant note of Seattle's unemployment rate, which was rising faster than stock prices had been two years before. Every day, the local papers were full of high-tech company bankruptcy stories. The writers grew weary of finding new ways to report the same old Dog Bites Man story, leading with ever-less-imaginative variations on "Another day, another dot-com collapse." When Indaba closed its doors in the midst of this carnage, the jobless rate in Seattle was hitting 12 percent—exactly double the national average—and my fellow losers, being younger, more skilled, and generally without families to support, were eminently more employable than I was. There wasn't a glimmer of hope to be seen no matter where I looked.

Not that I was looking, particularly. When you lose your job, you devote most of your waking hours—which include those hours you spend lying in bed at night—to self-loathing. It keeps you too busy to look for work. There is something almost bracing about the beating you give yourself for having so carefully arranged your life so as to leave you with a family to feed and no means of doing so at the time in your dependents' lives when they most need your money. You fill your days with visitations from your angry Inner Mother, who is given to shrieking: "How could you have been so stupid? So self-indulgent? So capricious? I mean, it's one thing to lead *yourself* so carefully down the road to ruin. It's just one loser more or less. But your wife and children? *What were you thinking?*"

The problem with this sort of energetic self-flagellation is that the high only lasts for a few days. And unemployment is forever.

I waited a week before telling my wife, who was in California, at Caitlin's college, seeing her through recovery from an emergency appendectomy. I got up every morning and went to work as if there was a reason for me to be there, a future to continue building, while I tried to figure out how to have the conversation with her about our financial ruin. ("Um . . . Honey, I left the career that was supporting us to follow two children I knew full well were headed for ruin.") I finally managed it when I was driving her back home from the airport. She said nothing for several minutes—I could hear the wheels in her head clicking away as she did the math, adding up the month's severance pay I would get, the $2,500 I would be reimbursed for having bought my stock options, the remains of our F5 stock, my unemployment compensation checks . . . then subtracting endless costs. We might be able to hold on to house, home, and respectability for four months or so. After that . . . all I could think about was George Orwell's *The Road to Wigan Pier*.

"Well, shit," she said.

She has a fatal tendency to look at the bright side, and rebounded with depressing speed. I should tell everyone we know, she said, about my downfall because someone might know of a job somewhere. She suggested that I explore every connection in the technology world that I had made through my writing.

The more she tried encouraging me, the more discouraged I felt. I couldn't bear talking with anyone about my humiliation. And I had been a relentless skeptic when writing about other high-tech companies, scorning scheme after scheme with a fervor equaled only by the fervor with which I had fallen in thrall to Squish and Joey and their stupid empire. It was sheer perversity, the way I was predicting the bursting of the technology-boom bubble even as I was enthusiastically diving into the bubble bath.

The month of sitting around the Indaba office in despair finally came to an end, and I settled in at home, looking at employment ads online, filing my weekly unemployment compensation claim every Monday morning, dutifully finding a way to send out three résumés per week so as to meet the requirements of the dole, walking down to the mailbox at noon, e-mailing various temporary-employment agencies to remind them that I was still pointlessly alive, and sitting bleakly in my basement office, my mood growing ever blacker, ever blacker.

I applied for work as a teacher, public-relations flack, technical writer, marketing writer, computer-user education writer, manager, editor of this, producer of that, and so on, sending various versions of my résumé off into the silence and nothingness, feeling eminently unqualified and unsuited for every possible job on modern Earth, except for bile processor.

Now I began measuring the passage of unemployment time in months rather than weeks. I could see fear growing in the eyes of my children, and saw how hard it was for them to ask what few questions they asked: "Will I be able to go back to college in the fall?" "Are we going to have to sell the house?" Anne told me one night that she had been driving Jocelyn and two friends somewhere, and the friends invited Jocelyn to go to a movie with them. Jocelyn answered evasively, telling them she thought she had to do something else that night. Then when she and Anne got home, she said, "Would it have been OK to say yes to them? Can we afford for me to go to movies anymore?"

I was three months unemployed when I got my first call from a prospective employer. "Is this Fred Moody?" a voice asked when I answered the phone.

"Yes."

"I saw your resume on monster.com, and noticed that it had been posted some time ago. I was wondering if you were still looking for opportunities?"

My heart kicked back to life, like an old boiler. "Um . . . yeah."

"Well, we're looking for someone to head up our technical writing department. I'm a recruiter for F5."

That was the call that brought me through simple suffering to the conviction that I was being tortured. I stopped talking to my family almost entirely. We sat through dinners in silence. The kids would bolt their dinners and flee, and on the occasional night when I was feeling particularly garrulous, I might, after they'd left the table, utter something like, "I sent out some more résumés today."

Then I would lapse back into silence, fighting back infuriating tears, counting down the days until our money ran out and my unemployment checks stopped coming, tuning out my wife's disgusting words of support and encouragement.

The only voice I would listen to was the one I could hear coming out of *Monstrance*. It sounded like Mr. Ed's voice. "It doesn't really matter what happens to you, you know. . . . It doesn't matter what happens to *anybody*. Humans! [Snicker, snort.] Someday I'll be looking out from here at pretty much nothing—no traces of human endeavor left! No trace of anything any human ever did on this Earth, except for what my sculptor did. Har. Har. Har. I'm gonna outlast *hewman* civilization!"

I came to regard my life as an exercise in monstrous irony: I had moved my family to the end of a dead-end street in a quiet, isolated neighborhood on a sparsely populated island in order to seal them off, protect them from all possible harm. Then it turned out that the only real menace to those nearest and dearest to me was . . . me. Me and my bone-headed outbreak of ambition.

I started narrating my life in the third person, the way Erin had done back in the happy times: "So, in a certain startup had worked a certain fuckin' moron . . ."; "The fuckin' moron woke from troubled sleep one morning to discover that he had turned into a monstrous vermin in the eyes of prospective employers . . ."; "What struck him most was the fact that from Monday on he would be a fuckin' moron."

The whole bust raging through Seattle, the legions of laid-off, the ruined lives—I saw it all as a story not about the city but about me. Everything boom-and-bust-related became part of my personal tragedy, ancillary details in the story of my suffering. I was Seattle's only chronically unemployed man. I couldn't encounter anything in the news without making it about me: Other unemployed were not suffering humans but simply competitors, obstacles to my finding work; George Bush's tax cut for the wealthy, enacted while he was aggressively taxing my unemployment checks, was an assault not on the undermoneyed masses but on me alone. I saw my life now as a ridiculous quest that began as a vain and pointless attempt to understand, to define, Seattle: What it was, what it was becoming, whether the magic that I believed to be unique to it could be saved in the face of material progress and a tremendous economic boom. That search gradually became more and more confused until I couldn't tell whether I was trying to define my city or myself. Whenever I asked the question, "What kind of city is Seattle becoming?" was I really asking the question, "What the hell am I turning into?" Did there come a time when I could no longer tell the difference between the two?

It wasn't just me, either—that question always seemed to be part of the news in Seattle, the main item on the public agenda. I decided this intense preoccupation among Seattleites with Seattle's identity—a preoccupation I believed to be unique to Seattle—was really a struggle on the part of its citizens to come to terms with the kind of adults they had grown up to be. I couldn't imagine Cleveland or Detroit having gone through this relentless self-examination when they were 150 years old. What was it about Seattle that made its people so self-absorbed?

All these city-as-self, self-as-city, what-is-the-meaning-of-every-little-thing-that-ever-happens-here questions and meditations spiraling around and around and around in my head came crashing to a dizzying halt on September 11, when I spent the day along with the rest of the nation watching replays of the same horrifying images, those planes hitting the World Trade Center towers and the towers collapsing. As Rick Anderson would point out in the *Weekly* a few days later, the towers were "engineered by Seattleites . . . designed by a Seattle-born and-schooled architect, built with Seattle-fabricated steel, and felled by Seattle airplanes." It is testament to the severity of my implosion that I regarded the event less as a global turning point than as a grotesque symbolic referendum on Seattle's pretensions and ambitions. I saw the catastrophe as the grim closing of a circle, the fulfillment of the prophecy uttered by Seattle's founders when they dubbed their new settlement "New-York-Pretty-Soon."

This would be more or less when I bottomed out. My vision started to collapse around me so that I could see little more than the patch of ground in front of my feet, or the patch of table between my elbows, as I stood or sat listlessly mulling over my lamentable condition. It was like looking out at the world through a hole in the wall of my black, lightless room.

Then one night, for no reason, I raised my head while we were sitting at the dinner table and looked out at my family for what felt like the first time in months. My eyes met Caitlin's—she was home for the summer—who was sitting directly across from me, her brows beetling, her lips pursed, her face set in a stern expression. I was about to be disciplined.

"You are the most self-pitying person I've ever seen," she said. "*Ever.*"

It was an amazing moment—one of the great experiences of my life. The blackness evaporated around me. I felt clouds part overhead and heard a chorus of angels burst into song, as is customary when humans undergo Revelation. It was almost unbearably trite. Everything and everyone around me vanished for an instant, replaced by pure glowing golden light and the vision of a shining path curving out before me, beginning to describe a circle.

I blinked and restored my home and family to their rightful places. My wife was sitting to my right, Jocelyn to my left, Caitlin across from me. We were all quietly eating as if nothing at all had happened. Had anyone heard what Caitlin said? Was she even aware that she'd said what I'd heard her say?

Now everything was different. My sorrows and fears had evaporated. I was Little Shat again, taken aside by Caitlin for correction, brought body and soul back to those pre-boom days of laid-back bliss. And now, I knew, all would be well.

Sodom and Tomorrow

I woke up the morning after Caitlin's pronouncement and resolved never to look back. I feared I would be turned into a pillar of salt by the Caitlin-mediated god offering me redemption. I pictured Seattle as a smoking ruin, to be instantly forgotten and fled in search of some relatively prelapsarian city—like Seattle before the boom—and I was wary of plunging into my self-pitying spiral again.

As if to acknowledge the wisdom (and maybe even the virtue) of my decision, a job suddenly materialized. One week to the day after my unemployment compensation ran out, after five months of unemployment, I began work writing newsletters, fliers, and Web pages for the King County Department of Transportation. Cosseting commuters. My office, it turned out, was in Maynardtown—a short walk through Pioneer Square from the ferry terminal—with a view out to the south, looking directly at two classically vulgar Paul Allen vanity projects: the new Seahawks football stadium and the new buildings around the Allen-restored old Union Station. I would have expected to view them as horrifying, if not downright threatening, encroaching as they were on the edge of the sacred center of Seattle. Instead, from the safety of my Maynardtown perch, in my new state of mind, they looked a world away—as harmless, now that the boom was over, as they were ostentatious. They looked more like the ruins of a fallen, bloated empire than new monuments to a new emperor.

In a way, they *were* ruins—the boom they pretended to honor had gone bust before the paint on the football stadium was dry, and Amazon, the primary tenant in the Union Square project, was laying off employees by the hundreds. It was as if Allen had built them not with the intention that they have a useful life before fading to ruin, but simply to be ruins. He wanted to leave a stain on the landscape that would immortalize him. I couldn't look at them without thinking of Jonathan Raban's line about the Pyramids: "Mr. Big was here."

In the cold cleansing light of the technology bust, all the boom-delivered dangers to Seattle looked faded, worn, weakened. Gleaming new office buildings were plastered with vacancy signs that looked like white flags of surrender. The big success stories of the boom—Microsoft, Starbucks—had become just another part of the corporate scenery. Their novelty worn off, their growth curves flattened, their competitive environments completely changed, their founders grown into middle age, they had lost their novelty, their charm, their power. They were reduced like their corporate elders to a kind of white noise in the background. They were faded celebrities—still there, still glittering, but no longer vibrant, no longer leading the way to a glorious future, no longer objects of fascination, no longer dangerous.

I saw firsthand one morning how precipitous the fall can be from glamorous startup to establishment white trash. I was standing in a Pioneer Square Starbucks, at the corner of First and Yesler, when I saw a tourist couple walk in. The man was a classic: in his seventies, sporting a straw fedora, loud shirt, oversized Bermuda shorts, and black socks and shoes. He looked like the result of a collaboration between Edward Hopper and David Hockney. He and his wife took only two steps into the Starbucks theme park before he stopped, enraged. "Let's go get coffee somewhere else!" he said. "I don't want to go to a *franchise*."

I came all the way to Seattle to have an alternative-coffee experience, dad gummit, and I'm damned well going to have one!

I found what he was looking for in the opposite corner of Pioneer Square, at Second and Jackson—across the street from my new workplace. Called Zeitgeist Art • Coffee, it was, according to its promotional material, an "out of the box" coffee house exhorting addicts to "support the spirit of Seattle's independent coffee houses." The first time I walked into the place—unfinished brick walls, the kind of massive wood beams that characterize so many of Pioneer Square's original buildings, that

classic Seattle preservation-as-revolution ambience, an art exhibit hanging on the walls, deliberately disenfranchised youngsters working behind
the counter—I felt instantly at home. I also noticed that the Zeitgeist was
crowded—far more so than both the Starbucks down the block and the
one across Maynardtown, where I'd encountered the disgruntled tourist.

How bad can things be in post-Starbucks/Microsoft/Tiffany's Seattle
if the thirst for alternative Art • Coffee can still be slaked?

A few months later, I encountered an exhibition mounted at Zeitgeist
of forty-by-fifty-inch "C-prints"—they look like color photographs
printed on canvas—composed by Chad States. I was particularly taken
with the print "Wrapping Up"—a self-portrait of States, down on one
knee in the dirt at the base of a tree. It is after dark. He has dug a small
hole in front of him—the discarded shovel is lying in the foreground, as
if flung down in haste—and he is furtively putting a small, red-ribboned,
bright-red gift box in it. He is looking a little off to one side. Surrounded by drabness—dusk, brown tree trunks, dirt, States's black clothing—the box is vivid, spectacular, tacky, and splendid. States, his face
mournful, reflective, intends to bury it and flee before anyone can catch
him in the act.

I see the picture as a depiction of precisely what Seattle is doing now,
in the wake of its ill-advised embracing of the boom: trying to hide its
gifts again, return to obscurity, find a way back to that peaceful cultural
isolation, the Golden Age of Ivar. Back when clams were clams. It was a
time when people knew what an amazing treasure we had here, and
strived to keep the ambitious at bay so as to preserve as much of the surrounding natural and spiritual splendor as possible, for as long as possible.

There were days in my new job when I felt like I was undergoing a reverse
Rip van Winkle experience, waking up in the distant past rather than the
distant future. I would walk through Pioneer Square, through a Seattle I
had thought long dead, and go to work among Seattleites of a sort I had
presumed long gone. My sojourn among the tech-boomers—which, I was
beginning to realize, had effectively been twenty years long—was a self-
imposed jail sentence, a wallowing in ambition and acquisitiveness, most
of the people I spent my time with having alien values and social skills.
For every person I met with aspirations beyond personal wealth and
glory—and I was surprised to note that I now ranked Bill Gates first
among them—there were hundreds scheming to get theirs while the getting was good. That certainly had become my ethic at the end: Give me

my options, get me to cash conversion as quickly as possible, cut me a big check, and cut me loose. At the height of the boom, that was the city's defining ethic.

Now I worked among people whose days were consumed almost entirely by efforts to help other people in ways large and small. Selflessness was the defining ethic. When I was given my first writing assignment, a flier about a bus route on Seattle's Beacon Hill, I was told, "Keep in mind that your audience is a Hmong immigrant grandma squatting with her groceries at a bus stop, squinting at this flier and trying to figure out what the hell is going to happen to her bus." It was the most empathetic portrait of a reader I'd ever heard.

I met transit planners who would ride buses to the far reaches of the county and back after work to see whether they had eased commuters' burdens with the routes they redesigned, or to see if there were ways to make buses serve people better. I overheard phone conversation after phone conversation in which my co-workers were listening to overheated complaints from callers, some of dubious sanity, and answering with epic patience, dutifully taking down every word, promising to pass it on to the appropriate department, then actually doing so. You would have thought helping a caller recover from a nearby road construction project or a bus driver's real or imagined slight was a life-or-death proposition for them— the equivalent of closing a $40 million venture-capital deal in the technology sector.

It was like being in Mister Rogers' neighborhood. I brought my wife in to the office one day to meet my new peers and she came away astounded that I had found my way back to the Seattle of yore. "I can't believe you work with people like this," she said. "You've never had it this good. They are *nice*, they care how you are doing, they listen to what you're saying, they respond appropriately when you talk . . ."

No longer fearful of looking back—convinced, in fact, that there was no point in having gone through what I'd gone through unless I looked all the way back and tried to make sense of it all—I began taking stock of the city, trying to assess its condition after the boom. Was there still a "Seattle" outside of Maynardtown? So much of the town had gone to glitz, it was undeniably more crowded, and its infrastructure had failed drastically to keep up with this last burst of boom-boosted growth. So many people—friends of mine among them—were still out of work. Seattle traffic, in a study that shocked the city, was revealed to be second-worst in the nation, after chronic offender Los Angeles. In the newspapers, traffic problems became the symbol of Seattle malaise. The *Seattle Times* posed the question, "Has Seattle lost its soul?" and 350 people answered, most of them with a doleful "Yes," many of them citing, as evidence, experiences they had had in their cars. Road-rage stories came to be more and more the trend in both daily papers, the theme in all of them being that it was to be expected in a normal American city, but never in Seattle.

One morning, a traumatized young woman stopped her car during the early-morning commute on the Interstate 5 bridge over Lake Union. The bridge was sixteen stories above the lake. She climbed over the railing and stood there, trying to work up the nerve to jump.

In due course, the police arrived and began attempting to talk the woman out of suicide. They blocked off a section of the lane behind her. Then, as traffic piled up, the police were horrified to hear shouts from motorists behind them, urging her to "jump, bitch, jump!" Desperate to keep the woman from hearing more, the police completely shut down traffic on the freeway at 8 A.M., paralyzing the city.

Ultimately, the woman did jump, suffering severe injuries. The story appeared in news outlets around the country, all of them posing the question, "What has happened to Seattle?" And Seattle itself went into a paroxysm of self-examination, wondering how on earth a city fabled for its civility could be capable of such monstrous insensitivity.

The episode came as no shock to me, in my heightened state of post-boom remorse. I was convinced that Seattle was tremendously corrupted by the boom and that its recovery was at least as much in doubt as mine was. I joined the legions of Seattleites sifting through statistics as if they were birds' entrails, looking for the answer to the question "How much has Seattle declined?" Second-worst-traffic-in-the-nation bad gave way to the more telling news that Seattle now had the fewest children per capita of any city in the nation save for San Francisco. There had been a time when Seattle, in thrall to Bobo, ruled by Ivar, had been a family town. Now I saw the new statistical ranking—the dubious realization of that distant *Seattle 2000* goal—as a sign that Seattle had been overtaken by the self-obsessed, chasing wealth and material acquisition at the expense of the sustaining values and joys that keep a civilization spiritually alive. A city that has no place for kids, I thought, is a city without hope. I connected the decline with the joyful defiant wit of Seattle's Sean Nelson, a young writer who had been fired by the *Weekly* in 1997 and went on to fame and fortune as the front man for Harvey Danger, among the most successful of Seattle's post-grunge rock bands. In the band's witty hit

"Flagpole Sitta," Nelson sings, "Been around the world and seen that only stupid people are breeding." I heard in the song a Seattle-bred singer's cry of exuberant despair, shouted out on behalf of his city.

One day, I paid a visit to Dale Chihuly, on the theory that I could measure the change in Seattle over the course of the boom by measuring the difference between the artist I had met back at the boom's beginnings and the world-renowned celebrity from twenty-first-century Seattle.

Chihuly had become an eponym by then, the name being pretty much generic—a term for gigantic, brilliantly colored glass sculptures that are variously viewed as grandiose, gorgeous, spectacular, gross, breathtaking, and egomaniacal. Until the turn of the millennium, the two most notorious were the "Chihuly over Venice" series of chandeliers temporarily suspended over the canals in that birth-of-glass-art city and memorialized in countless videotapes and books cranked out by the indefatigable Chihuly publicity machine; and the massive "Bellagio Ceiling," a sculpture, installed in the lobby of a Las Vegas hotel/casino, that is made up of 2,000 glass pieces weighing 40,000 pounds in all, held in place overhead by another 10,000 pounds of steel. (Chihuly does Vegas!). The piece covers 2,100 square feet—making it, Chihuly hastened to tell me during my visit, the *Guinness Book of World Records*-designated world's largest sculpture.

After those prodigious feats, Chihuly talked his way into the old Walled City of Jerusalem, where he installed towers (including one standing thirty-two feet and weighing in at twenty-five tons), chandeliers, and various other glass pieces in one of art history's grander gestures: *Jerusalem 2000*. Who but Chihuly, I wondered, would have the nerve to try putting his mark on the millennium by improving the look and feel of the cradle of Judeo-Christianity with his own artwork?

I met with him in his celebrated Boathouse, on the north shore of Lake Union, next to Ivar's Salmon House. He took me up to his apartment there, at the top of a twisted flight of stairs above the offices and display rooms at water level. I reminded him that I spent a few days with him in 1982, and his face registered shock. "A lot has happened since you saw me last," he said after we shook hands. "Now I'm a CEO, I guess." He sounded utterly exhausted, as if the prodigious efforts exerted over those nineteen years had finally caught up with him this very morning.

It is undeniably true that the small studio operation I saw when I first met him had become a corporation-scale enterprise. Chihuly now employed 120 people working in three different facilities: the Boathouse; a group of warehouses in Ballard where his huge pieces were assembled for approval by clients, then dismantled and packed for shipping; and a 75,000-square-foot warehouse on the Tacoma waterfront, from where his work was shipped out in containers to museums, galleries, and private collectors around the world. At any given time now, between ten and twenty Chihuly installations were under construction somewhere in the world, and he had, on average, two museum openings a month. It was reliably estimated that his enterprise brought in $1.5 million per month.

It was not surprising then that he had lost touch with most of the colleagues from his salad days. Chihuly the celebrity was viewed with disdain (or, said his friends, jealousy) by many local artists, and even those who praised his genius decried his estrangement from the "real" arts world. It was assumed in some circles in Seattle that he had earned his fame and financial success at the expense of his integrity, and that his art now was more eye candy than food for the soul.

Sitting that day with him in his apartment looking out over Lake Union, I felt a palpable sense of isolation. I had had to set up this appointment weeks in advance, and was ushered in to Chihuly, as if to the Master, by a businesslike young woman who met me in an office downstairs. And the Chihuly I encountered had changed in disquieting ways from the iconoclastic Barnum I remembered. His voice was much softer, his speech more halting; he ingested a prodigious array of vitamins and assorted other pills every morning; he moved slowly and awkwardly, as if coping with the aches and pains of old age; his hair, still artfully disarranged and tangled in that famous Chihuly do, was much thinner, and inexpertly dyed black, lending him something of the air of Gustave Aschenbach near the end of *Death in Venice*. He seemed markedly doleful and talked almost exclusively of business rather than art, his discourses on his work limited largely to comments about the outsized scale of his installations.

As we talked, he mentioned, along with the scale of the Bellagio project and the number of people and amount of heavy equipment he employed for *Jerusalem 2000*, the laboratory he is operating in Ballard, where he is experimenting with ways to make plastic look like glass—an initiative, should it succeed, that would allow him to construct works of even more staggering size. It grew increasingly clear that size mattered a great deal to Chihuly—he came back to the topic again and again. *"Blue Feather Tower,"* he said at one point, returning to discussion of *Jerusalem 2000*, "was sixty feet high and had more than three thousand parts . . . We used a two-hundred-foot crane to bring things into the castle, we had eleven forty-foot containers of glass, four thousand pieces, and I took about thirty people."

Gone were the enthusiastic and energetic paeans to glass as an artistic medium, to the mission of the glass artist, to the magical properties of glass in its delivery of color and light. I felt almost as if I were talking to an animatronic version of the younger, charismatic Chihuly—a figure who now was soullessly going through the motions of being an artist, particularly when he talked, as he did at great length, oblivious or indifferent to the symbolic implications, of his dream of moving from glass to plastic.

Chihuly interrupted my line of questions at one point to ask me how I felt about present-day Seattle. I commenced a long speech about how diminished I thought it was, how money and the quest for glory and celebrity had corrupted it, then stopped in mid-pronouncement when I noticed that Chihuly was staring at me as if he thought I was completely insane.

As our conversation neared its end, I felt myself falling prey to an overwhelming sense of gloom. I could not bring myself to admire the successful Chihuly anywhere near as much as I had admired—liked, really—the striving younger Chihuly. It made me wonder whether material success seen through eyes like mine—the eyes of an unregenerate Seattleite—could ever appear as anything other than a passage from dreamy, glamorous idealism to seamy cynicism. Sitting there, listening to Chihuly talk about the size of this exhibition and the size of that piece, about business and money and grandeur and Vegas and celebrity and attention and nearly everything but art, all I could think about was his passage from charismatic artist/visionary to chagrined old king in his tower, counting his money and boasting zestlessly about the size of his kingdom.

Finished now, we stood, walked down a flight of stairs, and made our way to a long room looking out over Lake Union. The room was a good hundred feet long, and scarcely wider than an amazing table, made from an old-growth tree cut lengthwise, that ran nearly its full length. I stood at one end and looked in some wonder at two hundred-foot rows of little Chihuly glass sculptures arranged on the table. They had been produced by the crews working all day long, day after day, in the huge studio behind the Boathouse. "I have to look these over," he said as he turned away from me, "to decide which ones are good enough to sign."

For a few minutes I watched him as he made his way down the rows of these mass-produced little Chihulys. He was walking slowly, a little stooped over. I was reminded, vividly, of the title character in Orson

Welles's *Citizen Kane*, shuffling disconsolately through his massive mansion near the end of his life. It was hard not to wonder whether Chihuly himself ever found his mind turning to similar disconsolation, and whether he regretted, as Welles's version of William Randolph Hearst did, the turn his life had taken from the capture of luster to the counting of lucre.

I keep seeing him now walking slowly down that row of his works, going through the motions less of an artist than of an executive, and wondering if I am seeing not so much a corrupted figure as one who simply is on the far side of success's curve. Is it the Seattleite in me who insists on seeing Chihuly's material success as moral failure? Am I looking at him through the distorted lens of my own willful losing? Do I see him as a personification of the boom I've decided to loathe? One minute, I decide that I am watching a great artist walking the length of this gallery, his genius and merit invisible to me because of my consistent embrace of failure. The next, I am convinced that Chihuly is the art-world version of Paul Allen.

There did come a time when I had to admit that the boom, once I looked beyond its real and imagined effects on me, me, me, was as much a good as a bad thing for the world, if not necessarily for Seattle. Bill Gates, his struggles with competitors and the federal government notwithstanding, began emerging from the smoke of the bust as a tremendous force of enlightenment, decency, and simple social good. He began doing exactly what he had said he would do with his fortune: taking great care in researching how it could be put to the best possible use, then giving it away.

In a February 2002 speech to the 9th Conference on Retroviruses and Opportunistic Infections, Gates demonstrated how well aware he was of the importance and potential of his money, and how intent he was on directing it at the world's most pressing problems—and those most neglected by mainstream philanthropy. By the time I came across this speech, he already had given $1 billion to fund college scholarships for racial minorities, for whom scholarship money and entry to college were being drastically reduced because of U.S. Supreme Court rulings on affirmative action, and a staggering $4.8 billion to "global health."

Gates had determined that efforts to eradicate disease—particularly HIV/AIDS—were misdirected. "Typically there's been a fifteen-to-twenty-year lag between the use of a new vaccine in the rich world and the poor world," he said in his conference speech. "Unfortunately, many of the needs of the world at large are not present in rich countries. So here we get what you'd have to call the greatest market failure of all time." He went on to describe what he called the "90/10 rule: 90 percent of the world's resources are spent on 10 percent of its medical problems and conversely 10 percent of the resources are spent on 90 percent of the problem."

Considering that Gates could best be described as a capitalist's capitalist, as enthusiastic a competitor in the marketplace as anyone in history, his remarks on the failure of capitalism to address the world's most pressing problems were relatively shocking. They set me off on a reading binge of Gates speeches posted on the Bill & Melinda Gates Foundation Web site. "When I first learned about world health," Gates says there, "I have to say that I was kind of stunned. I half expected that the United States and other governments and foundations were really taking these low-cost interventions [vaccines and other essential health-care initiatives] and saying that the value of life is the same throughout the world and really focusing on that problem. And yet the more I learned about it the more I realized that there is a real market failure here. There's a failure of visibility; there's a failure of incentives; there's a failure of cooperation that has really led to a very disastrous situation. In fact, the gap in health outcomes is growing very dramatically. While the rich world is cutting down in tobacco use, it's growing in the poor world. AIDS and TB are really a phenomenon of the poor world. When I say the poor world of course I mean the majority of the world, anything outside the enclave that most of us here are privileged to live in and the kind of vaccines and things that we take for granted not only for ourselves, but also for our children. . . . 95 percent of all new HIV infections occur in developing countries, 99 percent of TB and malaria sufferers live in developing countries. Yet where demand for health spending is greatest, supply is lowest."

His research almost took on the form of a philanthropist's search for an investment opportunity—the sector where he could get the most bang for his buck. "Rich governments are not fighting these diseases because the rich world doesn't have them," Gates said in another speech. "The private sector generally is not developing vaccines for poor countries because poor countries can't buy them. Of the $70 billion spent globally on health every year, only 10 percent is devoted to research on diseases that make up 90 percent of the total disease burden. . . . Market-based capitalism works well for the developed world, but our human values and compassion are needed to save these children. Markets alone won't do this."

Just as dire as the direction of markets is the direction of philanthropy. "People might ask why I am doing philanthropy that is largely targeting poor countries of the world. Many of the foundations around the world primarily target the same rich country where the wealth was earned and although I have no dispute with that—I think it's fine—I think the balance ought to weigh more heavily in favor of the true inequities that exist on a fairly global basis."

Gates decided that there were only two possible ways out of the conundrum. "I believe," he said, "that if you took the world and you randomly re-sorted it so that rich people lived next door to poor people—so, for example, people in the United States saw millions of mothers burying babies who had died from measles or malnutrition or pneumonia—they would insist something be done. And they would be willing to pay for it." That being a practical impossibility, he decided that it fell to him to pay for it.

I spent a lot of time reading and rereading these remarks. They are profoundly sensitive, and more thoughtful than I ever would have expected from such an ambitious, competitive, driven young American capitalist. Gates had parlayed his startup into the largest personal fortune in the world and now was dispensing that fortune in the most enlightened way possible. Where did that enlightenment come from? Was it something innate? A function of his intelligence? I decide to believe it is his Seattleness—he is the kind of "out of the box" corporate titan-turned-philanthropist that could come only from such a determinedly alternative place.

Days passed, each one increasing my distance and emotional detachment from the boom and its effects on Seattle, on me. I felt myself emerging—finally!—from the Dark Phoebus Erin had ushered me into twenty years before.

I had fallen into a new habit: tracking down people from the distant past to see how much they had been changed, damaged, helped, harmed, or left untouched by the boom. Connie Butler and Rick Downing were still living in their Wallingford house, working happily away at their same businesses—both of which had benefited indirectly from the boom—lavishing their love and lucre on their daughter, now six years old. Dick

Weiss and Sonja Blomdahl had married and were raising their daughter in the same Fremont home where I'd spent so much time with Weiss in the 1980s, when I was writing about and admiring glass art and artists. I walked up to that house one day and was surprised and thrilled to see that it hadn't changed at all. The living room was still packed with glass pieces by Weiss, Blomdahl, and their friends, Weiss still worked in a small studio built against the back of the house, still wrote up his invoices and letters on a portable typewriter, and still entertained guests in the small kitchen upstairs in their home. He was still working with rondelles, building beautiful, intricate, abstract flat panels for doors and windows, while Blomdahl was still making bowls containing what the *Seattle Post-Intelligencer*'s Regina Hackett calls "color that defies gravity."

I had the impression that Weiss and Blomdahl were living in a protective bubble, isolated from the boom, and hadn't even noticed it was out there.

Well, not entirely. Weiss took me out to his studio to look at his recent work and said, laughing, "What happened was that all these technology people around here turned up with all this money for big new homes—they've been keeping me incredibly busy for years!" Then he shrugged his shoulders, as if to add, "Go figure!" He seemed to regard the last twenty years as an enormous joke.

I realized later that he was the first person I'd come across in the course of my re-exploration who viewed the boom not as a marvelous transformation of Seattle from small town to world-class city, as Greater Seattle did, nor as an evil force destroying everything that was good here, as Lesser Seattle did, nor again as a get-rich-right-now opportunity, as the boom's progenitors and participants did. To Weiss, it was just something fate delivered—fortune to be endured whether it is good or bad. It comes your way and you make the best of it, doing what you do out of love for what you do, allowing outsiders to buy into it as much or as little as they want. The work and the joy is all that matters—the money comes and goes when it wants to, according to its own rules. The only difference the boom had made in his life was that he worked more steadily for a time.

Weiss seemed to have the same view of the boom that Seattle writer David Shields had about displays of ambition here: "[I]s it really all that terrible," Shields wrote in his 2002 *Enough About You: Adventures in Auto-biography*, "if Seattle is now (or was—pre-Nasdaq crash) a 'worldwide center of ambition'? Isn't that a good, or at least an amusing, thing?" In his previous two books, *Remote* and *Black Planet*, Shields had reveled in affectionately deriding what he called Seattle's "upbeat earnestness," left over from its Bobo/Ivar days. In *Black Planet*, he confessed that his greatest fear was that he was "becoming a Seattleite." (He had moved here in adulthood to teach at the University of Washington.) Then, ruminating in *Enough About You* about the self he inhabits and creates in Seattle, he wrote, "As difficult as I sometimes find to admit it, I'm a westerner and even, now, a Seattleite. I love being a resident of a remote state, where (we tell ourselves) we're disconnected from everyone else and therefore forced to make everything up on our own, feverishly hoping that what we come up with will somehow, magically, prove to be indispensable to the rest of the world which, hemmed in by tradition, hasn't thought of that yet."

Maybe that was true for me, too. Maybe it was more than greed after all that drove me Indaba-ward. Maybe I just got caught up in the Zeitgeist and set off with all the other silicon rushers intent on coming up with what the rest of the world hasn't thought of yet. It's just what Seattleites always do—and have been doing since the utopian days of George Venable Smith. (That's what startups were here—latter-day Washington Territory utopias.) What's the point of trying to figure out why, or agonizing over what went wrong and what went right?

And maybe too this exercise in self-examination is really just what Seattleites do all the time: try to sort out their individual selves from the group, in a city where the single unchanging, ongoing, consistent preoccupation on the part of the urban collective consciousness is a struggle to identify the city's self. What kind of town am I becoming? Seattle, I am convinced, is more caught up in this question, figuring out from minute to minute what it is, what it is becoming (laid-back? civil? overcrowded? mean-spirited? cool? big-league? world power? dropout?) than any city ever. Now I see Shields (and me, too, enough about him) as a distillation of his city. He is a writer who delights in plunging his brain into a milieu, like a mad scientist plunking a brain into a vat of chemicals, just to see what happens to it. "I'm just trying to be honest here: the only portraits I'm really interested in are self-portraits as well," he writes in *Enough About You*. "I like it when a writer makes the arrow point in both directions—outward toward another person and inward toward his own head." Terrified of becoming a Seattleite, he has plunged his brain into Seattle and seen it turn into . . . the brain of a Seattleite.

There came a day when the combined forces of new employment, Weiss and Blomdahl, Shields, Butler and Downing, my happy resurgent family,

Seattle's summertime weather, and a long-overdue devouring of books on Seattle history set me free from the infinite inward brooding spiral I'd trapped myself in when trying to make moral sense of my participation in the boom. I started adding up the boom-delivered blessings in my life and found them too numerous to count. *Monstrance for a Grey Horse*, which delivers constant inspiration to me, is in my yard because of money generated by a startup's IPO. The boom brought enough national attention to Seattle to goad publishers into paying me to write books. The *Weekly* thrived for years on boom-driven bucks, many of which it passed on to me. Directly and indirectly, boom money kept my family alive for years. Our family trip to Korea to explore and pay homage to Jocelyn's roots was brought us by the boom. And it was the boom that forced me out of the typesetting business at precisely the right moment: One day later, one day earlier, and we would have gotten the wrong daughter.

If anyone in Seattle can legitimately be said to be working at things the rest of the world "hasn't thought of yet," it is James L. Acord. After leaving Richland in 1998, his efforts at getting permission to use a nuclear reactor to create sculpture rebuffed, he set off on a worldwide quest for a reactor he could use in his transmutation art project. He secured an artist-in-residency at Imperial College of Physics, in London, and began negotiating with Rutherford-Appleton Laboratories and British Nuclear Fuels there for use of a reactor. After years of study, he had worked out the physics of transmuting technetium-99 (a byproduct of nuclear reactors that is a form of nuclear waste in this country and nuclear fuel in France) into ruthenium (a platinoid, it is among the rarest metals in the universe), and he wanted to use the reactor-transmuted material in a "reliquary" (traditionally, a receptacle for the storing of sacred relics—e.g., the bones of a saint—in the Catholic Church). He already had mounted an exhibit of three reliquaries—studies for the masterpiece he had in mind—and that exhibit began touring Europe in 1999. *Fourth Reliquary*, as Acord called his dream piece, was to be the culmination of this thematic exploration. He was fixated to the point of obsession by the transmutation, through art, of dangerous nuclear material into something benign, even inspiring. "Public perceptions of nuclear technology," he wrote in one of his proposals, "will never be clarified until that same technology is put into the service of art, where its various capabilities and parameters might be humanized and reconceived." He wanted to encase his transmuted material in a reliquary because "the containment, distribution, preservation and application of nuclear waste is as important today as the containment and distribution of holy relics was to the medieval Catholic Church."

Arts organizations loved this stuff; scientists and bureaucrats in charge of nuclear reactors were less enthusiastic. Acord spent a year in London being celebrated by the Imperial College and the London arts scene and being rebuffed repeatedly by the gatekeepers at British Nuclear Fuels. His London misadventure ultimately set him off on one of his more sustained downward spirals, hastened by the attention he was getting from the London arts establishment. What drove him over the edge was an opening in London of an exhibit of his work—the sort of educated-adult gathering that terrifies him. (A runaway at age fifteen, Acord never finished high school.) A sympathetic art critic cornered him at the opening and asked him to "contextualize" his work for her. (Acord tells this story over and over again now, italicizing *contextualize* as if it were the most frightening thing anyone ever said to him.) He begged off, ran to a pub with a group of blue-collar ironworkers who had helped build the reliquaries, and soon after was back in Seattle.

When it came time to return to London for his second year of artist-in-residency, Acord summoned me to the Red Door tavern in Fremont for an extremely sentimental good-bye on the way to the airport. A month later, he called to say good-bye again—he had gone out to the airport, then turned back at the last minute. I sat through sentiment-soaked good-byes with him four times over two months before he disappeared entirely—not, as I thought, to London, but to a life on the Seattle streets. On those rare occasions when I saw him, he would either be drunk to the point of incoherence, depressed to the point of incoherence, or both.

Acord is a psychologically fragile (and obsessive) man who has lived alternately on the fringe and in the gutter all his life. He told me once that for him "Life is a dark room full of sharp objects." He was incarcerated for a time in his youth in a "lockdown mental-health facility," and has a terrible time managing the day-to-day details that come as second nature to most people. He has no bank account, no driver's license, scarcely any possessions, no family, and only a few friends. He can endure a given social situation for no more than two hours or so. Since leaving Richland in 1997, he has not had a home—his last year in Richland was spent in the shed on the edge of town that was his studio—except for the apartment given him in London during his artist-in-residency. For years, he has carried around a set of seven keys that, he says, "can open nothing," being the keys to the home and life he lost in Richland. He throws them "like the I Ching," and makes beautiful, highly realistic color drawings of the result. He has done this hundreds of times over the last four years. "I'm going to keep drawing these keys," he says, "until they lose their aura. Then I'm going to throw them into the middle of Puget Sound."

Acord has been "trying to solve the problems" of *Fourth Reliquary* for years. He attacks problems of artistic composition by drawing constantly, the same shapes over and over and over again, trying to get at the result he knows is locked somewhere in his unconscious. He abets this effort with prodigious reading—usually math and physics books. During this particular long downward drift, though, he could not put together enough of a routine to do any kind of sustained drawing work. Staying in friends' homes, he could never get a dedicated space for drawing set up, and he felt obliged to make attempts at conversation and a social life with his hosts. And homeless shelters, of course, were impossible work spaces.

His deterioration during this period was extreme. I met him, at his request, in a Pioneer Square tavern one day and he was hopelessly drunk, shuffling through the envelope he carried around with him in an attempt to show me his library card, soup-kitchen card, homeless shelter card, and the beginning of a drawing on which he'd made no progress. I left him that day not expecting to see him alive again.

Acord availed himself of the public library's personal computers to work on art proposals, correspond by e-mail with the gallery in Italy that was trying to put together a tour of his new work, and write to his friends. He was one of the legions of derelicts you see hanging around those machines in public libraries everywhere. He has a characteristically terrible time with computers, as with almost everything else in his life—"The only thing I know how to do right," he said to me once, "is make sculpture"—and these library sessions often turned into fiascos, particularly since the librarians would limit his time on the computers.

In his struggles with computers as with everything else, Acord seems to travel in the opposite direction of most people—the more time he spends studying something, the less he learns about it. (Sculpture, of course, excepted.) He sent me a long and rather entertaining letter once describing a typically Acordean struggle with the material world. In order to furnish proof of his amazing and ingenious struggles with the English language—I received a letter from him once saying, with unintentional aptitude, that he wanted to "writhe and check in"—I have reproduced the letter here exactly as he typed it.

Mr. Fred Moody
Dear Fred Moody,

It isn't that you have been on my mind these past weeks. And I am hoping to see you for an in-person visit, hopefully at "Larry's Green Front" on First Avenue (which I haven't been to since I returned from London and is one of my favorite places) but I've just been having the greatest truble sending emails from my Eudora account. I received your telephone message at Andy Constant's out in Carnation just as I was leaving my 'house-sit' there. All my phone cards are used up and I feel I'm slipping behind staying in touch with my friends.

I opened this email account in London because I had to, and it worked flawlessly for weeks, and I got back to the States and my ability descended day by day until I couldn't do anything, not even print. I haven't even been able to open the "in box" letter I have from you—much less the other corrospondace from England (and, without putting to grave a face upon this, I do want to mention that the difference between being a tenured professor creating sculpture and being a street wino in Pioneer Square is significant to me). So Fred if you get this please send back a "I got it Jim" so I know.

Paul Luksch {I'm sure you remember him, he was the white-haired guy who helped us on the installation of Monstrance for a Grey Horse oout at your place) has been helping me with my computer problems. Paul is the perfect guys in that he and I are friends these many years now and he is very patience. I don't want to cop to that I'm hysterical every time I loose a document, but I am. Paul seems to have the patience to deal with that.

So it's past midnight on Tuesday the 21-st so it's really early morning of the 23rd and I'm riding in this morning with Don to Seattle at 4:15 AM which will put me in Pioneer Square about Fiveishs. I'm working from Don Carver's computer in South Everett. Don is not on line {sculptor, right? Telephone cut off years ago) so I'm going to try to copy this to my disk and take it to downtown Seattle. I'm going to met Paul at one o'clock PM today on the ramp of the ferry in Seattle from Baindgerge Island (or Bremerton, I can never remember which). Then he is going to help me send it from a Sesattle public library. Something a home-less person needs to know how to do if he needs access to a nuclear reactor in Europe.

So I'm dog tired, low on beer and almost out of cigarettes and Don is going to get up in the next hour and I'm headed for Seattle. I'm going to try and send this to you soon, like today. Now I have to save it to disk the process of witch has lost so many documents. If this is lost I'll still get together with you for a beer.

All Best,
James L. Acord

Post script: I did not succeed in saving this to disk. It is days later. I did not meet up with Paul at one o'clock this afternoon at a coffee shop near the Bremerton to Seattle ferry terminal. I relayed a message through Tom Putnam this afternoon to Paul that I now didn't have anything to send. the cost of phone calls from the AMPM phone booth to Tom Putnam's in Seattle from South Everett is $2.45. I made thre calls to Tom without getting through. Or getting my money back. That took all the last money I had (over seven bucks). In the end I caled Tom collect and Tom promised to call Paul to tell him I wouldn't make it. So, Fred, you're my frend and I'm going to hard-mail this missive to you. I still have some stamps.

All best,
Jim

Oh, yeah . . . let's give this guy a nuclear reactor!

But then one day a friend bought Acord a week's rent at a decrepit transient flophouse in Ballard, called the Starlight Hotel. The doors were secured with padlocks, the hallways and floors were crooked, the other denizens were addicts, hookers, and other people horribly down on their luck who paid their rent by the week and generally moved on or were carried out after only a few days. The place oozed dust like a wet sponge oozes water. It looked like the last stop for people on their way to hitting bottom. Acord rigged up a drawing table by propping a piece of plywood between his bed and the heater under a windowsill, and got down to work. Suddenly, some floodgate in his mind opened, and the creativity came pouring out of him. He started producing tremendous numbers of drawings of both the inner workings and the outer appearance of *Fourth Reliquary*. Aware that he was on to something, he started selling drawings to friends in return for another week at the Starlight. In e-mails and conversation during that month and after, he always referred to his month there, without irony, as "my artist-in-residency at the Starlight Hotel."

When he had tapped out all his friends, Acord went back on the street until I brought Joey King up to date on his problems, and Joey had me arrange for a three-month stay at the Starlight. This Acord came to call his "Fellowship."

From April into July, Acord worked feverishly, drawing and reading day and night. He was reaching the culmination of years of thinking and planning. He still looked like hell, but at least he looked like good hell. He had devised a way of building a machine that transmuted technetium into ruthenium a few atoms at a time, and encasing this machine in a stainless steel reliquary, approximately three feet high by two feet wide, with levers to be manipulated by the viewer. Turn the levers one way, and the transmutation was activated; turn them another way, and the transmutation was turned off.

The drawings he executed on the way to conceiving this work are gorgeous. In the squalor of his room, they looked not only particularly splendid but also like they belonged nowhere else. The inner workings of the reliquary are made up of small, delicate little machine parts and other items lifted from science labs, machine shops, smoke detectors, antique clocks, and beehives, among other odd places, all of these things meticulously drawn by Acord's hand. And the outside of the reliquary, which is to be welded shut when the innards are completed, is all rounded edges, like the outline of a cluster of subatomic particles, or a melted-and-misshapen statue of a fertility goddess.

Indeed, the reliquary's shape and function are based, Acord explained to me during a visit to the Starlight, on "three things: The Venus of Willendorf, a medieval chastity belt, and Heisenberg's Uncertainty Principle." This last had to do with the essential mystery of the sculpture: The user cannot tell whether he or she is activating or deactivating the transmutation by turning the levers because everything inside the sculpture is invisible. "It's Schrödinger's cat!" Acord told me excitedly. "The only way to find out what's going on inside the sculpture is to destroy it!"

Each day, Acord would walk from the Starlight up to the Ballard branch of the Seattle Public Library to correspond by e-mail with some physicists in London who had consistently championed his work and with the gallery in Italy that was putting together a show of his and other artists' new work, to be called "Atomica." It was scheduled to open in Switzerland in May 2003, then to tour Europe before closing in New York a year later. With the help and money of friends in Seattle, he was able to put together a compact disc of reproductions of his drawings and send them off to the gallery, and with the help of his friends in London he was able to secure a new artist-in-residency at Oxford University.

Acord woke up one morning near the end of his Fellowship at the Starlight and realized that he was finished—ready to build the sculpture he'd been trying to design for eleven years. He was to have the use of laboratory facilities in London and the help of a team of craftspeople to build *Fourth Reliquary*, and would have only to give one lecture a month to earn his keep. He would have to settle for using a particle accelerator instead of a nuclear reactor to create the technetium, at the rate of 1,000 atoms per hour, but he decided he could live with that compromise. It was not the amount of technetium being transmuted into ruthenium that mattered. What mattered was that the reliquary would contain the act of transmutation itself.

Acord, now ecstatic, spent August—he was to leave in early September for London—tracking down friends in Seattle to give them drawings and thank them. Joey and I met him at Larry's Green Front, where he presented Joey with a portfolio of drawings showing his progress toward the final design and thanked him profusely. "This is the best idea I ever had in my life," he said of *Fourth Reliquary*, "and this has been the most creative period in my whole life. What can I say? I get by with a little help from my friends."

Little more than a block away from Larry's Green Front is a tiny bookstore, called David Ishii Bookseller, that deals in used and rare books. It first opened in 1972 and has remained exactly the same ever since: dark, cluttered, and presided over by Ishii alone, who has been wearing the same floppy-brimmed fisherman's hat to work since the day his store opened. Ishii has never hired an employee; he sits in a chair with his back to the store window, doing crossword puzzles and reading newspapers, magazines, and books all day, and when he goes out to run errands or find lunch he closes up the store until he returns.

Ishii is both retiring and voluble. He never initiates a conversation with a customer; but if you ask him a question or direct a comment at him, his eyes pop open, turning exactly as round as the perfectly round spectacles he wears, and the words come pouring out of him—especially when the topic is anything from Seattle's past.

I walked in there one day near the end of my unemployment, when I was floundering, and asked for Emmett Watson's books, all three of which were out of print. Ishii had two of them, and said he would "call Emmett's daughter" for the third and have it there in a day or two. "I'll take these two now," I said, "and come back in a few days for the other one." Then I asked him if I could use a credit card to buy the books. "No," he said, "I don't take cards. You can either pay me with cash or a check, or if you don't have anything on you now, just take the books and send me a check when you get home."

Astonished, I stood there watching as he took the books, wrapped them in brown paper, and tied the package with a string, using no tape. I saw on the rolltop desk behind him a small portable typewriter and a rotary phone. I felt like I was standing in some place out of time— immutable, ineradicably charming, a little reminder of what Seattle used to be.

Ishii turned out to be a goldmine of Seattle history, of which I was entirely and inexcusably ignorant. As I made my way through the reading that would come to inform this book, I kept coming back to ask him questions—he seemed to have watched everything through his storefront window, from the settlers' landing at Alki to the technology boom—and to buy more books on Seattle's past. And again and again, I heard that same conversation with customers, many of them from out of town: "Do you take credit cards?" "No, I don't take cards. You can either pay me with cash or a check, or if you don't have anything on you now, just take the books and send me a check when you get home."

More than anyone else, it was Ishii and Acord who brought me round to the end of my ceaseless questions about Seattle. Only Seattle, I decided, could have kept Acord alive long enough to fight his way through to the completion of *Fourth Reliquary*. His survival said more about the essence of the city than all the new buildings and new money wreaking a transformation I now saw as superficial. I couldn't imagine him thriving anywhere other than here, and I saw his sculpture—in which all the intricate splendor, the proof of his genius, is hidden by a cumulo-geometric, stainless-steel shell shaped like cloud cover—as an unconscious artistic echo of Seattle's spectacular setting, with its magnificent mountain almost always hidden by clouds.

As for Ishii, I was talking with him one day when he suddenly veered off in a new conversational direction, as he was wont to do when he got on a verbal roll. "It was so funny," he said, pointing up at the floors above his store. "One day—it seemed like they all moved in on the same day—

all these technology companies moved in here. Kids. They were talking about how they were all going to get rich. Then it seemed like practically the next day they all moved out! I'd be outside and see people coming out with computers in their arms. 'Where are you going?' I'd ask. 'We're taking this stuff to be auctioned!' they'd say." He stopped for a second, shaking his head. "It happened so fast! Man, it was *so fast*! Really, really *fast*! Boom!—It was over!" Then he turned and went back to his chair, his back to the window, and picked up the crossword puzzle he'd been solving when I came in.

The boom and bust I'd spent years enduring, studying, wondering about, fearful that it had wrecked the city, had been little more than an entertaining blink of the eye to Ishii. And I realized that in the context of Seattle events, it *was* little more than the blink of an eye—only the latest in a series of similar blinks in the city's life. Out of ignorance, out of self-absorption, out of self-importance, I had missed the insignificance of the boom, mistaking an ordinary Seattle event for an extraordinary personal and world catastrophe.

Now I could see, through Ishii's magic window, those WTO riots I had waded through for what they really were: a rising up of the Ghost of Seattle Past to knock some sense into deluded Seattle Present.

Soon I would read somewhere that Seattle's economy is always either twice as good or twice as bad as the rest of the nation's. I was to come across that statement the same day I read that Seattle's unemployment rate, at 12 percent, was double the national average. I would soon discover how common, how constant a feature the boom-to-bust pattern was in Seattle history. I would come to understand that pattern first as a socio-economic expression of Northwest weather, in which we revel, through every July and August, in the irrational exuberance of strange hot constant sweet sunlight, then settle—disgruntled, resigned—into the long dark wet gloom of winter, which runs more or less from sopping October through drippy June. Every blessed year. And, ultimately, I would see that Seattle's boom-and-bust pattern was not the spiking and plummeting line you see on stock-market charts but was instead a repeating circle—a modern, vulgar version of the Hmong's eternal return.

In the immediate wake of the boom, confused, adrift, frightened, I had reveled in rage, self-loathing, loathing for everyone connected in any way with my misbegotten embrace of ambition: Squish, Sumi, Joey, Hartz Mountain Pet Foods, Brewster. I thought there was something extraordinary about what I'd been through. Now I could see the utter ordinariness of my experience riding through the boom to its crashing conclusion.

The boom was simply something we all had to cope with, like a natural disaster. Everyone—rich, poor, and ruined alike—was in one way or another victimized by it, and the bust was our cleansing opportunity, our chance to recover, to be enlightened, reborn, renewed.

It was my Oprah moment.

Now I believed I could see that Seattle was no more damaged by this boom than by any of the many other booms it had lived through, grown through, in its short history: the Alaska Gold Rush, the World War I shipbuilding boom, the World War II ship- and plane-building boom, the postwar aerospace-industry boom. It was just *life*—time circling back again and again and again as the city grew into itself.

All of us in Seattle did the best we could this time around. Few of us really had the tools to cope with or understand what we were contending with. Next boom time, I thought, I'll know better. And I hope I'll have the sense to do what the native tribes here used to do: melt into the forest and hide from those ambitious rival tribes until the invasion is over.

Where a few months before I had seen only wreckage, devastation, now I saw renewal. Ishii, Acord, the Zeitgeist . . . they were like those first tender green little shoots forcing their way up through the bare wreckage on the slopes of Mt. St. Helens a few months after the 1980 eruption. They testified to how the spirit unique to this place endures, through boom and bust and boom and bust, ineradicable, unalterable. I watch Ishii again wrapping another customer's book in that plain brown paper and tying it closed with string and I picture a city at peace again, ultimately indifferent to the storms and stresses the ambitious visit upon it time and time again. Throughout Seattle's short history, through all of its spasms of growth, there has endured something of that Northwest-traditional resignation, that essential disdain for ambition—a form of wisdom extending from those ambition-wary natives all the way to Ivar and beyond. Seattle, I decide, happy at last, always finds a way to knock itself off the perch of pretension it ascends every few decades or so. It is forever fixed in my mind as stellar Seahawk rookie running back Curt Warner on Opening Day 1983, bursting through that line of scrimmage against Kansas City, running sixty yards downfield with the hopes and dreams of Seattle fans rising exponentially step by step, no more losing, no more losing, until—spectacularly, gracefully, willfully—he fumbles the football.